CHURCHILL'S SECRET WAR

DIPLOMATIC DECRYPTS, THE FOREIGN OFFICE AND TURKEY 1942–44

In memory of
Alastair Guthrie Denniston
1881–1961

CHURCHILL'S SECRET WAR

DIPLOMATIC DECRYPTS, THE FOREIGN OFFICE AND TURKEY 1942–44

ROBIN DENNISTON

CHANCELLOR PRESS

Published in 1997 by
Sutton Publishing Limited · Phoenix Mill
Thrupp · Stroud · Gloucestershire · GL5 2BU

This edition published in 2000 by Chancellor Press,
an imprint of Bounty Books,
a division of Octopus Publishing Group Limited,
2–4 Heron Quays, London, E14 4JP.

British Library Cataloguing in Publication Data
A catalogue record for this book is available from the British Library

ISBN 0-75370-382-3

Typeset in 10/12pt Plantin Light
Typesetting and origination by
Sutton Publishing Limited.
Printed in Great Britain by
J.H. Haynes & Co., Sparkford.

CONTENTS

LIST OF PLATES

AUTHOR'S NOTE

Churchill's interest in secret signals intelligence (sigint) is now common knowledge, but his use of intercepted diplomatic telegrams (BJs) in the Second World War has only become apparent with the release in 1994 of his regular supply of Ultra, the DIR/C Archive. Churchill proves to have been a voracious reader of diplomatic intercepts from 1941–44, and used them as part of his communication with the Foreign Office.

This book establishes the value of these intercepts (particularly those Turkey-sourced) in supplying Churchill and the Foreign Office with authentic information on neutrals' response to the war in Europe, and analyses the way Churchill used them. Turkey was seen by both sides to be the most important neutral power.

Why did Turkey interest Churchill? This book answers the question by tracing his involvement with diplomatic intercepts back to 1914, and then revealing how the Government Code and Cipher School (GCCS) was empowered to continue monitoring such traffic until 1939, when 'Station X' was established at Bletchley Park (BP).

After tracing the interwar work of GCCS on the secret diplomatic traffic of most major powers and outlining Turkey's place among those powers, Robin Denniston concentrates on four events or processes in which Churchill's use of diplomatic messages played a part in determining his wartime policy, which was sometimes at odds with that of the Foreign Office. He examines the use Churchill and the Foreign Office made of BJs to persuade Turkey to join the Allies between 1940 and 1943, suggesting that the Adana Conference of January 1943 produced little change in Turkish foreign policy partly because of the lack of BJs, due to tight British security on the train. The Dodecanese defeat of 1943 is explained in the light of the signals intelligence Churchill was reading. A later chapter shows the results at GCCS in London of the theft of secret Foreign Office papers in Ankara from November 1943: whether actual BJs were included in these papers, how they were received and how they led to a breakthrough in reading the German diplomatic cipher, too late to be useful to Churchill.

Acronyms and Abbreviations

ADM	Admiralty
AM	Air Ministry
BJ	Secret signals intercept circulated in Whitehall in blue jackets
BP	Bletchley Park
BSC	British Security Co-ordination
'C'	Gen Sir Stewart Menzies, Head of the Secret Intelligence Services
C&W	Cable & Wireless
C-in-C	Commander-in-Chief
CCC	Churchill College, Cambridge
CIGS	Chief of the Imperial General Staff (Lord Alanbrooke)
COS	The (British) Chiefs of Staff
DEFE	Files of the Minister of Defence (Churchill) at the PRO
Dedip	Foreign Diplomatic Decrypts, accepted usage from 1943
DF	Direction Finding
DGFP	*Documents on German Foreign Policy* – see Bibliography
DIR/C	The files brought by the Chief of the British Secret Service to Churchill. Called HW1 in the PRO.
DMI	Director of Military Intelligence
DNI	Director of Naval Intelligence
FO	The (British) Foreign Office
GCCS	The Government Code and Cipher School
GCHQ	Government Communications Headquarters
GHQ	General Headquarters
GPO	General Post Office
IWM	The Imperial War Museum
JIC	Joint Intelligence Committee
ME	Middle East
MEW	Ministry of Economic Warfare
MI 1B	Military Intelligence (Cryptanalytical Section)
MI6	Secret Intelligence Service (MI6)
MTB	Motor Torpedo Boat
NAC	National Archives of Canada in Ottawa
NSA	National Security Agency (USA)
OTP	One Time Pad: an unbreakable code system employing pages of 5-figure numbers available only to sender and recipient
PRO	Public Record Office
RAF	Royal Air Force
SD	Sicherheitsdienst: the Intelligence Branch of the SS under Heydrich.
sigint	signals intelligence
SIS	Secret Intelligence Service (MI6)
sit rep	situation report
TA	Traffic Analysis
W/T	Wireless Telegraphy

Introduction

Whence did WSC get his more outrageous strategic ideas . . .? The answer is strictly and absolutely from his own brain.

Desmond Morton, 9 July 1960

The literature on Churchill's use of secret intelligence at war is large and growing, in the USA as well as the UK. This book studies his use of diplomatic intercepts, based on newly discovered files Churchill himself hoarded during his lifetime. These files – which came to him almost daily from his intelligence chief, Brig Stewart Menzies – contain a surprise, in that together with much Ultra traffic (high-grade or Enigma/Fish intercepts frequently referred to as 'Boniface') there was much more diplomatic material in what Churchill was reading than any historian has hitherto realised. It was widely recognised, of course, that he studied the military, naval and air intercepts supplied to him from 1941. But it has only recently become apparent that Churchill's absorption in the product of the government's deciphering department had its origins in the First World War. In November 1914, when First Lord of the Admiralty, he had written the original charter for the legendary 'Room 40 OB', ensuring that German naval intercepts were available to his nominees. This involvement with, and possessiveness over, secret signals intelligence continued unabated until 1945 when Japanese diplomatic messages between Berlin and Tokyo informed the war leadership that the time had come to drop atomic bombs on Hiroshima and Nagasaki. The intercepted telegrams he studied were diplomatic as often as army and navy traffic in and between both world wars.

Churchill had always been interested in Turkey, ever since intercepts supplied to him by the Director of Naval Intelligence, Adm Reginald Hall, told him he could have secured Turkish non-participation in hostilities in February 1915 and he chose to disregard this vital information. Later he backed a Greek foray against the Turks at Smyrna in 1922 in an episode in which intercepted diplomatic messages between the Turkish ambassador in Paris and Constantinople provided him, Curzon and Lloyd George with vital information on the attitude of the Turkish leadership. By 1940 he had convinced himself that he alone could bring Turkey into the war as an ally. Few people, then or now, agreed with him, but he took immense pains to develop British policy towards Turkey in a manner that would shorten the war.

Why was Churchill so interested in Turkey? He believed that Turkey, like the other major neutral powers, collectively and individually, had the opportunity to affect the outcome of the war. Turkey was the most powerful neutral, for historical and geographical as well as strategic reasons. So Turkey could help to determine which way the war would go. Other questions then follow: what effect did Churchill's interest have on Turkey's determination to stay neutral in the Second World War? By what means did Turkey exploit the international situation to safeguard its own sovereignty? In Whitehall, how did the policies of the Foreign Office and the War Office differ from Churchill's own policy in playing 'the Turkey hand'? And within the Foreign Office whose voice counted for most, and did the diplomats there speak with one voice? How did the government obtain authentic and timely knowledge of Turkish intentions? How did the diplomatic intercepts produced in London and Bletchley between 1922 and 1944 alter the course of British foreign policy in the eastern Mediterranean, and what use was made of them by the Foreign Office and Churchill?

In considering these and related questions, this book focuses on three specific events – the conference in January 1943 between Churchill and the Turkish leadership; the abortive British campaign to recapture the Dodecanese later that year, with its diplomatic consequences; and one of the single most spectacular spy coups of the war, the so-called 'Cicero' affair, on which new light is thrown by reference to Churchill's files of diplomatic intercepts in November 1943. All these events are seen against a background of international diplomatic intrigue in which Turkey's determination to stay neutral plays a central role.

The PRO has provided access (except where documents have been withheld by GCHQ) to files Churchill valued so highly that their contents had often to be reciphered and cabled to him – sometimes in the exact words (*ipsissima verba*) – whenever he was out of the country. Their recent arrival at the PRO means that diplomatic historians have had no more than a few months to review the material and undertake the dangerous counterfactual exercise of answering the question, how would Churchill and the Foreign Office have handled Turkey without the Turkey-sourced intercepts? An attempt is made here to strip out these messages from the general progress of Turco-British relations to see how differently Churchill would have played the Turkey hand had this material not been available to him, in its *ipsissima verba* state, in DIR/C.[1]

Little attention has hitherto been given to the British government's achievements in obtaining intelligence by intercepting letters and telegrams and by breaking the diplomatic ciphers of neutral and friendly nations, and its impact on the conduct of foreign policy during the Second World War. Such references as there are to the non-military side of the wartime secret intelligence have been made despite the fact that both the US State Department and Her Majesty's government have been unwilling until recently to disclose any diplomatic material. The arrival of DIR/C in the PRO means that a new source of secret information available throughout much of the war to the Foreign Office but hitherto unknown to most historians of secret intelligence can now be studied at least for part of the period during which Turco-British relations were a major concern of British foreign policy. This also raises questions related to the Foreign Office's perception of the Turkish mind which require answering.

I suggest that the intelligent reading and use of secret signals intercepts, in war and peace, by the major western powers, assisted foreign policy makers (notably Churchill) who understood their limitations as well as their potential value. But the corollary that diplomatic history might need to be substantially rewritten in the light of recent releases in London, Ottawa and Washington does not necessarily follow. Little now known from the released intercepts, and unknown or only partially known before, actually affects existing diplomatic history.

Turkey was a crucial case. The Foreign Office had been hard at work improving Anglo-Turkish relations since the early 1930s, but by 1940 this was reduced to Turkey's trade in chrome with Britain and with Germany. Without Churchill relentlessly seeking any opportunity to divert German armies from the Eastern Front and looking for an ally in the eastern Mediterranean, it is unlikely that Turkey would have loomed so large in Allied war strategy. At least two policies, therefore, towards Turkish neutrality in the Second World War can be discerned: those of Churchill and of the Southern Department of the Foreign Office which was responsible for Turkey. What united them was their common reading of Turkey-related diplomatic decrypts.

Within the Southern Department, the wartime minutes of George Clutton and John Sterndale-Bennett (nicknamed 'Benito' after Mussolini) predominate, but the observations of very senior diplomats such as the Deputy Under Secretary, Orme Sargent ('Moley') and the Permanent Under Secretary, Sir Alexander Cadogan, throw light on the different perceptions of Turkish neutrality within the government. The Foreign Secretary, Anthony Eden, himself played a part, marred by his too obvious concern with the consequences to his own political career of the success or otherwise of British Turkish policy. From Ankara the British ambassador, Sir Hughe Knatchbull-Hugessen, wrote informally about Turkish affairs to both Sargent and Cadogan. John Sterndale-Bennett and another even abler colleague, Knox Helm, were posted to the embassy in Ankara, thus ensuring co-ordination of policy between Ankara and London. This relationship can be traced by studying the FO 371 (general correspondence) and FO 195 (embassy and consulate) files of the period. While this book concentrates on DIR/C, these and other Foreign Office files have also been useful. There are drafts of Churchill's unsent letters to colleagues and to Roosevelt, relating to Turkey, in the PREM3 and 4 (Premier) files. Some War Office, Admiralty and Air Ministry files contain references to decrypt diplomacy which the 'weeders' have missed.

That a new theme in Churchillian historiography has thus emerged is due to the release of DIR/C. The evidence therein points up Churchill's enthusiasm for playing the Turkey hand alone and demonstrates his personally directed policy towards Turkey, despite this being the responsibility of the Southern Department under the Secretary of State. This book includes an attempt to assess:

- The importance to the Department of the diplomatic intercepts as distinct from other sources of information.
- How officials regarded and used them.
- How their advice, consequent on these questions, was received and adopted or otherwise by the framers of British foreign policy in the eastern Mediterranean throughout the war.

This study of Churchill's use of secret signals intelligence, before and during the Second World War, breaks new ground in several other respects. The role of the neutrals has never received much attention from historians.[2] In focusing on Turkey's remarkably resilient and subtle diplomacy towards Italy, Germany, Britain and, especially, the Soviet Union throughout the war, several significant themes develop. One theme is the alternating strategies of Germany and Britain towards the Balkans – the former involving an invasion of Turkey from Bulgaria to carry the Blitzkrieg to Egypt and Persia in 1940–41, the latter the opening of a second front in the Balkans from Turkey across the eastern Mediterranean in 1943, to divert German divisions from the Eastern Front and thus hasten D-Day in the west. Another is the predominating voice of Churchill in Allied war planning in the eastern Mediterranean. Since he was neither a commander-in-chief nor a head of state (as Roosevelt and Stalin were) his strategic ambitions could only be promoted through a cumbersome programme involving the Americans, the Russians and his own War Cabinet and Chiefs of Staff. Despite these handicaps, Churchill struggled with his allies and colleagues for what he saw as the best way forward from 1941, and Turkish involvement in the war was always on his agenda.

Why this was so leads to the third theme of this study – his lifelong interest in and use of signals intelligence.[3] Churchill had always read naval and diplomatic intercepts. As early as 1915 when he was First Lord of the Admiralty he had personally drafted the first charter of Room 40 OB – the navy's legendary decrypting department. Its longest serving member remarked scathingly of this charter, that 'to have carried out his instructions literally would, no doubt, have safeguarded the secret but must also have nullified the value of the messages' – because of the restricted distribution and the prohibitions attached to any mention of them.[4] This sentence, it may be said, neatly encapsulates the whole problem of how to use intercepts while protecting their security – not enough security and they cease to exist; too much and they cannot be used. Churchill's use of intercepts continued through the long interwar years of 'his War against the Russian Revolution' in 1920 and the Turks at Chanak in 1922.[5] At the approach of the Second World War he was reading diplomatic intercepts received from a friend in government (Desmond Morton).[6] He found the study of raw authentic intercepts, not gists or summaries or paraphrases, indispensable in formulating policy, and explained their importance to Lord Curzon in 1922. While this is now acknowledged, what he was reading between 1941 and 1945 has only recently been released and so has not yet been studied by historians.[7] His written comments and observations on many of these messages can be seen for the first time, both on Axis service traffic (Enigma) and diplomatic (medium-grade) traffic. They are a pointer to his daily study of the inner movement of the war through the voices of his enemies, and of the neutrals.

So far as Turkish neutrality went this was, of course, the responsibility of the Southern Department, not of the Minister of Defence. By reading the new (DIR/C) files alongside the FO files on wartime Turkey it is possible to discern significant differences in attitude between officials of the Southern Department whose Turkish remit was jealously safeguarded against GHQ ME, and against Churchill himself, who wished to 'play the Turkey hand' alone, and proceeded to do so in early 1943 much against the wishes of the foreign secretary and the rest of the War Cabinet. New connections can thus be drawn between Churchill and the FO over Turco-British wartime relations, themselves an organic development from the FO's prewar policy towards Turkey, ably set out by D.C. Watt in his *How War Came*.[8]

These causal connections cannot be fully developed without some account of two separate strands in British twentieth-century history. Chapter 2 describes the development of British cryptography from 1915, through the Russian, Turkish and Italian crises of the 1920s and '30s. This is followed by an account of Turco-British relationships between the Dardanelles crisis of 1915 and the Chanak crisis of 1922 up to September 1939. A bridging chapter (3) carries the story of Churchill, wartime signals intelligence and the progress of the war in the Mediterranean to the end of 1941, at which point the DIR/C files come on stream. Thereafter until January 1943 when Churchill made his surprise visit to the Turkish leadership at Adana – and beyond, until early 1944 – the files relating to Turkey are reviewed in the light of the changing nature of the war.

The Adana Conference was followed later in the year by two significant events – one disastrous, the other ludicrous. The disaster was the Dodecanese debacle of October 1943 in which British forces were beaten by better-officered Germans with a consequential loss of British credibility in the area.[9] The other was the theft, inside the British ambassador's residence in Ankara, of important Foreign Office papers by his Albanian valet, Eleysa Basna – codenamed 'Cicero' by the ambassador's German counterpart in Ankara, Fritz von Papen. Chapter 8 seeks to demonstrate that, since much of this material was identical with Churchill's own reading, and since captured German documents have demonstrated the great interest shown in it by Hitler, Goebbels and Jodl in Berlin, a revised account is necessary of what diplomats until recently have regarded as the biggest FO security lapse until Burgess and Maclean. This is written in the light of what we now know, fifty years later, about British cipher security, Churchill's use of deciphered messages, and the state of the war in 1943–44.

The Dodecanese debacle and the 'Cicero' affair conclude this study of Churchill's use of signals intelligence and the FO's policy towards Turkey in the Second World War. A year was to elapse before Turkey joined the Allies and in that year much diplomatic activity persisted, but the end was no longer in doubt and the focus of Churchill's interest moved to western Europe, and to Operation 'Overlord', the invasion of Normandy in June 1944. The concluding chapter develops the basic thrust of my argument – that while the release of the new files is to be welcomed as revealing interesting new connections between Churchill and his war work, it does not materially alter the history of the Second World War.

Wartime Turkey has been the subject of several ambassadorial memoirs (René Massigli, Hughe Knatchbull-Hugessen, Fritz von Papen) and spy memoirs (Eleysa Basna, Ludwig Moyzisch, Nicholas Elliot, Walter Schellenberg). The opening up of DIR/C is by far the most notable primary source, but does it add to or alter what is already in the books? Much was known before: Churchill knew it at the time because he read DIR almost every day. President İnönü of Turkey knew it because he was reading much of the same material, the reports his ambassadors sent to the Foreign Ministry in Ankara, which was pivotal in formulating Turkish foreign policy. Whitehall knew it. Hitler and Goebbels knew it. Turkey-related diplomatic intercepts corroborate the historical record but contain few surprises, since the narrative is already in place. While that does not reduce their importance, which is in relating the study of diplomatic signals intelligence to foreign policy in wartime Whitehall, Berlin and Ankara, it may provide a convincingly negative answer to the question previously raised of the requirement to adjust the record.

How the British came by the Turkish diplomatic telegrams is another question this book seeks to answer. British wartime radio and telegram interception and decryption at Bletchley Park have, of course, been the subject of a substantial literature of which Hinsley's monumental *British Intelligence in the Second World War* holds pride of place.[10] Prof Hinsley (with his co-authors) not only had full access to the files when writing, but was himself a key figure in running Bletchley Park from 1941 to 1944: originating, developing, modifying and operating the complex procedures which turned the raw messages which arrived at Bletchley at all hours of the day or night from many intercept stations scattered across the world into usable, relevant, topical material – still authentic despite the many processes they had gone through. Other BP veterans have written about signals intelligence in the Second World War including Gordon Welchman, Peter Calvocoressi and Ralph Bennett, but none of these, apart from Hinsley, had access to the diplomatic material which is the subject of this book.[11]

Churchill famously told his researchers that his own history of the Second World War was not history, it was his case.[12] Official historians, as will be shown, followed him, particularly in 1943 over the Adana Conference and the Dodecanese assault, not because he had put his 'case' together with his own selected documents before they had completed their task, but because they found that the files gave little extra useful information, and that what Churchill thought and did at the time, as recorded by him, remained the best source available. The Dodecanese affair is particularly illuminating, in that immediately after it Churchill ordered his personal staf to collect all his relevant memoranda and telegrams, in order to have 'his case' ready for publication. This was duly done and they appear as PREM 3/3/3 at the PRO and form the basis of his 'Island Prizes Lost' chapter in vol. 5 (*Closing the Ring*, London, Cassell) of his war history, published eight years later. They were published *in toto* in 1976 as vol. 2 of *Principal War Telegrams and Memoranda* (Kraus Thompson, 1976). It is rare for such a significant combined operation to be reported on by its principal participant, for his own actions to become, relatively without comment, the historical record. Nor did a subsequent generation of revisionist historians greatly alter the received, Churchillian, account of the years of the Second World War, as recent scholars have pointed out. The missing material for a definitive account of Churchill's 1943 war work is to be found in the diplomatic intercepts. Though they throw valuable new light on what Churchill was up to in his eastern Mediterranean policy (as this book hopes to demonstrate) they require little, if any, rewriting of history. To trace these intercepts, through Churchill's use of them, to his directives and memoranda – and then to his actual history, and on the lavish use made of them by both official and revisionist historians – is to gain a glimpse at last of how diplomatic decrypts infiltrated the historical record.

I should like to thank Professors Kathleen Burk and David French of University College, London, for help and guidance in the preparation of this book; and also Professors Christopher Andrew and Peter Hennessy for encouragement and information. Thanks are also due to Rupert Allason MP, Dr Rosa Beddington, Dr Selim Deringil, Ralph Erskine, Professor John Ferris, Margaret Finch, Tony Fulker, Randal Grey, David Irving, Professor Sir Harry Hinsley, Rachel Maxwell-Hyslop, Dr Joe Maiolo, Simona Middleton, Sir Patrick Reilly, and the editors at Sutton Publishing. Special thanks are due to the staff of the PRO at Kew, at the Churchill Archives in Churchill College, Cambridge, and at the National Archives of Canada in Ottawa. Extracts from the Ian Jacob and Denniston papers are published by kind permission of the Archivist at Churchill College. An early version of chapter 2 appeared in *Intelligence and National Security* (July 1995).

Robin Denniston

I am after the Turk
– Winston Churchill to Anthony Eden,
8 June 1942

[Churchill's] volatile mind is at present set on Turkey and Bulgaria, and he
wants to organise a heroic adventure against Gallipoli and the Dardanelles
– Lord Asquith to Venetia Stanley, October 1914

Turks are most awful brigands. We daren't threaten them, we can't bribe them
– Alexander Cadogan, 24 August 1942

Turing: *I am a code-breaker. I deciphered all the German codes and won the war*
single-handedly. That's top secret, of course, nobody knows
Ron [grinning]: *Just me*
Turing: *You and Mr Churchill*
– Hugh Whitemore, *Breaking the Code*

Reading the whole war . . . every day, from the enemy viewpoint, the British
being the enemy
– Christine Brooke-Rose on Hut 3, Bletchley Park, *Remake*, p. 108

The distribution of diplomatic intercepts throughout the chancelleries of many
powers between the wars suggests an interesting new angle on both the conduct
and the study of international diplomacy
– The author, 1996

It is said about Foreign Office minutes that if you read the odd paragraph
numbers and the even paragraph numbers in series you get both sides of the case
fully stated.
– WSC, vol. 5, p. 627

England has organised a network of intercept stations designed particularly for
listening to our radio. This accounts for the decyphering of more than 100 of our
codes. The key to those codes are sent to London where a Russian subject,
Feterlajn, has been put at the head of cipher affairs.
– Trotsky to Lenin, 1921

CHAPTER ONE

Why Turkey?

*Those who remember the operations of 1915 and 1916 in the Dardanelles and
Mesopotamia may be glad that the Turks, who were then against us, are now for us.
What is the cause of this change? It was because, during the same years in which the
Germans turned to thievery, the Turks turned to honest ways.*

R.G. Collingwood, *The New Leviathan*, p. 374

This chapter attempts to answer the question, why was Turkey so important
to Churchill in 1941? It brings together Turco-British international relations
from 1914 to 1943, relates Churchill's failed attempt on Turkish neutrality in
the First World War to his playing of the Turkey hand in the Second World
War; links his perceptions of, and intelligence on, Turkish foreign policy to his
war strategy, considers the balance of advantage of having Turkey as an active
and demanding ally, and then summarises Turco-British relations between
1940 and 1943 using newly disclosed diplomatic intercepts.

   The following pages also touch on the importance of Turkish
economics, geography and history in relation to world affairs since the
ascendancy of Atatürk. His successors shared with Britain (and probably
also with Germany) a common source of intelligence – ambassadorial
reports from most European capitals sent to Ankara for their guidance,
which were also intercepted and used by the FO in London. Churchill's
interest in signals intelligence generally is then integrated into the picture,
particularly that related to Turkey. His obsession with the Turks had
strong roots in the First World War, and thus can be seen to lead directly
to his unilateral decision to seek out the Turkish leadership on Turkish soil
in January 1943.

Churchill and Turkey in the First World War

To answer the question, 'Why Turkey?', some account of Turco-British
relations in 1914–15 is first required, for significant parallels can be
observed between British war strategy towards the Turks at the Dardanelles,
in part driven by Churchill as First Lord of the Admiralty in 1914, and
remarkably similar thoughts of a Balkan offensive launched from Turkey
harboured by an older if not wiser Churchill in 1942–43.

In August 1914 the German failure to destroy France following the 'miracle' of the Battle of the Marne induced the Reich to look at Turkey, then still neutral. A Turkish threat to distract Russian armies from Germany's Eastern Front would stop Russian trade through the Dardanelles, might hasten Bulgarian involvement and would threaten British imperial communications at Suez. The parallel with the Second World War, so far as Germany was concerned, was clear, and von Falkenhayn in 1914, as Jodl would do in 1943, promoted the view that a threat to Suez would weaken British forces in the west.

In Whitehall Winston Churchill urged the cabinet towards an offensive against Turkey – first conceived as involving a strong military contingent as well as the then all-powerful Royal Navy, subsequently a navy-only operation. The generals and admirals – ill-prepared culturally for the onset of total war – failed to deliver unequivocal support. On 30 October the Germans provoked the Turkish navy to shell the Russian Black Sea Fleet and provided Churchill with his opportunity in the Mediterranean. He unilaterally – and unconstitutionally – ordered the Royal Navy to shell the Turks stationed round the Dardanelles. This obliged the Turks to strengthen their defences, though their ammunition remained in short supply.

Churchill's advocacy of an attack on the Dardanelles was based on the perception that a successful result would give Britain the chance to dictate terms at Constantinople. However, he knew (as he would know about the Dodecanese assault in 1943) that the venture would be both costly and risky. In 1914 he found insufficient support for his plan: an attack on Turkey would only relax pressure on Russia, it was said, and play the German game. But he did have support from Adm 'Jacky' Fisher, the First Sea Lord, who wrote on 3 January 1915: 'The attack on Turkey holds the field, assuming a strong body of British troops to achieve a continued assault.' In the event, this was unforthcoming but Churchill pressed on, despite Fisher's view, expressed to the Dardanelles Commission in 1917, that the naval operation alone was doomed to failure.

The consequence of the confused leadership structure in Whitehall and of the First Lord's determination to play the Turkey card himself, led to disaster for Britain. This remained in the collective memory as a stigma to be born by Churchill for the next twenty years.[1] That leadership structure was no less confused at the outbreak of the Second World War, except that Churchill was in undisputed command by June 1940, and not compelled to work entirely through advocacy. A parallel situation with regard to Turkey quickly developed in the stricken years of 1940–41 but before that Turco-British diplomatic relations had taken a turn for the better. To see why, Turkey needs to be seen in a European context.

Turkey in Context

The dismemberment of the Ottoman empire in 1879 followed the successful Russian siege of Erzerum five years earlier. Previously extending to the Adriatic in the west and the Danube basin in the north-west, the empire had been in decline since 1690. By 1878 new nation states had grown within the Ottoman boundaries; Bulgaria had thrown off the Turkish yoke in a revolt backed by fellow Slavs in Russia, to whom thereafter she was tied by race, religion and gratitude. Despite their victory over the British at the Dardanelles, the First World War proved disastrous for those in Ankara reluctant to face the realities of the post-Ottoman world.

The Treaty of Versailles left Turkey with no European territory, and western leaders, in particular Lloyd George, were determined to exclude her from the Continent. She was disliked and feared by the international community. The dislike stemmed in part from a deep-seated anti-Muslim prejudice, partly explained by the residual predominance of Christian prejudices in the chancelleries of the great western powers. The legacy of Ottoman oppression and corruption had left Turkey the sick man of Europe and something of a pariah. The fear arose from Turkey's strong tradition in arms, weakened but not allayed by being on the losing side in the First World War.

The rise of Atatürk signalled to the architects of Versailles a recrudescence of Ottoman imperialism, symbolised by Turkish victory over Greece at Chanak in 1922. Greece, backed only by Britain and in spite of British public opinion, was repelled from Turkish territory amid some savage ethnic cleansing.[2] A severe earthquake then compounded the problems of the Turkish leadership. Thereafter Atatürk was to prove a friend of the west, and Britain in particular, thanks in part to the close friendship he established with the British ambassador in Ankara, Sir Percy Loraine.

The world longed for peace, and thus good relations with the nascent, etiolated Turkish state became the cornerstone of the Balkan policies of all the western great powers – of none more so than Britain. Additionally Turkey's foreign minister, Ismet İnönü – later to lead the Turkish nation through the Second World War and beyond – proved to be a formidably successful negotiator at the Lausanne Conference of 1923. While Lord Curzon was perceived to be the ablest tactician of the great power statesmen present, it was İnönü who won for his country significant modifications to Versailles, including parts of western Thrace which made the Straits in effect a broad river through Turkish territory, much to the chagrin of generations of Russian and Bulgarian diplomats.

Chanak in 1922 and Montreux in 1936 were significant moments in the development of Turkish foreign policy in the interwar period. British attitudes to Turkey were affected by two factors which bound Turco-British relations together for the next twenty years. One was the presence of Winston Churchill back in government after serving in a sort of honourable disgrace as a battalion commander on the Western Front. Churchill was passionately in favour of the Chanak provocation in 1922, pressing information derived from Turkish diplomatic intercepts on his colleagues to show which way the wind was blowing. The second, arising from the first, was Britain's access to Turkish military and diplomatic ciphers continuously from 1916 to 1945. These informed Churchill how he could have taken advantage of the shortage of Turkish ammunition and the willingness of the Turkish banks to accept bribes to intervene: thus informed, he could have averted the Dardanelles fiasco. Seven years later he read the intercepts which spelt out the chances of the success of the Chanak provocation and, twenty years after that, he plotted each step in Turkey's plans to stay neutral in 1941–43. Thus the relationship between Churchill, Turkey and diplomatic intercepts can be traced over twenty-nine years, which helps explain why playing the 'Turkey hand' was so important to him in the Second World War.

Some account of Turkey's economic and political developments will serve to bridge the interwar years. The crises and conferences which brought modern Turkey into being created an essentially non-viable state, lacking the infrastructure and resources of other Middle Eastern countries, settling uneasily for a centralised one-party state on Portuguese lines but with a commitment to some form of eventual social democracy which was slow to come and over which the Turkish leadership procrastinated, often with good reason.

Turkey's strategic position at the eastern end of the Mediterranean and the southern shore of the Black Sea meant that it was a target of constant surveillance by Whitehall, but in fact the country was split, not geographically but ethnically and culturally, into two quite distinct groupings. Turkish discrimination against Armenian, Azerbaijani, Kurdish and Greek minorities obscured the fact that many Turks shared more in common with populations between the Caucasus and the Caspian than with their Balkan neighbours. The huge Anatolian hinterland was comparatively undeveloped, and schools, roads and amenities generally were scarce. The economy was fragile, illiteracy extensive and taxation yielded insufficient revenue to support not only a large standing army but by 1939 a massive call-up of reservists and a state of emergency. Foreign trade was hard to come by without credit, or barter, or state intervention. Here was a third world country in which a million peasant farmer producers had become consumers through the call-up, as Prime Minister Saraçoğlu explained in the Turkish National Assembly in July 1941.[3] A wealth tax, introduced as a consequence, caused widespread alarm, particularly among the non-Muslim minorities in the west of the country, against whom it was targeted and who involuntarily contributed 85 per cent of the additional revenue raised. After a good harvest the peasantry regularly worked on the roads for additional subsistence, and thus gradually opened Anatolia up to the internal combustion engine.

Looking east and south, to Mecca and Arabia and central Asia rather than to Europe, the 18 million population had no wish to fight the Germans, the

Russians or anyone else, except perhaps the Bulgarians. Only Muslims could bear arms and many of the minorities suffered discrimination. Dissent was discouraged and the press followed the government line with only mild differences of emphasis depending on whether the proprietor or editor inclined to national socialism or democratic capitalism. All alike were afraid of Russia, until Mussolini's interventions in Africa, Spain and Albania made Italy Turkey's chief problem.

İnönü knew that his army was equipped to fight and win on Turkish soil and elsewhere in Asia but not against the Wehrmacht (German army) with its new weapons and frightening new ways of carrying out *Blitzkrieg* (lightning war). On Atatürk's death in 1938 İnönü had been appointed his successor in the presidency. He concentrated his attention on foreign policy, to maintain his predecessor's priorities, holding Turkey's new borders inviolate, keeping her hard-won rights in the Straits, buying only from nations that bought from them, making wary non-aggression noises to her equally fragile neighbours – Romania, Greece and Bulgaria – ignoring the Arab world and the Jewish refugees from Eastern Europe, and maintaining friendship, albeit on their terms, with the great powers, particularly Britain. And he based the policy on the reports of his ambassadors which were invariably delivered straight to him.

At the start of hostilities in September 1939 Turkey's major enemy was Italy, whose advance into Albania two months previously was seen as further evidence of Mussolini's neo-imperialist policy, already condemned by the League of Nations, though later condoned. It was clear to the Turks that Mussolini's ambitions were by no means fully realised, and his occupation of the Dodecanese islands might prove to be the prelude to sharp fighting in the eastern Mediterranean. But elsewhere İnönü followed Atatürk in seeking to ensure the balance of power in Europe was maintained. So Germany's ambitions in eastern Europe, already realised in Austria, Czechoslovakia and Poland, loomed menacingly, although German diplomats then and thereafter, on Hitler's orders, treated Turkey with politeness and care. The British approach by way of reciprocal guarantee in April 1939 came as the climax of several years of diplomatic activity designed to keep Turkey sweet. The formalities were completed by the Franco-Turco-British Pact which guaranteed Turkey's borders from any threat in the west – but the FO files reveal that almost no one understood what the pact really entailed, and in particular what would happen if a belligerent country attempted to sail its ships through the Straits. And it was never put to the test. French influence, hitherto dominant,[4] was severely eroded by the unmoving nature of the French position which failed to maintain her *mission civilisatrice* in the Middle East, and was effectively eliminated when France surrendered to the Germans in June 1940.

Thus preserving Turkish neutrality required all İnönü's concentration and formidable negotiating powers. Conflicting concerns swirled round the politicians in Ankara, and historical and ancestral memories skewed the negotiating processes. Fear of Russia was compounded by the widespread fear of international Bolshevisation – which by 1938 threatened to bring parts of northern Spain into the Russian orbit – with a growing awareness of what Stalin's purges were doing to the officer class there. With France immobile and Italy flexing its muscles, with Germany enticing her into trading dependency and Britain unable to deliver what she promised, Turkey also had potential problems on her eastern borders where in Persia and Afghanistan unstable regimes, tribal loyalties and oil complicated international relations. Many Turks – sometimes İnönü himself – hankered for a recrudescence of panturanism – the re-establishment of the wider frontiers and spheres of influence of the declining years of the Ottoman Empire – and longed at least to fight the Bulgarians, their erstwhile vassals. Control of the Straits was maintained only through the terms of the Montreux Convention which were widely resented by the other Black Sea littoral powers.

Such was the geopolitical reality for Turkey in 1939. This was the situation Churchill manipulated constantly, though in the end unavailingly. He was kept informed of Turkish military thinking by Adm Howard Kelly whom he sent to Ankara where he struck up a friendship with Marshal Kakmak.[5] Kelly's manuscript diary entries covering these years are at the National Maritime Museum. The Turks, he reported, admired German efficiency. He went on unauthorised walks near strategic installations and was constantly being arrested. In 1940 he noted that it was evident that Turkey had no intention of going to war except for the protection of her own interests, but Churchill disregarded his view. Despite his knowledge of Ottoman history and the wounds left by the Dardanelles venture, Churchill's wish to get Turkey into the war was not based on geopolitical reality but on a mixture of hope and desperation. In 1940 when France fell he had no one else in Europe to turn to, and when a year later Russia joined the Allies, and America six months after that, neither partner went along with his Turkish ploy, though such was his influence until mid-1944 that the other two sometimes pretended to do so.

He went about bringing Turkey into the war by proposing a platonic marriage, based on mutual convenience. He ignored Turkey's fear that the success of any great power would threaten the balance of power in Europe and her own territorial sovereignty. By 1940 Germany was almost at Turkey's doorstep, Russia was a less than friendly neighbour to the north, whose plight in 1941 raised the spectre of a plea for help against the German invader. Russia's later successes displaced Italy and Germany as the major threat, as the prospect rose of Germany being rolled back by a newly victorious Soviet Union, still suspected of promoting Bolshevism internationally. And when British successes in the Mediterranean seemed likely to throw the Axis out of the region, Turkey grew to fear yet another imperial superpower would displace Italy as a potential aggressor. Thus Germany, Russia, Britain, Italy (and France until mid-1940) had all constituted a direct challenge to Turkish independence.

In 1941 all Churchill had to go on was the Turco-Franco-British guarantee of mutual assistance of 1939, effectively nullified in 1940 by the collapse of France. But he had something else which only Hitler, Ribbentrop and a handful of FO officials in London and Berlin shared: he had intimate access to the formulation of Turkish foreign policy through the secret diplomatic intercepts from Turkish ambassadors abroad to Ankara. These told him in great detail when to press his platonic marriage suit and when to quench his ardour; when President İnönü might be ready to receive him, and under what conditions and with what agenda and with what outcome; what Axis pressures were exerted on Ankara and how they were received; how the Turks reacted to German successes in 1940 and 1941, and the Russian successes thereafter; their suspicions of American intentions, their fears of the Bolshevisation of Europe, shared by the Iberian countries, their scepticism of his own good faith – would the British, could the British, deliver what they were promising: both success in fighting the Germans and sophisticated new weaponry for the Turks to defend themselves against the Bulgarians.

He had little help from his colleagues. Anthony Eden, Secretary of State for Foreign Affairs, did not like the Turks and was not liked by them. Harold Macmillan was assigned political responsibility for most Mediterranean littoral countries, but specifically bound out of Turkey.[6] The British generals were too assertive, the admirals only marginally less so. Turkey should be handled by London, Churchill ruled. And London meant Churchill, and only Churchill had the diplomatic intercepts.

As for the other Allies, neither America nor Russia shared his enthusiasm for Turkey – but for different reasons. To the Americans Turkey looked like a part of a plot to set up a second front as far away as possible from the British or imperial homelands, in the Balkans, an area they regarded as an exclusively European can of worms. In November 1940 the Russians had urged on their Axis partners a carve-up of the world: Molotov wanted Russian expansion at the expense of Turkey and proposed that Moscow and Berlin should impose these claims by force. But a year later the Russians, fighting for their lives, had no time for or interest in the Turks. They could not understand why the British continued to court them after Adana and though they agreed it was important they join the Allies in 1943 they cooled to this project, as indeed to Turkey, when they saw the diplomatic game the Turks were playing so successfully.

So Churchill had his platonic marriage of convenience, a stick and carrot method of proposing it (if you don't you'll be invaded by someone, probably Russia, perhaps Bulgaria; if you do you'll get the best new weaponry and maybe the Dodecanese) and his Turkish diplomatic intercepts. Given such a poor hand he may be thought to have played it with panache and skill and an endearing lack of self-importance. All present at Adana thought so. The conference itself took place amid scenes of amazing friendship and conviviality. But the British could not or would not deliver as promised, while the Turks were reluctant to accept and make use of what did arrive, for fear of provoking the Germans. A stalemate developed thereafter and a year of diplomatic gerrymandering began, until President İnönü quite unexpectedly removed his reputedly pro-German foreign minister, Numan Menemencioğlu, stopped sending chromite to Germany, forbade passage of German naval vessels through the Straits and ultimately, with one week to go, entered the war. By that time the fighting was almost over. Despite the malingering and some consequential ill-tempered remarks, Churchill persisted in his attachment to his idea of Turkey and was personally instrumental in bringing her into the United Nations in late 1945.

If Churchill thus failed basically to secure a useful ally in the Turks, it was because there was nothing in it for them. The Turkish leadership called his bluff, very politely, and the German bluff (perhaps the more honest of the two). They also called the Russian bluff when in 1945 Molotov proposed a revision of the terms of the Montreux Convention.

The Turkish ambassadors, attachés, diplomats and foreign ministry officials kept their president *au courant* with the progress of the war, mainly by means of the diplomatic reports, which were systematically intercepted, decrypted and read assiduously in Whitehall and the Wilhelmstrasse – and by none more assiduously than Churchill himself, as we shall see. These Turkish officials were all remarkably and genuinely united behind İnönü in working for continued Turkish neutrality at almost any cost. They all refused to think seriously about becoming a belligerent unless and until Turkish sovereignty had been infringed. It never was.

Churchill's Secret Source

Two factors can now be seen to tie Turkey umbilically to Whitehall in the interwar period. One was Churchill at the Dardanelles and at Chanak; the other was the secret signals intelligence that the British obtained, unknown to the Turks, which gave them easy access to the reports from European capitals on which the Turks themselves, and İnönü in particular, relied in shaping foreign policy.[7] This form of intelligence had always been highly regarded by Churchill and some account of his early use and appreciation of it now follows.

Churchill's direct involvement with the product of the cryptographers did not start in 1940 when he became prime minister or even in the latter days of peace when Maj Morton kept him *au courant* with what the intercepts were saying to the government.[8] It started in 1915 when he was First Lord of the Admiralty and Room 40 OB was born. He himself wrote the rules and procedures whereby naval decrypts – wireless messages and telegrams – should be processed. He decided who should see them, apart from himself, and more significantly who should not.[9] He dealt with Room 40 through successive DNIs – first Sir Alfred Ewing, then Adm Sir Reginald 'Blinker' Hall. His relationship with Hall was not easy because they were both mavericks. It was Hall[10] who without cabinet authorisation fixed the price on receipt of which the Turks would withdraw from the Dardanelles. His negotiation was aborted by Churchill who was too preoccupied with his own agenda, and looked Hall's gift-horse in the mouth. Hall's use of signals intelligence in the First World War went on to include the spectacular success of the disclosure of the Zimmermann telegram[11] – bringing the USA into the war – a feat Churchill may have envied as well as admired, and for lack of a similar intercept in the Second World War he had to wait many anxious months before the United States was forced into the war by Japan and Germany.

So diplomatic intercepts, or blue jackets or 'BJ telegrams' were familiar to Churchill over nearly thirty years in and out of government. What they were, where they came from, how they evolved from the routines of those manning Room 40 Old Buildings in the First World War, who read them and what they thought of them – and what was done with them, at the time and afterward – all throw light on their use in the Second World War.[12]

Diplomatic as well as naval intercepts were decrypted by Room 40 in the First World War and became part of foreign policy making in 1919 when decisions were made to maintain an intercepting and decrypting facility based on cable censorship and the identification of appropriate diplomatic traffic. Similar work continued in Germany, the USA and the USSR. The British specifically targeted traffic to and from the USA, France, the Soviet Union and Japan.[13] Italy, Spain and Turkey followed later.

The fledgling Government Code and Cipher School (GCCS) eavesdropped on all major countries except Germany, which adopted supposedly unbreakable machine encipherment, and the Soviet Union, which used the labour-intensive but secure ciphering technique known as the One Time Pad (OTP) after British politicians had revealed that they were reading her secret messages.[14] Japanese and Turkish diplomatic traffic proved to be of particular interest and importance. The lack of naval and military traffic was an inevitable consequence of peace. Targeting Japan proved clever or lucky or both, for the penetration of Japanese diplomatic and naval signals yielded vital wartime information on the state of Germany to the Americans and Russians as well as the British. The importance of this will emerge in the pages that follow.[15] Turkey's diplomatic messages were targeted by Cable & Wireless in Constantinople, and were also read in Berlin and probably Moscow.[16] The Spanish Civil War released valuable Italian naval material including Enigma intercepts which enabled GCCS to study machine encipherment. Access to the German naval traffic was limited to traffic analysis (TA) until June 1940, but the analysis of the volume and direction of enemy traffic developed new cryptographic skills based on wireless telegraphy, which eventually provided most tactical signals intelligence. During the Second World War service traffic was obviously the main priority, and has subsequently dominated the literature of secret intelligence. But in the 1920s there was no military or naval traffic, only diplomatic telegrams. The Spanish Civil War yielded a bonanza of Italian military and naval traffic, all successfully read by GCCS, and the Abyssinian war of 1935–36 produced readable Italian material both military and diplomatic.

The changing nature of GCCS's product mix affected relations between GCCS and its client ministries. These varied. Through its own Room 40 operation, the Admiralty had a long-term interest since 1914, and continued to control its own assessment and distribution. The army had its excellent decryption department, MI 1B in the First World War, and the arrival of Brig John Tiltman to liaise with the army at GCCS strengthened links with the War Office, because he was not only a first-class cryptographer but an effective diplomat who became a founding father of Anglo-American signals co-operation.[17] The RAF with its shorter history had, in consequence, a less possessive attitude to the handling of signals intelligence derived from sources other than its own. It provided GCCS with technical facilities. Outside the peacetime service ministries, the chief client was the FO, but a separate 'commercial' section of GCCS emerged in 1937 and later became crucial to the Ministry of Economic Warfare. This section monitored German imports of vital minerals especially from Spain and Portugal. Maj Desmond Morton, Churchill's confidant, was on the circulating list of BJs in the period covered by DIR/C[18] and therefore, as head of the department which evolved into the Ministry of Economic Warfare, would have seen prewar BJs from the Commercial Section of GCCS.

It was, of course, diplomatic traffic which predominated throughout the interwar period, and the importance of Turkey to the FO in the 1930s suggests that Turkish traffic, in any case easily available, would have formed a significant fraction of the intercepts, continuing through 1939 and the 'guarantee' period till 1941 when DIR/C, now available, shows Turkey still in a leading position as suppliers of BJs.[19]

The BJs (in French) were sent to and read by the Turkish president and foreign minister, and formed the basis of their subtly changing attitudes to both Axis and Allies. Perhaps it was because both Britain and Germany were reading their messages that Turkey was never pressurised by either belligerent. Both knew the high cost of equipping a major new ally's large army. German as well as British commanders knew that a Turkish alliance might be more a liability than an asset – as one Field Marshal Lord Wavell summed up Turkish involvement – and courtship rituals seemed preferable to rape. Churchill used his daily access to DIR/C to advise, threaten and cajole his colleagues in the War Cabinet and the Chiefs of Staff to accept his view of how the Allies could beat the Axis. His conviction that a second front in the west would be unsustainable until the Russians had seriously reduced the fighting strength of the Wehrmacht on the Eastern Front led him to promote several alternative second fronts, of which an Aegean initiative in conjunction with Turkey – entering the war on the Allied side – would be the most likely to head off the insistence of Stalin and Roosevelt on an early launch of a second front in the west. Few people, then or now, agreed with his Turkey policy and by 1944 it was off the agenda.

Why was Turkey so important to him? Several clues have already been noted. He was believed by the Germans to be obsessed with his personal responsibility for the British failure at the Dardanelles in 1915. In 1941 he saw a pro-Allied Turkey as guardian of the imperial route to India, the Far East and Persian oil. He dreamed of a million hardy Turkish soldiers joining the exiguous divisions of Britain and the inexperienced Americans. He was starved of allies after France fell in 1940, and in his determination to keep the fighting away from the shores of Britain, he lighted on Turkey, and worked unceasingly, against opposition and indifference from his new allies after 1941, and against his own government colleagues, to bring her in.

While this can be substantiated from the existing Churchillian historiography, there is another aspect of his playing the Turkey hand. Churchill's insistence on seeing intercepts 'raw' on a daily basis gave him a unique insight into Hitler's war planning in the Caucasus and on the Eastern Front, as well as in North Africa. The Turkish diplomatic intercepts significantly augmented his picture of how the war was seen by others. He made no secret of his personal commitment to Turkey, and this can be seen in the manner in which he later wrote his history of the war. 'This is not history,' Churchill told one of his assistants working on his multi-volume history of the Second World War, 'it is my case.'[20] He selected and reproduced, often *in extenso*, his own directives for the conduct of the war and the policy that he believed HM government should adopt towards Turkey. His use of his own documents, especially those relating to Turkey, makes his history arid reading but his selection of documents becomes of new interest when correlated with DIR/C and his attitude towards Turkey. This can now be seen not with his own hindsight when he was writing after the war but as the war developed. This is particularly true of the autumn of 1943, when he personally drove the British Dodecanese assault using intercepts and rhetoric for lack of a proper plan of campaign, and the senior officers able to carry it out successfully.[21] It is difficult to learn much about the 1940–41 period before DIR/C came on stream in the autumn, by which time the war had been nearly lost. But from September 1941 until mid-1945 DIR/C provided Churchill with diplomatic decrypts which formed the basis of the British government's foreign policy towards neutrals – that is to say its attitude to those who were neither former friends (France, the Low Countries, Yugoslavia, Greece) nor enemies (Germany, Japan and Italy). Turkey provided the most.

If this is but a provisional answer to the question 'why Turkey?' a clearer picture may be gained by identifying the common ground offered by DIR/C, Churchill, the FO and Turkey's understandable wish to stay non-belligerent. Churchill himself bulked large in this scenario. Most of the other characters are half a dozen Turkish ambassadors, and an equal number of ambassadors of other countries posted to Ankara. Why did they report what they did – was it because they wanted to impress, to alert, to alarm, to press their own cause, to win favour at home, to advance their careers by saying what they thought their masters wished to hear? Or were they routine communications by a run-of-the-mill diplomat? Only a full reading of items over a sustained period could give Churchill then or historians now the flavour, the *nuances*, the context to make meaningful judgments on which politicians could make decisions. In fact cumulatively they read less like formal diplomatic exchanges and more like a novel – by Benjamin Disraeli, perhaps, or even Leo Tolstoy – or sometimes Jeffrey Archer. The question is answered by incorporating the new source, DIR/C, into the history of the war and by analysing the prime minister's position on and use of this daily file, and testing the hypothesis that the new source provided crucial information to him and many departments in Whitehall. The emergence of Turkish foreign policy as a major factor in British strategic planning from 1941–45 confirms the view that Turkish neutrality deserves further study. Since the Turkish leadership based policy decisions largely on the reports received from their diplomats in foreign capitals, and since intercepts of many of these appear in DIR/C, it is theoretically possible to construct a hidden dialogue between Churchill and the three Turks who together conducted Turkish foreign policy – İnönü, Saraçoğlu and Menemencioğlu.

In order even to guess at how GCCS's main client, the FO, used its most secret source in relation to Turkey, Chapter 2 traces the development of the techniques of British interception, decryption, translation, assessment and distribution of the secret diplomatic communications of foreign governments in the prewar period. Since Turkish material is prominent in both, the case for a special study of Turkey emerges naturally. Other FO files reveal that intercepts illuminated many patterns of decision making in Ankara, the nature of Turkish strategy and its diplomatic relations with other countries, especially the USSR and Britain.[22]

While Turkish wartime foreign policy was in the hands of no more than three men, British policy by 1940 was conducted by Churchill, despite Secretary of State for Foreign Affairs Anthony Eden and the staff of the Southern Department of the FO. What diplomats in both capitals were relying on as well as reports by Turkish ambassadors, chargés and attachés from most of the capitals of Europe and some of America and Asia, were directives and circulars from the Turkish foreign ministry on foreign policy and neutrality, and reports sent from Ankara by representatives of European countries covering the war situation in the eastern Mediterranean and on the Eastern and North African fronts in general, and official high level Turkish reactions thereto. Far from being restricted to the news and views of non-Turkish neutrals, the wartime BJs revealed (for instance) the Iberian terror of the impending 'Bolshevisation of Europe', the effect of Mussolini's resignation on the Axis conduct of the war and the neutral overreaction to it, on the conflicting agenda of the Big Three after Casablanca at Moscow, Tehran, Cairo and Yalta, on the reasons for the defection of Hungary and

Bulgaria from the Axis, and on the reasons why Russia did not declare war on Japan till 1945, on the reasons for the defection of Hungary and Bulgaria from the Axis, and on many other diplomatic concerns.

DIR/C differs from other intelligence sources, and the BJs required a different form of appreciation from all other sources of information, as Churchill knew.

Churchill and Turkey

In trying to answer the question, 'What light does DIR/C throw on the FO, Churchill, Turkey and the relation between all three from 1941–45?', it is not clear whether the new material adds to or alters what is already on the record. Churchill understood the changing diplomatic situation at the time because he was reading it almost every day. İnönü knew because he was reading some of the same material. Hitler, Goebbels, Kaltenbrunner and Ribbentrop knew about it too. By concentrating on the British archive and correlating DIR with the files relevant to Turkey during the war, it has proved possible to make new connections between the Southern Department of the FO, the policies which officials advocated towards Turkey, and the key part played by Churchill in using the Turkish gambit to hasten Allied victory.

Why the Turkish gambit should have loomed so large in British war strategy in 1942 is a question answered in Chapter 3. The Joint Planning Staff, after consultation with Churchill, expressed the hope as early as December 1941:

> that the offensive against Germany will take the form of large-scale land operations on the Russian front, large-scale bombing operations supplemented by amphibious raids of increasing weight from the United Kingdom and a gradual tightening of the ring round Axis-controlled Europe by the occupation of strategic points in the Atlantic Islands, North and West Africa, Tripoli and Turkey. Every opportunity will be taken to try and knock out Italy as an active partner in the war. These operations will be followed in the final phase by simultaneous land operations against Germany herself, from the West by the British, from the South by the United States and from the East by the Russians.[23]

A minor amendment was made later but essentially this remained Britain's grand strategy. It was not until 8 October 1942 that Churchill told Eden: 'I am after the Turk'. However, grand strategy, British historians now agree, is something of a misnomer for what was actually going on in the minds of the Chiefs of Staff and the prime minister. For Churchill, instinct or rhetoric would be a more accurate word. What is noteworthy is the important role that Turkey was playing in Allied war planning at this early stage, and without any evidence that she would be a willing partner. That it was

Churchill who introduced the Turkey factor can be asserted with confidence, since Turkey was neutral and thus belonged, in Whitehall terms, to the FO and subject to the wiles of British foreign policy, rather than belonging – as an ally – with the war planners. While Churchill was only an important voice in the latter debate, he did not have to argue his case in foreign policy matters.[24]

By 24 July 1942, Churchill predicted that 'our second front will in fact comprise both the Atlantic and the Mediterranean coasts of Europe, and we can push either right-handed, left-handed or both-handed as our resources and circumstances permit'.[25] Churchill's approach to war planning was characteristically, and realistically, opportunistic. How could it be otherwise in 1940 when Britain was at the mercy of the German *Blitzkrieg* in southern and eastern as well as western Europe, Germany was well on the way to becoming master of Europe, defeated but for a moment in the Battle of Britain, and so full of enterprising and aggressive new schemes that hastily reactive and provisional half-measures were all that were practically available to the Chiefs of Staff.

In July 1940 Churchill told the Russian ambassador, Ivan Maisky, that his strategy was to get through the next three months. He wanted Turkey in the war because only thus could German troops in large numbers be diverted from the Russian front, to assuage the Russian need for a second front immediately, while the RAF could bomb the oilfields and refineries of Romania, Austria and Hungary which he and others believed to be vital to Germany's war effort. Turkey had a large army, a million men. Churchill's instinct at that time drove him to make common cause with the Turks, suspecting that it would always be difficult to beat the Germans in close combat. The Turkish soldiery – cheap, plentiful and expendable – were already under canvas and might account for 500,000 invading German troops as well as providing a fierce and reassuring comradeship in arms.

German aggression in Poland in September 1939 soon gave Russia the large portions of eastern Europe she acquired by signing the Nazi-Soviet Pact. The Baltic states, valuable mining areas of eastern Poland and Bessarabia, Moldova and Buckhovina fell to Stalin. The Soviet Union in one bound had closed on Turkey's borders. Russia joined Italy in joint first place on the list of Turkey's bogeymen. Meanwhile British catastrophes in Norway in the spring of 1940, the overrunning by Germany of the Low Countries, and particularly the fall of France, resounded menacingly in Ankara. Hitler had triumphed, almost without opposition, over what was believed to be the world's greatest army – the French – in a matter of weeks and his Greater Germany policy brought the victorious Wehrmacht to the borders of Turkey, while his need for oil, wheat and minerals was now satisfied by the adherence of Romania to the Axis and the opening of new oil wells in Austria. Thousands of tons of war equipment were left behind by the Allies at Dunkirk. In June Italy declared war on the Allies and France sued for an armistice with the Axis. What Germany had achieved by

Blitzkrieg in the west she could as easily achieve in the Near East, and if that meant invading Anatolia en route to the oilfields of Persia, the Suez Canal and the borders of India, even that might seem possible after the rout of France.

France's fall created strong anti-French feeling in Ankara. One signatory of the Turco-Franco-British Pact having already defaulted, Turkey signed a commercial agreement with Germany in July 1940. Japan joined the other Axis partners to sign the Tripartite Pact on 27 September. Japan was a long way from Turkey but fear of the 'yellow peril' was only dormant in diplomatic circles, as the BJs constantly attest. On 7 October Germany entered Romania and on 28 October Italy attacked Greece. German aircraft and Italian troops were stationed close to the Thracian border by the end of the year. Though Turkey stayed friendly with Britain, Ankara little doubted that Germany would shortly be master of Europe.

For Britain the worst was not over. Germany occupied Bulgaria in March 1941 and Yugoslavia in April. German armies invaded Greece and defeated Greek and Commonwealth troops there. The brief Allied occupation of Crete was brought to a bloody end when the remaining troops were evacuated. While British successes against the Luftwaffe (German air force) in the Battle of Britain and against the Italians by land and sea, as well as her still powerful influence in Persia and Egypt, bolstered her prestige among unaligned nations, German military supremacy was by now the dominating concern of Turkish diplomats. Where would Germany turn next? She had proved unbeatable everywhere, though containable momentarily when Hitler called off the invasion of Britain. The RAF's success against the Luftwaffe in the Battle of Britain seemed only a temporary setback to Germany's unstoppable ambition for world domination. Turkey had to align herself with the future victor.

On 22 June 1941, however, Germany invaded Russia, and Turkish diplomats speculated to each other whether Hitler had finally overreached himself. Turkey was relieved because pressure from both Germany and Russia would be eased so long as they were locked in mortal combat with each other. Germany had opted not to threaten or cajole Turkey to join the fray by allowing German troops and *matériel* through Anatolia towards Egypt and Persia. But the breathing space was short-lived. For the rest of 1941 the fragile alliance between Britain and Russia, celebrated by their joint occupation of Persia in August of that year, and promoted almost single-handedly by Churchill, did little to mitigate the results of the military disasters suffered by Britain in North Africa, or the crippling of her Atlantic supply lines by German U-boats.

For Turkey these setbacks meant that British offers of friendship in arms were irrelevant to her real needs. Diplomatic efforts by the British ambassador in Ankara, Sir Hughe Knatchbull-Hugessen and Foreign Secretary Anthony Eden were politely shrugged off. A British offer to mediate between Turkey and Russia was ignored. On 10 October 1941 Jodl noted: 'We have won this war'. It was a war which Turkish diplomacy, given sufficient skill and nerve – and İnönü had plenty despite his frail appearance, deafness and lack of popular appeal – would keep her doing nicely out of it rather than in it, rather like Sweden and Switzerland. As indeed it proved.

For readers of diplomatic decrypts, the early months of 1942 saw Rommel driving the British relentlessly eastwards in North Africa and a new enemy, Japan, striking south as the Germans had done in Europe so that Malaya, Burma and Indo-China were soon part of the East Asian Co-Prosperity Region. The Japanese were dominant in the Indian Ocean, talking of invading Australia and/or India, and of linking up with their Axis partners somewhere near the Persian Gulf. The world war had become a reality and few doubted who would be the victor, for Allied shipping losses in January–June 1942 were insupportable. The Germans had intercepted and read British codes and ciphers and knew the whereabouts of all convoys of importance while it took the British a further year to crack the German naval code.[26] While the Turkish leadership was not to know the full extent of Allied defeat, it knew from its ambassador that Churchill was in a deep and understandable depression. On 12 February 1942 the British surrendered at Singapore, and Sir Alexander Cadogan in the FO noted 'it was the blackest day of the war'.[27]

In Ankara Sukru Saraçoğlu had just become prime minister and shortly afterwards Numan Menemencioğlu was appointed foreign minister. March saw Turkish diplomats abroad reporting armistice approaches between Germany and Russia with sometimes Turkey, sometimes Sweden, sometimes the Iberian nations named as would-be mediators. İnönü proclaimed Turkish neutrality. Diplomatic intercepts yielded signs in March and April that Germany would attack Turkey as part of her spring offensive, while in Berlin Japanese ambassador Hiroshi Oshima confidently predicted global German victory. May saw further evidence of possible peace negotiations between Russia and Germany. The Spanish thought the Allies had decided to occupy Turkey. Molotov, visiting in Washington, called for a second front in the west in 1942. In June a delegation of Turkish arms dealers were treated by Hitler to a lecture in international history and to his assurances of undying friendship between the two countries. In June Tobruk fell to Rommel with the loss to Britain of face and booty. The intercepts were full of it.

While the Turkish leadership was slowly adjusting to the prospect of German omnipotence and the inevitability of a Russian request to revise the terms of the Montreux Convention, Churchill was still hankering after Turkey. From the intercepts he could observe others failing to handle Turkey effectively. The Turks resented the arrogance of British soldiers, Eden failed to impress his counterparts in Ankara and Hugessen wrote long reports but failed to make headway against the Turkish diplomats resolved to stay neutral. The Germans had decided to leave Turkey in a state of benevolent neutrality monitored by their ambassador, Franz von Papen, and the Russians had other matters on their minds. The Turks suspected that the British neither could nor would keep their promises about the supply of equipment for the army. The Turkey hand was being played, in fact, rather ineptly; Churchill's concern with Turkey, testified to by his doctor, his colleagues, and himself in his account of these traumatic months of the war, was so intense that he would play the hand himself. And at the end of January 1943 he did.

It was not until the end of 1942 that the tide of war turned – El Alamein on 4 November and Stalingrad on 23 November. Meanwhile American successes in the Pacific were followed by Allied landings at Casablanca and Oran. BJs of the period buzzed with these events. A new belligerent, the United States, was as worrying to Ankara as the new Soviet successes in the south, bringing Soviet claims as a Black Sea littoral nation back into the minds of the Turkish leadership. Pressures on Turkey to join (or not to join) the Axis or the Allies continued till October when Soviet successes in the Caucasus and in the north eased German pressure on Turkey. By the end of the month the neutral Portuguese diplomats reflected that Germany, who had lost the First World War through exhaustion was now likely to lose the second in the same way.[28]

This was the background to Churchill's Turkish visit in January 1943, the hidden trick in the Turkey hand. We have seen that his interest in Turkey was out of all proportion to Turkey's likely usefulness on the Allied side in a combined operation. The Foreign Secretary joined the Chiefs of Staff and the rest of the War Cabinet in attempting, and failing, to head off Churchill's Turkish trip en route from the Casablanca Conference in January 1943. But despite what followed, or failed to follow, from that extraordinary encounter in the railway carriages parked in the wasteland in the slush and snow of the Mediterranean winter, Churchill's instinct seemed vindicated, and Turkey's views of the comparative merits of friendship with the Allies or the Axis were never the same again.

Post-Adana there was much martial activity in Turkey but the course of the war in the eastern Mediterranean remained static until the resignation of Mussolini in June 1943. This caused a flurry of Turkish ambassadorial reports to and from Ankara. Would the Allies achieve a quick victory? Would Italy make a separate peace? Would Japan insist on a reassertion of the Tripartite Pact? Would Germany invade the Dodecanese and arrive on Turkey's doorstep with one eye on the pipelines of Persia of which only Turkey now stood in the way? All the Balkans were as shocked by Italy's collapse in 1943 as by the fall of France in 1940. In fact it presaged an early Allied victory which never quite came off. For the Allies it proved a false dawn, as their conquest of Italy dragged on and the Germans retook the Dodecanese.

The war took on a different aspect in Ankara after January 1943. Protestations of friendship were followed by two British military missions, to bring Turkey into the war by providing equipment and training. It was not an easy agenda and it was not successfully carried out. Britain failed to provide what was needed. Direct American involvement ensued. Whether for this reason or as part of a complex strategy to maintain her neutrality, Turkey's demands escalated. Reconditioned Hurricanes were rejected for new Spitfires which had been promised. Guns urgently needed elsewhere could be ill spared to a country which perhaps could not use them and might never need them. Churchill himself goaded his reluctant Chiefs of Staff partly to save his own credibility, but his own powers were less than total and all he could offer the Turks when begging in America was his moral support. The second front in the west had to be postponed again, not once but twice. Stalin's ill-concealed fury found outlets in threats of patching up peace between the Soviet Union and a battered Germany – something regarded with equal dread by the Turks and the British. It was not until 6 June 1944 that the second front finally became a reality, and Turkish neutrality at that point ceased to be interesting or relevant to final victory.

CHAPTER TWO

Churchill's Diplomatic Intercepts

All the years I have been in office since it [Room 40] began in the autumn of 1914
I have read every one of these flimsies and attach more importance to them . . .
than to any other source of knowledge at the disposal of the state.

Winston Churchill to Austen Chamberlain, November 1924
(in Chamberlain's papers at Birmingham University library)

Any analysis of Churchill's use of diplomatic intercepts must start by an attempt to answer the question of how those intercepts came to be in the possession of the British government in the first place. The first section of this chapter tackles a cognate question: who produced them, and how?

Diplomatic eavesdropping in Britain in 1922 was not a new or recent practice, but the coming of wireless telegraphy (W/T) at the turn of the century gave access, via interception and decryption, to greatly increased volumes of traffic. Much of this would have been worthless, emanating from chancelleries without power or influence to affect the course of European affairs. But not all. For the victors in the First World War and from the signing of the Treaty of Versailles, British, French, Italian and American code-breaking departments were reinstated or established.[1] In Britain the history of signals intelligence, or sigint, has concentrated on the Admiralty code-breaking department in Room 40 OB (Old Buildings) from 1914 to 1918, and the interwar abuse of Soviet cipher insecurity, fuelling the anti-Bolshevik scares of the 1920s and precipitating a Soviet change to a more secure cipher system. The year 1939 brought not only a new world war but a new dimension of cryptanalysis involving breaking machine-enciphered messages. The Enigma breakthrough and what followed therefrom has been well documented. This chapter traces recent research into non-service – i.e. diplomatic – traffic, some of which was enciphered by systems which predated machine encipherment. The period covered includes the interwar years.

The nature of prewar intercepts can be identified by the diplomatic component of the files that came to Churchill from MI6 from late 1941 to VJ-Day. It was called DIR/C, and in the Public Record Office system it is known as HW1. This material (still described by retired government officials as the 'intercepts') can now be assessed, because Churchill was not only a prime user of diplomatic sigint but a compulsive hoarder of any and all papers that came his way, and it is his daily files of intercepts that have been released. They provide the first, and almost only, indication that diplomatic eavesdropping, on friends, neutrals and enemies, was an important part of the British cryptanalytical war effort. Churchill's use of it, particularly in 1943, and particularly the Turkish messages, is the main theme.

Extrapolating backwards it is possible to discern some of the prewar work, undertaken under the auspices of the FO by the SIS, which had to be done to make possible the wartime achievements of Bletchley Park. Unlike the war period, now extensively documented and researched, the evidence for the prewar period remains scanty and the literature somewhat specialised. While most war historians are familiar with the work of Bletchley Park, in particular the breaking on a continuous basis of the German machine cipher Enigma and the distribution of the resulting decrypts in a process called Ultra, few scholars so far have more than anecdotal evidence for the history, the people and the evolving processes within the British secret establishment which enabled Enigma to be read and Ultra to function from 1940 onwards. What and who made this achievement possible in the years before 1939? The claim made here is that a small group of non-established civil servants lodged in the FO and working on diplomatic intercepts from 1917 (and on naval and military messages since 1914) rose to the occasion in 1941 to provide the British war leadership with invaluable information on the state of the enemy. If that is proved true, it will answer an important question about Churchill's contribution to Allied victory.[2]

The Classical Cryptographers

The main sources for what follows consist of two documents, one handwritten until typed in 1994, covering the First World War, the other the interwar period, both deposited in the Churchill Archives in Cambridge.[3] By linking the names which appear in both documents, and the cryptographic processes described in them, it becomes possible to sketch the progress of British cryptography from 1915 to 1939 from a primary source, part of which has not hitherto been referred to in print.[4] The First World War document, which bears no signature, was written by Cdr Alastair Denniston to answer an enquiry put to him by Adm Sir William ('Bubbles') James, who wished to include a chapter on Room 40 in his autobiography, which was eventually published as *The Skies Were Always Blue*. The second, also written by Denniston in 1944, also unsigned, was to rebut an assumption made by the then head of GCCS, Gp Capt Eric Jones, that GCCS had failed to prepare effectually for the cryptographic needs of the Second World War.

Cryptography lies at the heart of secret signals intelligence. It is a misleading word, though used by 'the classical cryptographers' of Britain's codebreaking operation,[5] because it implies only the creation and security of codes and ciphers, whereas the key part of the job, carried out by all the major European powers since the establishment of W/T, was the reading of the secret diplomatic ciphers of other nations. And reading them (i.e. successfully and continuously solving them) was only part of an operation which started with interception and the channelling of raw, authentic, relevant Morse messages to a central decryption unit, manned by 'specialists' (i.e. cryptographers), and concluded with translation, assessment and distribution in suitable form to the appropriate clients. Each part of the total process was essential for the production of useful signals intelligence. Yet all these aspects were embraced in the one word cryptography. This extended meaning will be used here. Efficient interception and intelligent assessment both proved as important as decryption in the total cryptographic process whereby wireless intelligence on the activities of foreign nationals was made available to named departments and individuals within the British government who could use the information in foreign policy reports and recommendations.

This chapter charts the work done on diplomatic cipher messages between the wars by the classical cryptographers which brought both Ultra and medium-grade diplomatic intercepts from 1941 till VE-Day. The interwar activities of these cryptographers, learning from their own experience and mistakes, despite their exiguous resources, made possible the successful handling of the exponential increase in traffic occasioned by the breaking of the Luftwaffe Enigma cipher (using hand methods) in January 1940, which in turn played a key part in turning probable British defeat in 1940 into Allied victory in 1945.

It was a group drawn from different backgrounds – academia, the aristocracy, business, the stage, teachers, servicemen, university graduates and GPO trainees. All were linguists and most were proficient in mathematics.[6] All practised critical analysis. Some had worked on naval and diplomatic intercepts in the First World War. Other key figures joined when GCCS was set up in 1919. A Russian refugee joined in 1925. Only two women, one the wife of the Director of Naval Intelligence, Adm Godfrey and the other the sister of 'C' (Adm Sinclair), were specialists, showing the closed circle of initiates. Two had made the Zimmermann telegram readable in 1916. It was their common perception of the interlocking requirements of the service, enabling them to deliver relevant messages on time to the right people, which may justify the use of the word 'group' in describing the informal, collegial approach to their clandestine work from Room 40 in 1914 to Bletchley in 1942, work which played an understated part in turning defeat into victory.

This section has introduced the cryptographers who made Churchill's reading of diplomatic intercepts possible. But he was no stranger to the interception of German naval signals, as the next section makes clear.

Churchill's Intercepts: the First World War

At the beginning of the First World War German wireless signals were being easily intercepted but no one knew what to do with them. Under Sir Alfred Ewing and Adm Reginald 'Blinker' Hall[7] the founder-members of the group helped to solve that problem. Whether Winston Churchill, then First Lord of the Admiralty, was a help or a hindrance is a moot point, but his understanding of the importance of signals intelligence in the Second World War, which no one now doubts, can now be matched with his enthusiasm for the naval intercepts of Room 40 from 1914 onwards.[8] For it was he who as First Lord of the Admiralty directed, on 29 November 1914, that a particular naval officer[9] selected by the Admiralty to monitor the German messages that were pouring in, was:

> to study the telegrams with a view to finding out the general scheme of the enemy, and tracing how far the reports of the telegrams have in the past been verified as recorded facts . . . The telegrams when intercepted will go direct and exclusively to COS.[10]

Churchill had immediately spotted the political value of these golden eggs, and the need to protect the goose that laid them, though his rules of procedure had to be drastically changed. Characteristically, he steered them past the new Director of Naval Intelligence, Hall, and would not leave the procedures to the people doing the work.[11] The arrangements he made in 1914 for handling naval intercepts bear a strong resemblance to the orders he gave out for getting Ultra to him in 1941.

Very early in 1915 Churchill, together with Adm 'Jackie' Fisher, the First Sea Lord, made a disastrous decision with consequences which affected British standing in the Near East for a generation. Never one to enjoy sharing knowledge that brings power with anyone, and particularly not with one, like 'Blinker' Hall, as enterprising and ambitious as himself, he received from Hall information which would have averted the Dardanelles campaign fiasco. Hall had despatched two emissaries to persuade or bribe the Turks to break with Germany and allow the Royal Navy a free passage through the Dardanelles.[12] Negotiations were protracted and not helped by the alternative agenda of the FO, but on 13 March Hall read an intercept:

From Nauen to Constantinople.
12.3.15. Most Secret. For Admiral Usedom. HM the Kaiser has received the report and telegram relating to the Dardanelles. Everything conceivable is being done to arrange the supply of ammunition. For political reasons it is necessary to maintain a confident tone in Turkey. The Kaiser requests you to use your influence in this direction. The sending of a German or Austrian submarine is being seriously considered. By command of All Highest. v Müller.[13]

Hall took the intercept to Churchill who said, 'that means they [the Turks] have come to the end of their ammunition'. Hall then updated Churchill on his private initiative to buy off the Turks. His emissaries were Griffin Ender and Edwin Whittal. They met a Turkish emissary at Dedeagatch on 15 March 1915. Hall informed Hankey of these negotiations on 4 March. Much later (on 7 October 1937), he sent his account of the episode to Capt (then Sir Herbert) Richmond, adding:

> I had no cabinet authority for the money then. Because of the Turkish shortage of ammunition and the inability of the Germans to make good the shortage for at least a week, victory to them seemed inevitable.[14]

In his Churchill encounter in 1915, Hall went on to add, 'If we were to get peace, or if we were to get a peaceful passage for that amount [up to £4,000,000] I imagine . . . [the cabinet] would be glad enough to pay.' This money paid into a Turkish bank would have split off the Turks from the Germans and allowed the Royal Navy a free passage through the Dardanelles, thus averting the catastrophe that threatened. Churchill refused to sanction the bribe, the campaign duly started, and this may have accounted for his subsequent unavailing pursuit of a Turkish alliance in the Second World War.[15]

Between the Wars

The armistice in 1918, followed by an acute cash crisis in Whitehall, threatened the continuity of Room 40 and its military counterpart, MI 1B, but not for long. Unlike the State Department in Washington, the FO continued to monitor peacetime diplomatic messages into and out of London and as many European capitals as could legitimately be targeted by cable scrutiny as well as by intercept stations. Funds were made available, procedures and priorities were established, and the Government Code and Cipher School (GCCS), was formally set up on 1 November 1919.

The key to the whole operation was, and is, interception. Without interception there can be no intercepts and no clandestine eavesdropping. The British seem to have been alone in adding cable interference as an additional means of reading messages – though telephone tapping became standard international practice in the 1930s, and tapping into other peoples' landlines may also have been practised. The operation of censorship is impossible to track, for lack of any references in the files. But the building of intercept stations in the interwar period in England, Scotland, Iraq and India was on a substantial scale, whose funding has only recently been identified.[16]

GCCS was the responsibility of the Head of the Secret Intelligence Services, but for reasons of security became the 'adopted child' of the FO, of which it was in fact a department. Both parents valued this unacknowledgeable child. In the case of the head of SIS, Adm Hugh

Sinclair, the evidence for this is largely negative. Sinclair allowed GCCS's distribution of Russian commercial and diplomatic intercepts to be used politically to expose the horrors of the revolution, thus compromising the work with the result that the Soviets resorted to the OTP which made their traffic unreadable for many years to come.[17] Sinclair has been almost entirely weeded out of the FO files but, despite his Russian blunder, those who worked for him (and his sister) held him in such respect and admiration that the group must have forgiven him; and under him GCCS continued to function effectively up to the time that he bought Bletchley Park for the nation in 1938, and his death in November 1939.[18]

The role of the FO as foster-father is easier to trace from the record but more difficult to evaluate. The cultural climate of the prewar FO was many-layered but at the top lay, like thick cream on a trifle, an Eton, Winchester and Oxbridge elite. For these people integration would have diluted their privileges by association with the Consular Service and the refugee specialists, linguists and ex-servicemen of GCCS. The crossover between the FO and GCCS may also have been limited by the absence of any career structure in the latter, as well as by its formidable linguistic requirements. But the FO could recognise value when they saw it, as they did as early as October 1922, when the distribution of Turkish diplomatic intercepts within Whitehall kept the authorities au fait with the dangerous Turkish and Greek military build-up in Thrace which resulted in the Chanak crisis.[19]

These 1922 intercepts, shared by those in power in Britain, revealed the extent of Turkish anger at the unprovoked bellicosity of the Greeks, from whom first Italy and then France withdrew support, leaving only Britain to back an untimely attempt to keep Turkey out of Europe. A year later GCCS's successful reading of the Soviet diplomatic cipher brought about a diplomatic crisis which nearly precipitated a confrontation with the Bolshevik leaders.[20] Both these crises were managed by the cabinet on the basis of the diplomatic decrypts of GCCS. In 1922 Churchill and Lloyd George regularly discussed their content and implications, while Sinclair, who as Head of the Secret Intelligence Services saw them routinely, encouraged their use as a means of expelling two leading Bolshevik diplomats then in London, though he later regretted this.[21] Fifteen years later when the Italians uncharacteristically erupted south-east into Abyssinia and west into participation in the Spanish Civil War, increased volume of diplomatic and naval traffic, mostly Italian, enabled GCCS not only to break machine and other ciphers but to contribute to foreign policy. Anthony Eden, to whom historians have not been kind, then personally drafted a successful request to the Treasury for funds to cover GCCS's enhanced activities in 1936–37.[22] The War Office lent its support to the expansion: 'This form of intelligence must be thoroughly organised in peace and . . . the cost entailed merely represents a small insurance premium.'[23]

At the end of 1919 GCCS employed 66 staff. This number went up to 94 in 1924, of whom 65 were support staff. By 1935 there were 104 on the payroll, of which 67 were support staff. The Abyssinian War produced a temporary need for Italian specialists, some of whom were laid off when the emergency receded, but the remainder supplied a firm basis for Bletchley's outstanding Italian section. A few were allowed to stay on because other and larger shadows were looming. In 1939 there were 125, of whom 88 were support staff. Of the 37 senior and junior assistants recruited between the wars and employed in 1939, many served throughout the war and into the Cold War period – testimony to the success of the informal and even eccentric method of recruiting practised by the head of GCCS.

Little is said about formal training, which perhaps tells its own story. About training the War Office early on took the view that 'the only way a man can learn to be a cryptographer is by devilling for an expert. A training programme would be an impossibility.'[24] The senior assistants were all proven cryptographers with a track-record of achievement and expertise stretching back in some cases to 1915. Cryptography (or cryptology, to use the American word) has a history which goes back to ancient Egypt, and in the USA formal cryptanalytical training, including the history of the subject, was promoted by the Head of Army Signals Intelligence, William Friedman.[25] He had studied the subject academically as well as being an outstanding practitioner. Other than Oliver Strachey's notes of his lectures to GCCS recruits in Churchill College, Cambridge, there is little evidence of similar training in the 1920s, which suggests that training was mostly 'on the job', and this is confirmed by the memoirs of recruits to Bletchley Park between 1940 and 1943.[26] By then the techniques were changing so fast, and the work to be done was so urgent, that formal training may well have been impossible. In the prewar GCCS the head and his deputy and the senior assistants were considerable cryptographers, but regarded their job as too hush-hush even to give it a name, much less a pedigree and academic respectability. They referred to 'special work' as opposed to 'administrative duties'.

The age and previous experience of most recruits, until the arrival of Oxbridge graduates in the mid-1930s, would indicate that a career structure within GCCS would have been impossible anyhow. Within the FO and Diplomatic Service as a whole there was, of course, a clear structure. GCCS's staff, both senior and junior, was explicitly bound out of this. Any crossover between the Diplomatic Service and GCCS, was minimal.[27] Yet to achieve what GCCS undoubtedly did required intelligence, dedication, discretion, flair, self-discipline and self-motivation of an uncommonly high order. The dichotomy between what was needed and the lack of incentives, both for recruits and experienced staff, was acknowledged by the head of GCCS:

It must be remembered that beyond a salary and accommodation vote GCCS had no financial status; it became in fact an adopted child of the Foreign Office with no family rights, and the poor relation of SIS whose peacetime activities left little cash to spare.[28]

GCCS's relations with other parts of government changed when Sinclair died on 8 November 1939. He held the trust, loyalty and affection of all the staff, and his death at such a crucial moment was the worst possible news for them. Denniston himself never recovered professionally, and found it difficult to share problems with his successor. 'The Admiral' was, indeed, irreplaceable: he understood the high degree of autonomy essential to cryptography. He ensured that the specialists worked in conditions appropriate to the intellectual strains of their work. He moved confidently in the highest Whitehall circles of power. Menzies's role as Director of Bletchley Park is more difficult to assess, and outside the scope of this chapter. He certainly kept Churchill supplied with intercepts, and regularly annotated them in green ink right through the war. He successfully protected their security.

By whatever means and to whatever effect, GCCS had developed a capacity for diplomatic eavesdropping on every major country except Germany, enhancing traditional practices in the light of experience and the intelligent application of critical analysis. The recruiting of cipher-brains destined to play a vital part at Bletchley might have appeared haphazard and restricted but the results must with hindsight be said to have been remarkable. Prof Peter Hennessy, the historian of Whitehall wrote:

> Commander Denniston, head of GCCS and one of the best-informed people in Whitehall when it came to events in Europe, was . . . at his desk in Broadway that Sunday [3 September 1939], drafting a letter to the Clerk's Department in the Foreign Office which controlled his manpower. Referring with sublime understatement to the activities of Hitler, he wrote: 'For some days now we have been obliged to recruit from our emergency list men of the professor type who the Treasury agreed to pay at the rate of £600 a year. I attached herewith a list of these gentlemen already called up together with the dates of their joining. I will keep you informed at intervals of further recruitment.'

The first list included Nigel de Grey, one of the Zimmermann telegram codebreakers, and Professors E.R.P. 'Vinca' Vincent and Tom Boase, both Italian specialists who worked at BP throughout the war. The second list 'was even more glittering with some of the greatest names ever to work in the trade'.[29] They included E.R. Norman, John Jeffries, Gordon Welchman, Frank Adcock, Hugh Last and Alan Turing. Of these at least three were to become crucially important to the work of Bletchley Park. The belief of the seniors at GCCS that trawling Oxbridge for bright graduates was not just the only but the best way to solve the new cryptographic problems led to the assembly at Bletchley by the end of 1939 of 'the ablest team of cryptographers and intelligence analysts in British history'.[30] But even before they joined in late 1939 GCCS had made significant strides towards providing a total cryptographic service to those in government able and willing to use it. How this took place is the subject of the section that follows.

While the relationship of GCCS to the FO is documented, it also had a totally secret relationship to the Secret Intelligence Services (SIS) whose interwar head, Adm Hugh Sinclair, had acquired responsibility not only for GCCS but also Interception and Direction Finding.[31] This enabled GCCS to develop a number of intelligent enhancements of their strictly cryptographic work. The first of these was Traffic Analysis (TA).[32] This was the scanning of a targeted subject's wireless activity when the actual messages could not be read but the volume and direction of them might indicate future activity. TA was acceptable when the cryptographer was temporarily unproductive, because the scale, intensity and direction of signals emanating from a targeted station could yield trustworthy information. TA played an important part in tactical planning, and indeed led in 1942 to a whole world of Y (or low-grade tactical) sigint.

The second was Direction Finding (DF), whereby the origin of a stream of signals and the location of a targeted enemy signals station could be worked out mathematically, by tracking the volume and direction of messages and applying co-ordinates. DF and TA were not useful in relation to diplomatic as distinct from service traffic. Diplomatic signals all came from fixed sources and the ups and downs in its volume did not reveal much. However, the work of GCCS and its outstations between the wars on TA and DF developed into the successful and secret Radio Security Service, which provided continuous useful traffic for all three branches of the British armed forces from 1941–45.

Perhaps even more significant was the evaluation of what should be fully processed and circulated, and what should not.[33] Eighty-five per cent of traffic processed was never distributed. The credibility of what was circulated depended on eliminating the inessential, the marginal, the boring and the irrelevant. Keeping the customer happy was an essential part of this assessment, and required an intimate knowledge of the workings of Whitehall minds.

A conviction arising from GCCS's response to interwar diplomatic eavesdropping was that apart from secure machine encipherment only the OTP would stay impervious to cryptanalytical attack. OTPs are essentially codes only available for one message, and known only to sender and recipient. The sender indicates the page, the column and the line where the message is to start in the first group of the signal. Other groups of numbers are added, and once used the whole page is torn off the pad and destroyed. GCCS between the wars promoted OTP, which became standard procedure for British diplomatic and Most Secret Source traffic throughout the war.[34] One disadvantage of OTP is the scale of the printing requirement. Oxford University Press was the chief supplier of OTPs to the government, through HMSO, in the Second World War. Since it had unfilled capacity and a deserved reputation for discretion it proved a valued supplier.[35]

Some of the classical cryptographers and their support staff, with their different backgrounds and skills, working in close proximity with each other over the years, formed a group, became friends, played golf together and got to know the wives and children of other members. GCCS became known humorously as the Golf Club and Chess Society, a soubriquet bestowed on it by Dilwyn Knox. To what extent is the word 'group' applicable? Nigel West takes the view that for more than twenty years 'Denniston essentially *was* GCCS'.[36] An alternative theory emerges from the foregoing that under his leadership a group of like-minded but differentially talented civil servants evolved together a strategy which, while dealing adequately with the needs of the 1920s and 1930s, successfully anticipated the wartime requirements of a greatly enhanced cryptological bureau, and thus enabled Churchill and his government to read German intentions on a comprehensive basis from January 1940 till May 1945.

There is sufficient evidence that group-thinking prevailed from 1933 till 1940 to evolve the systems and practices which led to the successful breaking of Luftwaffe Enigma and its distribution on a continuous basis from January 1940. That in turn led to other Enigma successes, and to Ultra, which got the messages at speed to Churchill and the other relevant users. And that played a significant part in the Allied victory against the U-boats, and in Europe and the Far East. There is a strong microcosmic resemblance between the cryptographic structures and working practices of the First World War and the interwar period on the one hand, and the greatly expanded but still recognisably similar work of the 'huts' at Bletchley Park 1939–45.

Diplomatic Intercepts in the 1930s

By 1936 the substitution of German aggression for the Bolshevik threat was high on the FO agenda and GCCS was correspondingly required to reallocate its resources accordingly. While the German diplomatic cipher 'Floradora' remained unrecovered, Italian and Japanese traffic, together with that of Turkey and other countries, enabled GCCS to keep its masters fully informed of the approach of war. But who read the intercepts? How did the GCCS product figure in the minds of the Secretary of State, the mandarins at the FO, politicians in the know and service chiefs who preferred their secret intelligence brought to them by their own people? The evidence for the prewar period is slight, but in practice anyone above the grade of Third Secretary had access to them.[37]

What is even more difficult to discover is what the FO made of its intercepts. The head of GCCS does not mention what happened to BJs after they left his office. The distribution lists of wartime BJs indicate that the head of the Civil Service, Sir Edward Bridges, received a copy of everything circulated.[38] Under the rules of its establishment GCCS delivered selected material to the FO and later to the service ministries. Sir Robert Vansittart

had his own sources of secret intelligence and must have read BJs. Eligibility
to handle them was a function of FO bureaucracy. Ordinary outgoing and
incoming telegraphic correspondence were treated differently from the
receipt of intelligence from SIS and GCCS. The former was dealt with in
the Communications Department, ciphered or deciphered, typed and
circulated. There was a distinction between the 'circulation' and the work on
the telegrams in the separate departments. The circulation of all but
telegrams classified Secret or Most (later Top) Secret was very wide
throughout the FO. But incoming telegrams (as other incoming
correspondence) would be 'entered' in the appropriate registry and
submitted by it to the department which it served. In the department all
papers would go to the junior in the 'Third Room' (who could be a second
or even a first secretary) responsible for the subject in question. Material
received from SIS and GCCS came direct to the office of the permanent
under-secretary and distributed from there under the direction of the latter's
private secretary, who was responsible for the FO's relations with GCCS
and MI6. BJs relevant to Turkey, for instance, would then go to the
Southern Department which had been carved out of the old Central
Department in 1932. The increased Italian traffic produced important
information in the mid-1930s which would have been evaluated in the
Southern Department, and would 'be taken into account in forming
judgments on situations or making recommendations for action. Their
contribution could, of course, be very important.'[39]

It is impossible to be more specific about prewar BJ reading, and this
makes difficult the assessment of the direct value of intercepts in the
formation of government foreign policy before the advent of Churchill. The
question is indeed unanswerable because they were but a part of the
information-gathering service on which the FO based its advice to ministers.
Moreover GCCS was making only slow progress on the German diplomatic
machine cipher, of vital importance to the FO, until 1943. FO officials, like
most other civil servants, read what was brought to them without too many
questions about what could not be decrypted. They would have had
preconceived ideas of what was important. They might reject whatever
relevant information conflicted with these ideas. In general, their classical
education made them philhellenic, which may by the same token have
disposed them to be anti-Turk. Moreover, they had other sources of
information on international diplomacy, privileged news and views, both
clandestine and semi-official, in addition to BJs.

To the reports of British military, air and naval attachés in most European
capitals could be added the results of monitoring foreign press and
broadcasts, covering much of the same ground as the BJs. The value of BJs
was their pristine quality. Without any mediating factor beyond GCCS's
decision that they were worth circulating, they conveyed what Britain's
friends and enemies, well-wishers and ill-wishers, thought about the coming
hostilities. In the main, judging from wartime diplomatic intercepts, they

would have been ambassadorial reports on conditions, events and comment on the countries for which they were responsible. But interception was a limited option since most European countries safeguarded their cipher security by using landlines for their communications. The Germans invested heavily in machine encipherment. Targeting Japan, Italy and Turkey so effectively produced important information, in the case of Turkey through cable scrutiny at the Constantinople headquarters of Cable & Wireless, in which the British government was a major shareholder, thus empowering itself to read Turkish traffic on a 'complete coverage' basis. After the Montreux Conference of 1936, Turkey became a prime target, from which the FO learned many patterns of decision making in Ankara, and the nature of Turkish diplomatic priorities, particularly in relation to Italy, France, Germany and Britain.[40]

GCCS's Interwar Achievements

Against a background of recently released files which reveal strong criticism in 1945 of the prewar GCCS's pessimistic attitude towards the breaking of German machine codes, it may now be appropriate to summarise the four major interwar achievements of GCCS.[41] The first was the deep penetration of the diplomatic codes of Turkey, Italy, Russia, Japan, Iberia and the USA. The Turkish traffic already referred to, obtained in full, with minimum delay and without any 'corrupt groups' thanks to Cable & Wireless's efficient service, deserves singling out. A file in the House of Lords' library contains copies of the actual Turkey-sourced BJs on which Churchill, Curzon and Lloyd George relied in attempting to thwart Turkish aggression at Smyrna in October 1922.[42] These intercepts were translated from the French by the fledgling GCCS in Melbury Road, Kensington. In all essentials they are identical to later BJs which were sent to named individuals in government from then on continuously until 1945. According to the Lloyd George files, copies of the intercepts went routinely to a printed distribution list which included the directors of service intelligence, senior ministers including Lloyd George, Curzon and Churchill, and Sir Basil Thompson (head of security at the Home Office). All through the Chanak crisis of October 1922 the diplomatic messages from the Turkish ambassador in Paris to Constantinople were the required reading of the policy makers.[43] Thus BJs were, even at this early stage, at the heart of British foreign policy.

The second achievement was the coverage of the total process of sigint from interception to distribution without which any one aspect was unable to fulfil its function. It is this second achievement which this chapter seeks to underline, because without a worked out functional system, acceptable to all, available to the Enigma specialists at Bletchley in 1939, the results of their achievement – usable high grade sigint or Ultra – might have been unavailable to the British armed forces by mid-1941.[44]

By September 1938 GCCS was on a war footing and under Sinclair had completed a successful dummy run, simulating war conditions, at a time when the appeasers still thought they had bought peace in their time. At the FO the diplomatic intercepts GCCS distributed round Whitehall told a different story, requiring a different policy, promoted by the Deputy Permanent Under-Secretary, Sir Orme Sargent, who acquired such a reputation as an anti-appeaser that he was nicknamed 'Moley' by his colleagues, after the character in *The Wind in the Willows* who could not let his friends off with easy answers. Sir Alexander Cadogan and most other ranking mandarins with access to the intercepts were of the same mind. Relations between GCCS and the FO can only be guessed at because no files survive, all intercept material was burnt immediately after reading and all references to GCCS and its product required modification to 'special' or 'reliable sources' before appearing in governmental minutes. Despite this reticence there must be a strong thread joining the diplomatic intercepts and the now famous FO opposition to Chamberlain's policy towards Hitler. This is the third of GCCS's interwar achievements.[45]

GCCS may have had its own political stance towards the German menace. Its members rallied round Vansittart whose views on the German menace they preferred to Cadogan and Eden, whom in turn they preferred to Halifax. Reading intercepts with this background would have produced a more radically anti-appeasement view even than that of the FO. Also discernible in the sparse literature is a significant difference in the group's attitude towards its clients.[46] Among the service ministries the Air Ministry, the newest and most flexible in its mindset, was judged the best customer. The Admiralty still had its own intelligence assessment department, using raw data from GCCS, while the War Office only realised the importance of sigint in the field during the fighting in North Africa in 1942. These attitudes are important because they formed the basis of the assessment of what should be circulated and to whom. Knowing your customers' character as well as his needs was part of GCCS's expertise. This, in turn, was a function of GCCS's autonomy, which had become such an accepted feature of the Whitehall landscape that it extended right through the Second World War. GCCS had won for itself the power to decide what its customers should read and hence influence policy. Without having established this degree of authority over all aspects of the total sigint operation in the years between the Spanish Civil War and the outbreak of hostilities on 3 September 1939, GCCS could not have developed its wartime role with so little delay. That is the fourth achievement of British cryptography before 1939.

The interwar period culminated for GCCS in two visits paid to mainland Europe in 1939 by GCCS's head – the first to Paris in January and the second to Poland in late August. Denniston, Knox and Menzies himself travelled by ferry and train across France and Germany to Poland. At Pryr, near Warsaw, the British and French parties learned that the Poles could read Enigma (though not currently) and would give two Enigma machines to France and Britain, knowing their chances of survival were slight. An Enigma machine was brought from Warsaw to Paris, thence via London to Bletchley, where a new generation of British cryptographers soon achieved amazing results on an almost daily basis, culminating in the breaking of the Luftwaffe cipher in January 1940.[47]

These four achievements together with the successful reading of the diplomatic ciphers of many countries and the recruiting campaigns of 1937–39 made possible the activities of Bletchley Park in 1939, which became by June 1940 vital to Churchill's conduct of the British war effort. Enigma was then, after many agonising difficulties had been overcome, integrated into GCCS's existing but enhanced structures and practices, while Ultra was a natural development of the interwar distribution system.

The process was immensely demanding and there were casualties. But there was no alternative. In 1940 and 1941 Britain did indeed stand alone. Her armies had been outclassed in Norway, France and Libya, while the Royal Navy had failed to protect convoys carrying vital war *matériel*. If the RAF had not defeated the Luftwaffe over British air space in September 1940, Hitler would have launched Operation 'Sealion' and Britain might well have been occupied like Denmark, like Hungary, like Romania. A British government-in-exile would have been established in Canada. A gauleiter from Berlin might have installed himself at Whitehall or Buckingham Palace. With access to British war factories, radar and the still formidable navy, Germany could have contemplated the unbelievable and become – what some Germans already felt themselves to be – masters of the western world. It is neither rhetorical nor sentimental to assert of Churchill that he was the saviour of the nation.[48] How he did it has been endlessly discussed. But the part played by Bletchley Park and the geese that 'laid the golden eggs and did not cackle' can be illuminated by tracing both eggs and geese to their point of origin, first in the Admiralty, then in the FO in the twenty years before war was declared.

Churchill's wartime achievement might have been significantly diminished had not British cryptographers served him and the country so effectively from his days as First Lord of the Admiralty in 1914, through the Turkish crisis of the early 1920s, the Russian, Spanish and Italian crises of the 1920s and 1930s, through the period of Hitler's European supremacy, to the breaking of Enigma and the creation and daily working of Ultra all through the war, until 8 May 1945, when the Germans surrendered unconditionally to the Allies.

CHAPTER THREE

Before the Deluge: 1940–41

If the British knew in detail about us everything we know about them [from interception] it could have very grave consequences.

Goebbels, 28 April 1942

Meanwhile she [Germany] is waging a war of nerves with Turkey in the hope that no military action will be necessary.

WO 190/893/22832

The previous chapter has shown the government fully aware of the importance both of diplomatic intercepts and, since the Abyssinian crisis, of the breaking of the Italian naval machine ciphers with its consequential provision of full and immediate information on Italian ship movements in the Mediterranean. This breakthrough was of more immediate use to the service ministries, and in fact became the basis of Enigma and Ultra which developed at Bletchley Park from late 1939. It is upon the implications of the former that this chapter now concentrates. It is divided into two parts, the first reconstructing Churchill's and the FO's view of eastern Mediterranean affairs, and the second attempting to show the results of DIR/C becoming available to Churchill from September 1941.

The Foreign Office and Turkey

Anglo-Turkish relations were a high priority for the FO throughout the 1930s and were developed by Sir Percy Loraine, the British ambassador who preceded the ill-fated Sir Hughe Knatchbull-Hugessen in Ankara. At war with each other in 1914–18, seriously at odds during the Chanak crisis of 1922, both parties realised that there were many advantages in Turco-British friendship. For Britain Turkey would provide a hedge protecting the imperial trade route, Persian oil and a defence against either German or Russian incursions into Egypt; for Turkey, Britain was still unquestionably a superpower, still with a great navy and a great empire.

The FO knew little about the actual economy and government of Turkey outside the main cities and embassy staff rarely ventured into the interior. The few who did reported back on the primitive state of the roads, railways, towns, villages, schools and peasantry. Illiteracy was almost universal, despite Atatürk's social engineering. Only Muslims could bear arms or become magistrates. Democracy was more a matter of good intentions than of actual implementation of policy, which suited both the government and the people. There was never any significant opposition either to Atatürk's reforms or İnönü's more directly dictatorial rule. None of this seems to have affected the traditional FO view that 'Johnny Turk' could be relied on in emergencies, and so in the spring of 1939 a guarantee was offered, similar to those already made to Poland and Romania.

In Ankara the chief government ministers had to balance the advantages of unconditional friendship with Britain against a number of complex and contradictory possibilities: a multilateral alliance with France, whose *mission civilisatrice* had made Turkish society francophone as well as Francophile; with Italy, a powerful and uncertain Mediterranean power under Mussolini; with Russia, feared in its new Bolshevik clothing as well as for its czarist ambitions in the ancient Near East, which had only been discarded momentarily by Lenin in the early 1920s – and with Germany, Turkey's ally of the First World War and now becoming the main force in Europe. There were good but different reasons for staying on friendly terms with all the great powers.

However, Halifax and Chamberlain delayed their approach to Turkey until it was almost too late, and reactions in Ankara to British diplomatic activity in Europe throughout the early months of 1939 grew sceptical. Hitler's Germany was disliked for its arrogance and both feared and admired for the overnight success of its Czech invasion of March 1939. In Britain the Southern Department of the FO continued to assume that Turkish friendship was on open offer, to be taken up as and when required – a dangerous assumption for which the British embassy in Ankara should have taken some blame.[1]

At the FO, first under Eden then Halifax then Eden again, two departments were studying Turkish foreign policy. One was the Southern Department, the other was GCCS. The latter regarded Turkish diplomatic messages as of prime importance because in 1919 and 1922 Turkish and British government leaders read Turkish diplomatic telegrams and based their policy upon what they read. These messages were extracted by GCCS from the full cover of Turkish diplomatic telegrams intercepted by the government-owned Cable & Wireless. These were delivered complete and at speed to GCCS and may only have needed translation from French and assessment by them before distribution.[2] Thus they formed a significant part of the total BJ traffic distributed which might have been out of proportion to their actual importance.

The FO files suggest that Eden inherited this Turkish policy without Churchill's enthusiasm, presumably because his concern over Italy dominated Mediterranean policy. Later he showed little finesse in his dealings with the Turks. After the Italian adventures in Africa and Albania he realised that a benevolently neutral Turkey had become a strategic necessity, but as Minister for War there was little he could do to expedite the

Anglo-Franco-Turkish Pact of 1939.[3] The FO's policy towards Turkey in the run-up to the start of hostilities in 1939 can thus be seen to have been a somewhat haphazard product of a close study of what Turkish diplomats were saying to each other and a hazy conviction, often overlooked when more important countries flexed their muscles, that a friendly Turkey was a useful protection for the imperial trade-routes to the Far East.

Churchill had a more romantic attitude to Turkey while out of office. He had long been interested in the country as an ally in any future world war, remaining as ignorant until 1945 of the true nature of the country's economy and willingness to fight outside its own borders as the FO. Moreover he had been a consistent advocate of the use of diplomatic signals intelligence in its raw, authentic form, as the best means of assessing the intentions of the major powers. Through his friendship with Maj Desmond Morton who had regular access to BJs, he would have been nearly as well informed of Turkish attitudes towards friendship with Britain as the Southern Department itself. By 1940 these two strands in Churchill's thinking – the importance of Turkey and the significance of their diplomatic intercepts – came together. His reading Turkish diplomatic intercepts, several a week before the war, would probably have influenced his Mediterranean view as soon as he became prime minister in May 1940. There was, as has been shown, a twofold reason why Turkish BJs were of particular significance: one was that Cable & Wireless supplied them in full cover, so a complete picture of Turkish international diplomacy was available to the FO on a daily basis. The other was that the Turkish leadership used them as the basis of its foreign policy.

Turkey was governed by a small clique of French-speaking statesmen and diplomats; ambassadors in the main European capitals regularly reported to Angora (as the FO still called the new Turkish capital), and their reports had become the chief source of intelligence for foreign policy decisions. These reports, and the responses of the Ministry for Foreign Affairs, illuminated patterns of decision making in Ankara, the nature of Turkish strategy and its diplomatic relations with other countries, especially the USSR and Britain.[4] Churchill's developing view of the importance of a wartime alliance with Turkey can thus be seen as a somewhat bizarre scheme of an out-of-office politician, while the FO, with daily access to Turkish diplomatic messages, may have underestimated the importance of Turkey. Both shared the regular supply of Turkish intercepts, which made them unusually well-informed of the reactions of an important neutral to the dire results of deep German penetration across Europe in the immediately following months, but their interpretation may have been different. The consequences of German success, however, were so dangerous to Britain, whose survival was seriously in doubt, that Turkish attitudes became of secondary importance to Churchill's expressed strategy, which was to get through the next three months, as is made clear in the section that follows.

The Phoney War

The nine months of the 'Phoney War' constitute a black hole in Turco-British relations. The FO files are sparse, Germany was about to spread its claws all over Europe. The French were keener than the British during this period on aggressive forays in the Near East, to reduce Germany's war effectiveness by bombing the Baku oilfields, as recommended by Adm Darlan and Gen Weygand on 22 February 1940.[5] France also wanted to make a pact with Turkey similar to the Turco-British Guarantee but the Turks would only agree if Britain was party to this also. Thus the Turco-British-French Pact was agreed, on the basis of which Dr Carl Clodius (the German trade negotiator) later tried to persuade the Turks to let Germany have the chrome otherwise due to go to France, by then a defeated nation.

In London Cadogan worried about Turkey. He and the COS, reading Turkey-related BJs, believed Turkey to be the northern bastion of the British position in the Middle East.[6] These considerations and German success in Norway ruled out the French project of an attack on the Caucasian oilfields.

None the less neither the Axis nor the Allies could keep their hands off Turkey. The Russians, then uneasy allies of both Germany and Italy, thought they could incapacitate Turkey and thus safeguard their southern flank: Molotov proposed this.[7] Meanwhile in April 1940 three plans had been made by the British COS to thwart three possible German moves: an attack on Turkey from Bulgaria, the seizure of the Bosphorus and the Dardanelles and a crossing into Asia Minor. The first, codenamed 'Leopold', was the setting up of thirty British observer groups in European Turkey and Anatolia. The second, 'Tiger', was for three British fighter squadrons to operate in Asia Minor. The third, 'Bear', was for an expanded air defence programme if German pressure on Turkey mounted: the despatch to Turkey of five squadrons of ten aircraft each, capable of attacking German air bases, lines of communication in Bulgaria, southern Romania and southern Yugoslavia.[8] Churchill pushed through 'Leopold' within a fortnight of becoming prime minister.[9] Further plans in case of a German attack on Turkey were completed by 20 July but not implemented as the Turks refused the proffered help. Churchill told the Defence Committee on 31 October that the Germans might seek to drive through Turkey to the Suez canal and a Turkish resistance 'might greatly delay the German advance'. He speculated on deploying as many as fifty-five Turkish divisions by the end of 1941, showing how Turkey stirred his imagination.[10] The COS wanted Britain to do all in its power to encourage and assist the Turks to resist any German advance. But if this was not enough, plans were to be made for the demolition of Turkish communications. Moreover an intelligence centre was contemplated at Ankara, and a plan to use the Polish navy to stop the Germans shipping oil across the Black Sea from Batumi to Burgas was canvassed because Poland was not a signatory of the Montreux Convention which bound its signatories not to undertake aggressive action in the Black Sea on pain of Turkish counter-aggression.

Before the fall of France, French Prime Minister Paul Reynaud tried to rush Turkey on to the Allied side, as Orme Sargent wrote to Hugessen on 26 March 1940, the object being to strike at Soviet interests in the Caucasus.[11] Although the sequence of events remains a murky affair, it seems fairly clear that Turkey was sounded out as to her likely intentions if the French initiative was activated. Turkey's traditional enmity with Russia was thought to facilitate an approach by the Allies, and Gp Capt R.A. George, the assistant military attaché in Ankara promoted a plan for joint Turco-Franco-British action if Turkey was threatened either from the west by Germany and Italy or from the east by Russia. But George noted there was no asphalt on Turkish runways so air strikes from Turkey to the Caucasus would be hazardous if not impossible.[12] The FO thought Turkey would not fight against Russia unless directly threatened but if Russia realised Turkey would work with the Allies this would not provoke but deter them. In the FO Sargent and his friend the recently appointed ambassador in Ankara, Sir Hughe Knatchbull-Hugessen, agreed that anything we did do against the USSR depended on Turkey. Hugessen responded by speculating that Russia's recent poor fighting performance in Finland might decide Turkey to attack the Baku and Batumi *oblasti*, whose populations were largely Turkish-speaking.[13] Speculation about possible Turkish moves ceased on 9 April when Germany invaded Denmark and Norway. On 10 May, the day Churchill became prime minister, Hitler commenced the offensive against France and Belgium.[14] Dunkirk followed less than three weeks later. A German-Norwegian armistice was signed on 9 June and by 22 June France too had signed an armistice. On 9 June Italy declared war on the Allies. 'This rendered operational Turkey's obligation under Clause 1 of the second article of the Treaty with Britain.'[15] But the Turks had decided well in advance that they would try by all means at their disposal to stay out before admitting any obligations.

The Turks were both alarmed and impressed by the scale and speed of the German advance. They were even more alarmed when at the end of June 1940 the USSR had acquired the whole of Bessarabia and Bukhovina. Romania, Hungary and Bulgaria were soon to fall within the Axis orbit. Turkey found itself with its former partners, Britain and France, in a state of near paralysis. Meanwhile the Germans were openly planning an assault on the Suez canal and the empire trade route by further invasions of countries certainly including Turkey. And the Russian foreign minister, Vyacheslav Molotov, having recently snubbed the Turkish foreign minister in Moscow as well as signed up with Germany, was talking about revising the Montreux agreement. There was little chance of Churchill putting his reading of diplomatic intercepts to good use in Turkey, which in July had signed an agreement to supply the Axis with chrome. In August the USSR declared the Baltic states socialist republics, the RAF triumphed in the Battle of

Britain and Hitler started doubting the wisdom of invading England. In the eastern Mediterranean any further thoughts of getting Turkey into the war were muted by Field Marshal Wavell's perception that Turkey would be more a liability than an asset, given the poverty of equipment and training of the soldiery and the passivity of most of the generals.[16] Hugessen, Halifax and George Rendel (recently promoted from the FO to be Minister Plenipotentiary in Bucharest) corresponded about the Turkish situation. In August Rendel wrote: 'I don't think the Turks have a Balkan policy, except being nice to Greece.'[17] On 20 August Sargent minuted that 'we are not in a position to dictate to Turkey' and the latter had made it quite clear that 'she does not intend to make the attempt at buying-off Russia.'[18] Yet on 5 September Halifax wrote: 'Turkey will remain the keystone of our policy in the near East.'[19]

The FO was responsible for Turkey, but no one there, not the Secretary of State, nor the permanent under-secretary or his senior aides, nor the British ambassador, could bring together a coherent policy which took the realities of the Turkish economy and the daunting facts of German expansionism into the Balkans into proper account. This had to wait until Churchill took over Turkey personally, still some months off. To what extent the Turkish diplomatic intercepts acted as a spur to keep Turkey high on the priority list of the FO in this period is difficult to assess, but given the pace of world events and the imminent possibility of a further German victory in the west – one that might send the whole FO off to Canada – it is unlikely that the intercepts were given much weight.

Germany Triumphant

The Phoney War was over by April 1940 when the Germans invaded Norway. It was not until 27 September that the Axis partners signed the Tripartite Pact. At that point Turkish foreign policy was hardening up in the face of this alarming evidence of a German victory. Her intentions were not kept particularly secret and Gen Franz Halder, the German Army Chief of Staff, wrote in his diary on 26 October that 'if anything conclusive is to be achieved, Bulgaria and Turkey have to be subdued, if necessary by force, especially in the case of the latter, to leave the way open through the Bosphorus to Syria'.[20] And a month later: 'If Turkey does not keep quiet in the event of an attack against Greece, she must be thrown out of Europe.'[21] Halder was only repeating what Hitler had just said to him.

On 1 November 1940 President İnönü of Turkey declared Turkey was out of the war, which precluded any use of her sea or air space by any of the belligerents. He wrote later: 'The situation of the Allied front was clear. France had collapsed. Britain had gone into this war unprepared. According to Marshal Petain Britain would not last long. In this situation, to make a declaration implying commitment to the alliance would be a grave mistake . . . As far as I was concerned the alliance was annulled *de facto*. It was not necessary to explain this.'[22] By the end of the year Hitler had decided against taking on Turkey and was turning towards 'Barbarossa'. Halder noted on 24 November that 'we have come to the considered decision to avoid conflict with Turkey at all costs'.[23]

The FO's interest in Turkey meant that Turkey became in effect the focal point of diplomatic pressure by all three belligerents: Germany, Italy and Britain. This became apparent when the Germans surged through the Balkans and occupied Bulgaria, Turkey's ancestral foe, bringing their troops within firing distance of Thrace. By January 1941 the Luftwaffe was flying into Bulgaria in force. Churchill had sent Eden twice to Turkey. On his January 1941 visit to Ankara Eden wrote that his policy towards Turkey was 'marked by a series of regressions'.[24] Churchill had also requisitioned Lt-Gen Sir James Marshall-Cornwall, about to take up his command to defend the south-west sector of the Home Front, to 'parley with the Turks' – in Churchill's own phrase. The general was the only high-ranking British officer with a certificate as a Turkish interpreter. He met the Turkish Chief of the General Staff, Gen Assim Gubnuz, on 15 January and spent a week fruitlessly trying to galvanise the somewhat torpid Turkish High Command, accustomed to easy soldiering in the long years of peace, and despite the state of emergency reluctant to learn about new methods of warfare or to retrain on the new equipment offered by the British.[25] Marshall-Cornwall was so keen on greater British co-operation with the Turks that Eden nervously minuted that he wished the soldiery would keep out of politics. On 29 January 1941 Churchill offered RAF squadrons to President İnönü of Turkey, who refused them.[26]

The month of January 1941 saw much ado about Turkey, involving the Russians, Greeks, Bulgarians and Italians, as well as Turks, British and Germans. Already by 6 January 1941 Churchill had written to Gen Ismay, 'We must so act as to make it certain that if the enemy enters Bulgaria Turkey will come into the war'.[27] It took four more years for Churchill's hope to become reality. Two days later Ambassador Hugessen reported to the FO: 'The Turks' faith in ourselves and France, particularly France, was considerably shattered by our asking them to join in.' The next day Halder recorded a major Hitler Conference on 'Barbarossa' and Bulgaria occupied by German troops.[28] In Berlin the Foreign Ministry was plying Hitler with Turkish diplomatic intercepts similar, perhaps identical, to those circulating in the FO, including reports on possible British reactions to the entry of German troops into Bulgaria.[29]

Churchill thought Hitler would turn east. On 20 January the COS wondered whether, after Bulgaria, Germany would operate against Britain or drive into the Ukraine and the Caucasus.[30] On 17 January the Soviets protested to Germany about the presence of German troops in Bulgaria. Two days later a German attack on Greece through Bulgaria was expected to be opposed by Turkey. On 21 January Field Marshal Sir Archibald Wavell, British C-in-C Middle East, was ordered to build up a mobile force of four infantry and one armoured divisions for use in Greece and Italy. On

23 January the Turkish ambassador in London thought any German attack on Russia would be a deception to mask a German invasion of Turkey.[31] On 26 January Churchill wrote to Wavell about 'infiltration [into Turkey] . . . before any clear-cut issue of invasion has been presented to the Turks who will then be told [by the Germans] to keep out or have Constantinople bombed'.[32] Three days later he offered İnönü RAF aircraft: the offer was refused. Meanwhile Ribbentrop was writing to the German Foreign Office: 'England will try to forestall German troops [in Bulgaria] to occupy the Straits to start military operations against Bulgaria in alliance with Turkey.'[33] On 30 January Military Intelligence predicted that Germany would attack Turkey.[34]

Finally, on 31 January, Churchill wrote to the Turkish President: 'Germany is preparing to repeat on the frontiers of Turkey the same manoeuvre as she accomplished on the frontiers of France in April and May 1940 . . . You and I, Mr President, should repeat in defence of Turkey the same measures the Germans are taking over Bulgaria.' Churchill went on to offer İnönü 100 AA guns and crews, a major commitment during the Blitz yet proof of the slenderness of British resources. He also asked to be allowed to station 100 RAF squadrons on Turkish soil.[35] The same day Churchill wrote to the COS that 'Air support promised to Turkey cannot be delayed.' The Graeco-Turkish operation takes precedence, replied the COS.[36] On 1 February a British military mission inspected the only three Turkish tank regiments while the Germans invaded Romania with 680,000 troops, monitored at Bletchley Park by the readers of Luftwaffe Enigma. Thus Churchill and the COS were kept informed of German troop movements in the Balkans but had little scope for action to counter, still less forestall, them. On 7 February the War Office speculated that twenty-five [Turkish] divisions would be enough to hold off Russia if Germany attacked Turkey.[37] Three days later Germany and Russia signed a treaty establishing the new German/Soviet borders in eastern Europe. On 14 February British war planners speculated on Germany's aggressive approach to Turkey, and (three days later) that Germany's entry into Bulgaria would be matched by Turkey's into Greece.[38] On 16 February Turkey signed a non-aggression pact with Bulgaria, the French urged bombing raids on the Baku-Batumi *oblasti* to eliminate the oil wells, not realising the offence that would cause in Turkey; the CIGS and Foreign Secretary went to talk to the Turks – without getting far – and Rommel became C-in-C of all German forces in North Africa.[39]

In Britain, the FO could do nothing to stem the German menace except to attempt to stiffen resistance in Turkey. How this was achieved is outlined in the section which follows.

Different Views on Turkey

It can be seen that the War Office was looking at Turkey as a future battlefield while the FO still thought that the Anglo-Turkish Alliance could achieve the same results – safeguard the imperial sea-routes and contain German expansionism in the area without hazarding Turkish troops in aggressive forays beyond their own borders. This section attempts to show the confused British tactical response to the German threat in south-eastern Europe, using a variety of sources, including Enigma and diplomatic intercepts, plus valuable reports from a senior Czech intelligence officer working for the Abwehr (German Military Intelligence Organisation) in Prague who supplied the British with vital information on German plans in the east.[40]

The FO, Ministry of Economic Warfare and the War Office appreciated the Turkish situation differently. On 3 February the Minister for Economic Warfare, Dr Hugh Dalton, noted 'some gloom over Turkey'. His comment suggested some government ministers were dissatisfied with Hugessen's presence in Ankara.[41] To put such an important and delicate problem into the hands of any diplomat would worry both politicians and military men, and Hugessen as a diplomat did not carry the weight of people like Loraine in Rome or Samuel Hoare in Madrid. The military establishment turned its mind to other Turkish options. On 6 February a War Office appreciation noted the possibility of Germany attacking Turkey, then Egypt:

> It is probable that Germany might defeat the Turks in Thrace and reach the Straits in not more than six weeks after the occupation of Salonika – say by the middle of May. But a further advance through Anatolia would be a big undertaking from the point of view of communications and the establishment of landing grounds; and although it might be possible for a German force to establish itself south of the Taurus by the end of July – this depending on the degree of Turkish resistance – it is estimated that eight divisions (increasing to 12 after two months) could be maintained through Anatolia for an advance via Syria on Egypt, and with Turkey hostile a considerable additional force would be required for protection of her lines of communication . . . A German invasion of Turkey would not aid her main thrust which is the invasion of Great Britain. Turkey would take action against any German force from Greece which crossed the Turkish border. But Turkey would take no action against German forces advancing further to the west against Greece.[42]

Where did Churchill stand, between these two ways of playing the Turkish hand? It is hard to say. Perhaps he was not alone in anticipating a poor Turkish military performance unless she was repelling an aggressor from within her own borders. Certainly, on 7 February, the day of Gen O'Connor's destruction of the Italian Tenth Army in North Africa, Hugessen wrote to Eden:

> I am convinced of extreme importance of increasing military supplies without delay. The President [İnönü], who spoke still more strongly on

this, said to me that, if Turkey had all that we promised, we might have had a different answer.[43]

Two days later Churchill wrote to ACM Sir Charles Portal, Chief of the Air Staff: 'You proposed sending ten squadrons to Turkey, which the Turks have not yet accepted . . . I am in it with you up to the neck. But have we not in fact promised the same pig to two customers?' [i.e. to Greece and Turkey].[44] Three days after this he wrote to Wavell: 'Both Greece and Turkey have hitherto refused our offer of technical units . . .' and assessed 'the chances of Turkish intervention . . . There will always remain the support of Turkey.'

On 12 February Pierson Dixon of the FO was told to be ready to leave for Ankara as part of the British diplomatic mission which would bring Turkey to the brink of war. The next day he reported on British foreign policy towards Turkey. Dixon told Eden later that 'the first question to decide was whether our forces should be offered to Greece or to Turkey . . .'[45] On 19 February Dalton noted worries about Eden's visit to Turkey. The same day Hitler learned that Romania, now Germany's ally, would no longer supply Turkey with oil. The Turkish minister re-stated Turkey's position that she would only enter the war if her own borders were attacked.[46] Two days later Churchill wrote to Smuts: 'The Russian attitude has undermined the Turks', and to Eden: 'Commitments made to Ankara . . . would tie your hands about the Greeks.'[47] Two days later the War Cabinet in London decided to support Greece, even without Turkey and Yugoslavia.

On 26 February Gen Sir John Dill, the CIGS, and Eden flew to Ankara for talks lasting well into March. Dill had gone out to Cairo firmly believing Wavell's British Expeditionary Force should go to Turkey, not Greece. Two days later Eden wrote to Churchill:

They [the Turkish leaders] thought Turkey's turn would come next . . . the common cause would be better served by Turkey remaining out of the war until her deficiencies had been remedied. They felt concerned lest the Russians should attack them if Turkey became involved in a war with Germany.[48]

It was now clear that in the uneasy months that followed the Phoney War, events were moving too swiftly for the British response to be anything but hastily reactive, and based on hope rather than fact. The part played by the BJs in bringing some hard information out of the chaos reigning in the eastern Mediterranean can only be guessed at, since none have been released. But Hinsley refers frequently during this period to 'neutral diplomatic intercepts', which suggests they were available to those in the FO seeking to formulate British foreign policy towards Turkey. However, secret intercepted neutral traffic can affect policy only when the receiving government has some scope to take initiatives and set priorities. When nothing, or too much, was happening, such traffic played little part in the policy making process. It was to be another two years therefore before BJs significantly aided Churchill and the FO.

Moreover it is difficult to exaggerate the intense fear aroused by Germany's military successes in this period. Millions and millions of Europeans felt (and many were) individually threatened by Hitler. All our hours had come in the summer of 1940, and despite the Battle of Britain it was to be nearly two years before fear of Nazi aggression could finally be dispelled. Because of this the FO continued to target Turkey in the months that followed, and Turkey constituted a major part of the Southern Department's workload. Diplomats there expected Germany to attack Turkey, while the Yugoslavs expected Germany would insist they join the Axis. The Turkish army had a million men called up and reservists amounting to another 1.5 million. Their purpose was clear: to keep all comers at arm's length.[49]

On 1 March Churchill wrote to Eden: 'The obvious German move is to overrun Bulgaria, further to intimidate Turkey by threat of air attacks . . . after which Turkey can be attacked or not, at their hostile convenience.'[50] Churchill noted a growing pessimism in Turkey, which he must have derived principally from reading the Turkey-related BJs of the period.[51]

Hitler had been keeping a wary eye on Turkey through his own intercept reading, but had concluded that an invasion of the country, as a preliminary to an assault on Egypt, was possible but difficult and ultimately pointless. He correctly assessed the geographical and socio-economic factors discouraging an invasion of Turkey. But Churchill's intercepts could give little indication of the way Hitler's mind was working, and then only at second or third hand through the reports of Balkan and Japanese diplomats to each other or to their respective foreign ministries.

On 6 April 1941 Germany attacked Yugoslavia and Greece instead, and stirred up trouble in Iraq and Iran. Churchill wrote to Eden: 'We have no power . . . to avert the fate of Greece unless Turkey and/or Yugoslavia come in, which seems most improbable.' The loss of the Balkans would be 'by no means a major catastrophe for us, provided Turkey remains honestly neutral'.[52] Three days later Hitler gave Halder his views on Italy, Spain, France and Turkey, for on 10 March he noted: 'Turkish attitude not clear: ?bribed by British.'[53] Two days later İnönü told Hitler: '[Turkey] cannot allow her sacred right to inviolability to be judged from the point of view of the victory of any foreign country.'[54] The same day he refused likewise to commit Turkish friendship to Britain, while German aircraft were already arriving in Turkey's neighbours' airfields, in Syria and Iraq.[55]

The next day Churchill wrote rather disingenuously to Eden in Ankara, where he had been sent to sort out the confusion caused by the Germans' invasions of Yugoslavia and Greece: 'Turkey requires stimulus and guidance as events develop. No one but you can combine and concert the momentous policy which you have pressed upon us and which we have adopted.'[56] On

18 March Eden met Saraçoğlu in Cyprus and Dalton noted that the Turks were complaining about non-delivery of the arms promised to them. On 23 March the Greek army capitulated, and Turkey broke off talks with the Yugoslavs, whose government had temporarily capitulated to the Germans.[57] Not everything was going the Axis way, because on 26 March the Italian navy suffered a major defeat at Cape Matapan, thanks to Dilwyn Knox's achievement in breaking a new Italian naval cipher at Bletchley Park.[58]

Eden was not doing well in his approaches to the Turkish leadership, so on 27 March Churchill himself wrote to İnönü: 'Surely now is the time to make a common front from which Germany will hardly dare assail.'[59] The same day, the Serbians having rebelled against the Axis, Churchill wrote to Eden in Turkey:

> This is Turkey's best chance of avoiding war . . . the Germans may . . . turn their whole striking force rapidly against Turkey in Thrace . . . There have been suggestions of this *in various telegrams* . . . The mass of Turkish troops gathered in Thrace would soon be driven back in confusion upon the Chatalja lines and the Bosphorous . . . The Turks' greatest danger is to be taken on alone jammed up in Thrace.[60]

Turkish involvement seemed to be reaching crisis point. By the end of the month, GCCS provided evidence of Germany gearing up to attack Russia, Churchill had watched Germany overrunning Yugoslavia, invading Greece, and defeating both Greeks and British there, all in the hectic space of twenty-four days. None the less, he told Roosevelt that Britain would be content if Turkey remained neutral.[61] But informed sources were by now confidently awaiting a German attack on Turkey.[62] On 8 April Halder noted 'The Balkan campaign begins.' By 11 April Belgrade was a mass of ruins.[63] Yugoslavia capitulated on 21 April. On 25 April Turkey signed a trade agreement with Germany. Four days later the COS thought Germany would continue through Greece, across the islands and invade Turkey. On 24 April Raschid Ali of Iraq appealed to Germany for help against advancing British forces.[64] On 26 April Churchill thought the war may spread to Turkey and, on the last day of the month, with Rommel on its border pounding Tobruk, he concluded that 'British failure to win Egypt will force a decision on Turkey.'

The pace of events in the Mediterranean was astounding, and Germany was still making the running. On 22 April a War Office appreciation noted that the Turkish army had been mobilised for many months, Turkey and Germany were talking trade, and many German businessmen were spending time in Turkey.[65] It was thought probable that Germany would force transit of her troops on the Turkish government and would then occupy Syria and thus isolate Turkey.

It can be seen that the War Office, through General Headquarters, Middle East, had a distinctive view of Turkey's potential to bolster the inchoate British military and diplomatic reactions to German aggression in the Mediterranean: on 30 April, the day the BEF finished its evacuation of mainland Greece, one option the chairborne soldiery considered was 'based on a hostile Turkey'. They, like the rest of the world, were paralysed by the speed of German armour through mountainous Yugoslavia and Greece, and despite the equally poor state of the roads in Turkey they thought the Germans would achieve 20 miles a day there if they were to invade Anatolia (seen as more probable than Thrace).[66]

By May the Turkish government had agreed with von Papen's offer to negotiate with the Germans. The same tough bargaining the Turks used against the British was now brought to play against the Germans.[67] In Greece the British, close to collapse, asked the Turks to occupy the islands of Chios, Mytilene and Samos, a provocation against Greece as well as a protection against the Germans. The Turks understandably said no. Instead, the Germans occupied the first two on 5 May and had completed their grip on all the Aegean islands a week later. Churchill told Roosevelt about his growing pessimism over Turkey, and on 12 May the Turks announced they could not under current conditions commit themselves to friendship with Britain. On 4 May, with BJ reading before him, Churchill reminded Roosevelt that the attitude of Spain, Vichy, Turkey and the Middle East may be finally determined by the outcome of the struggle off Turkish coastal waters.[68]

The Turks had offered to mediate between the Allies and Axis over Iraq, but Churchill wrote to Wavell: 'There can be no question of accepting the Turkish offer of mediation.'[69] This offer, if accepted, would have substantiated her neutrality claims, which was not at all what Churchill had in mind. On 8 May Luftwaffe aircraft landed at Mosul, in Iraq, and three Heinkel HeIIIs came in to land at Baghdad on 12 May, though one was shot down in error. They were joined by Italian formations on 17 May. This Axis effort, staged via Vichy and Syria, proved too late to sustain Raschid Ali.

On 20 May Germany had moved significantly closer against Turkey by the invasion of Crete. Churchill read an Enigma intercept providing a complete picture of exactly where the Germans intended to land there and wished to send the intercepts raw to Gen Freyberg, C-in-C British Forces Crete, but was overruled.[70] 'Had the Germans learnt that Britain was decrypting the Enigma messages, the single most important British advantage of the war would have been irretrievably lost.'[71] On 18 May Ribbentrop offered 'frontier rectification in return for transit facilities' to Turkey. The next day Churchill learned that the Iraqi situation was not secure and that a big German movement into Syria was impending.[72] Churchill told Roosevelt that the fate of Turkey hung in the balance, and Turkey told the British on 21 May that she was not ready to resist Germany. On 24 May Vichy asked for transit facilities for reinforcement of her garrisons through Turkey to Syria.[73] In Berlin on 25 May Oshima predicted a German advance towards India via Turkey and the Middle East.[74] On 30 May Crete fell and Germany acquired much British war *matériel*.

Despite this, by 31 May Baghdad had surrendered to the British and GCCS was intercepting messages confirming the certainty of Operation 'Barbarossa'. This period of German ascendancy in the Mediterranean concentrated minds at the FO on the possibility of a German victory which left Turkey's role in the war a minor affair. During the subsequent two months' events in eastern and south-eastern Europe swept Churchill's plans for Turkey aside.

Although the DIR/C series for this period has not yet been released, Hinsley refers regularly to 'Axis diplomatic sigint'. As early as the summer of 1940, the PM had required 'authentic documents . . . in their original form' to come to him through Maj Morton.[75] Since many of these authentic documents were diplomatic decrypts, and many of these referred to or emanated from Turkey, it is reasonable to assume that Turkey was still a high priority for him, despite the many other calls on his nervous energy. The evidence of his involvement in BJs is provided in Hinsley. The FO tracked Hitler's ambitions in the Balkans in detail through this period in case he decided to switch his combined forces back to invading Britain.[76] But by June he was about to launch 'Barbarossa' instead.

By 1 June Crete had been cleared of British forces. The Luftwaffe was to be withdrawn from Iraq and the British and Free French advanced into Syria on 8 June. On 4 June Halder noted that Turkey was weaker because of British decline and a week later that the conclusion of a German pact with Turkey was likely. On 6 June von Papen was reported by a US source in Bucharest as hinting that the Italian-owned but formerly Ottoman Dodecanese could become Turkey's after a German victory, and the Germans and Turks agreed to German *matériel* passing through Turkey towards Iraq and Syria, but not troops.[77]

The climax of German supremacy in the region arrived on 18 June when the Turco-German treaty of friendship was signed.[78] The Turkish press was made to work hard to create an auspicious atmosphere for the treaty. The press gave the treaty a warm welcome and underlined that 'Turco-German friendship was not a new thing'. But on 21 June Turkey refused passage of French troops across the country.[79]

This section has tried to present the bifurcated British reaction to German successes in south-eastern Europe from June 1941 till March 1942. Secret information available to the British was crucial at this time, and led directly (according to Hinsley's account) to the striking British victory over the Italians at Cape Matapan. Unfortunately the actual messages for the earlier period have not yet been released, and consequently reliance is confidently placed on Hinsley's account of these months of the war in the Mediterranean.[80]

Churchill's Secret Intelligence

Churchill was already receiving the intercepts he needed to mastermind the British war effort in the eastern Mediterranean, and 'to play the Turkey hand': by 24 June 1941 the first DIR/C came on stream and is available to the historian.[81] In London the service ministries were now receiving Enigma but only summaries of BJs, while the FO studied BJs but had no access to Enigma/Ultra until later in 1943.[82] Churchill of course had both, but would not allow anyone else, including those on his private staff, John Colville for instance, to see them. Since there was overlap in content and a complementary aspect to the two different sources of information, it can be seen that Churchill was putting himself in an unrivalled position as Britain's warlord: a position he did not intend to share with anyone. It was an impressive example of the need-to-know principle. He made most effective use of his personal resource from mid-1941 to mid-1944. After D-Day his role in war planning was diminished, but BJs remained vital reading to him and others planning whether and how to drop atomic bombs on Japan and thereby finish the war. In this early period, however, his frequent annotations, instructions to 'C' and others on cipher security, concern for the battles being waged on the Eastern and North African fronts and at sea, all show that his use of intercepts was a crucial factor in his conduct of the war, and his attitude to the neutrals.

On 27 June GCCS broke the German Abwehr Russian Front code. The very next day Churchill was upset at not having been shown a document from Hut 3, despite two copies going to Maj Morton, and protested directly to 'C' who offered to 'submit all naval material to you in future . . . if you so direct.' The PM replied, 'Yes, if not pure routine.' The document was in fact an account of the German admiral commanding U-boats [Adm Doenitz]. Churchill's appetite for authentic detail was insatiable. Two days later he asked Hut 3 via 'C' to say whenever possible tonnage and whether northbound or southbound 'of ships in the Mediterranean'. On 26 June Hugessen reported that the Turks in general and Saraçoğlu in particular were 'in a very touchy frame of mind' and Churchill, who was making his pitch towards Russia, despite Turkish sensibilities, was discreetly told by the FO to moderate his newly pro-Soviet speeches. But in Ankara Menemencioğlu told Hugessen Turkey did not want another treaty with Britain when 'the whole world was bound by treaties to maintain peace with Turkey'.

On 2 July a Soviet–Japanese neutrality pact was signed. The next day Halder noted: 'Germans will advance through Anatolia to Syria, concentrating her forces in Bulgaria . . . there will be political pressure on Turkey to grant German transit facilities.'[83] On 6 July Oliver Harvey noted in his diary: 'Our slowness is having a devastating effect on Turkey, on USA and on all our friends.'

By 11 July the American State Department protested to Turkey over her supplying chrome to Germany and so wanted to cut off US supplies to Turkey. The FO, with its own agenda, took a different line. Britain would sell on Lease-Lend to Turkey, to save dwindling gold reserves. George Clutton noted that the 'USA incensed by Turco-German Pact'.[84] Technicians and experts were reluctant to be seconded to Turkey in case the country was invaded – and their firms were reluctant to release them. The FO made much play of the close ties between the two countries: 'we more or less run their air force'. Eden briefed Halifax on Turkey.

On 15 July a report to Ankara by the Turkish ambassador in Moscow on the attitude of Turkey to the German-Russian conflict, was intercepted by the Germans and shown to Hitler.[85] Six other Turkish intercepts were passed by Hitler to Goebbels. A German descent on Turkey appeared imminent.[86] Few doubted he could do it, but Hitler himself began to doubt if it was worth doing when he could get so far without such a dangerous extension of his supply lines.

On 24 July, in London, Harvey noted in his diary 'an encouraging telegram from Ankara'. Turkey wanted to talk to Britain and was anti-German. Though Eden had always backed the Turkish front, nothing came of the Turkish approach. The next day von Papen reported the Turkish-speaking Azerbaijanis were stirring, and Hitler learnt from an intercept that the five-week-old Turco-German treaty meant nothing to Turkey.[87]

Stalin was only slowly waking up to the fact that his countrymen had the fight of their lives on their hands. On 28 July he told İnönü he had no territorial interest in revising Montreux, and put Turkey aside for the time being. On 2 August, an Italian diplomatic decrypt showed that the Italians were suspecting that Germany had been talking to the Persians about the territorial expansion of Persia in the event of a Soviet collapse.[88] On 6 August Eden complained to the Persian government about thousands of German spies – 'tourists' – in Persia. Presumably they came via Turkey, which had become the international espionage centre of the world. Six days later the Italian diplomatic service, decrypted at Bletchley Park, quoted Raschid Ali as believing that the Persian government was 'substantially favourable' to the Axis and would throw off the mask as soon as German troops appeared in the Caucasus.[89] The possibility of a German attack on Turkey had also been reported in September 1941 by A-54, a well-placed Czech agent working for the Abwehr in Vienna.[90]

In Berlin Ribbentrop did not share his master's determination to keep Turkey. He set up a committee to exploit panturanism, while guaranteeing Turkish territorial integrity. Meanwhile his underlings were carrying out a number of subversive activities throughout the Middle East.[91] If Turkey made light of her recent treaty with Germany she also remained suspicious of both Russia and Britain.[92] On 22 August an Italian diplomatic decrypt reported that Germany was continuing to transport arms and ammunition to Iran via Turkey. The next day Hugessen in Ankara reported that Turkey was considering building a lorry route through Anatolia to help the process.[93] Churchill told Stalin on 29 August: 'We are trying . . . to provide for Turkey so as to bring her in on our side.'

From then on Turkey was a prime target for the diplomatic cryptographers of both Germany and Britain, and the study of her ambassadorial reports became part of Churchill's daily workload. The continued neutrality of the Turks from the end of 1941 to the beginning of 1945 is a theme of several of the chapters that follow. Their success in staying out of the war, despite the threats and blandishments of von Papen in Ankara and of Churchill and the FO in London, which resulted in the Adana Conference of January 1943 is, of course, already familiar to war historians of the eastern Mediterranean region. Nothing in the new secret diplomatic intercepts substantially alters the Turkish wartime scene as already recorded, but some new light is shed on how Churchill himself conducted British foreign policy towards Turkey in those years.

At the beginning of this chapter, two questions were asked: one was, how important was the work of GCCS on Turkish messages between May 1940 and October 1941 and 1939 to the FO? The answer is that the expansion of GCCS from its mainly diplomatic work to its decryption of service traffic was of overriding importance to Churchill and the COS in 1940, so BJs figured less prominently than Enigma during this period, and their use by the FO cannot be realistically assessed from current data.

This chapter has provided a provisional answer to a further question about the quality and quantity of Turkey-sourced BJs in 1941: the evidence is to be found in Hinsley's history of secret intelligence. Though Churchill's mission to save the world from German expansionism benefited greatly from the work of Bletchley Park in the early years of the war, reliable information on Turkey from Turkish sources did not elevate Turkish participation in the war in Churchill's mind: he had other and greater problems to deal with. It should be added that these answers must remain speculative, given the non-availability of BJs before September 1941.

In the next two years, Churchill's concern with Turkey can be scanned in conjunction with his reading of diplomatic intercepts in a way which suggests the intercepts underpinned as well as infused his playing of the Turkey hand.

This chapter has sought to establish the context in which Churchill was able to use DIR from 1941 till VE-Day. The next two chapters are devoted to a study of Churchill's use of Turkish diplomatic messages in his eastern Mediterranean policy between 1941 and 1943.

CHAPTER FOUR

Turkish Neutrality: Liability or Asset?

Churchill loved the decrypts . . . as one who had been fascinated by cryptanalytic intelligence from 1914 onwards and who regarded it as of the utmost importance. Churchill alone enjoyed this overall view of intelligence. At this stage there was no integration of the material except in his head. It was a state of affairs that did not appeal to the military departments or the Foreign Office . . . especially when the PM was liable to spring on them . . . stuff they had not read or known.

Andrew Hodges in *Alan Turing: The Enigma of Intelligence*

Churchill and Turkey 1941–43

This chapter charts the developing relationship between Churchill and the Turkish leadership in the months before the Adana Conference. Germany was predominant in the eastern Mediterranean until the spring of 1942, but in the months before January 1943 the balance of power had swung towards the Allies, who had been victorious in North Africa, displaced the Italian dictator, while the Russians had achieved a massive victory at Stalingrad. It shows the extent to which Turkey, as a leading neutral, observed the signs of a possible separate peace – between Italy and Britain at one point, and between Russia and Germany all through the period till 6 June 1944. Linked to the possibility of a separate peace were the questions whether, when and where a second front would be launched. Speculation on this among the neutrals continued throughout the North African campaign, the invasion of Sicily and the Italian campaign. This was important because gauging neutral sensibilities gave Churchill, and other readers of BJs, an unrivalled entry into the mindset of those countries, Spain, Portugal, Switzerland, Sweden, Brazil, Chile, the Vatican, Vichy France and above all Turkey. These neutrals collectively had the power to alter the course of the war. That was why they were important. Turkey was the most important, so questions affecting Turkey's continuing policy of neutrality led Churchill and Eden in London, and Hitler in Berlin, to realise that Turkey could decide which way the war would go.

Churchill's own strategic objectives were materially affected by his daily reading of DIR/C. His only long-term strategic objective was to defeat the enemy, so his intercept reading resulted in strong and often otherwise inexplicable hunches. The much discussed Balkan offensive launched from Turkish territory across the Bosphorus to Greece and up the Danube to attack the German heartland recurred annually between 1942 and 1944, though it was never more than a figment of his imaginative way of looking at possibilities, fuelled by Balkan information from BJs. It was quite beyond the competence of the Anglo-American commanders to bring such a project into the realms of the possible. Churchill was a great extemporiser – and in late 1941 he could only react to what the enemy was doing, or might be planning to do next. The Turkish march was one theme on which he extemporised with many variations. First, as has been shown, he asked the CIGS, Sir John Dill, to send Gen James Marshall-Cornwall to Ankara on a one-man military mission to get Turkey onto the Allied side in late 1940 and early 1941. Marshall-Cornwall made two trips to Ankara. He did his best but he knew his job was impossible. On 19 February 1941 Field Marshal Lord Wavell, the C-in-C, told him 'the policy of our government is to build up a Balkan front'.[1] It was for this reason that Churchill then sent Foreign Secretary Anthony Eden twice to Turkey in 1941 to bully or lure the Turks in. The results were negative. Between Eden's second visit and Churchill's own arrival on Turkish soil in January 1943 the war developed in other theatres, but from May 1942 onwards Churchill set his sights on his personal intervention into Turkish foreign policy, partly as the start of a great Balkan second front to aid the Russians at Stalingrad, but more because he badly needed the comfort of the formidable Turkish army at his side, and his study of the diplomatic messages told him the time was ripe.

In Washington the leadership disliked pressurising Turkey, while in Whitehall Turkey remained the province of the Southern Department of the FO, instinctively opposed to anything as rash as Churchill's Turkish initiative. For over two decades it had been responsible for developing British friendship and trade with Turkey, it was proud of this not very difficult achievement and defended its right to look after the Turkish agenda. The War Cabinet, following Eden, took the same view as the Southern Department, while after 1942 the COS had their minds on the western Mediterranean and never looked favourably on a Balkan initiative from the east. In this they echoed the views of the Americans, who only saw trouble in stirring up Turkey and opening a Balkan front. Sir John Dill, now in Washington, who had sent Marshall-Cornwall to Ankara in 1940, tried to explain the problem of the American leadership to Churchill in early 1944:

Can I suggest without offence that you look [at Turkey] from the US Chiefs of Staff point of view, with their vast responsibilities in this great democracy, which are much more direct and more publicly recognised than in our country, and then do as you would be done by.[2]

What no one identified was Churchill's determination to do everything possible to postpone 'Overlord' until the Allies were capable of delivering it. This was the only credible second front. It was this instinct rather than any long-term plan of attack on the European heartland from Bulgaria that drove Churchill into the welcoming if hesitant arms of the Turkish oligarchs at Adana in January 1943. Churchill himself must have realised that, from the moment Hitler re-armed the substantial Bulgarian army with the latest German weaponry in 1941, this option did not exist; if so he kept his own counsel.

The view from Ankara in 1941 was rather different. Turkey was beset on all sides. To the east a joint Russo-British invasion of Persia from the north and south respectively had cut off both oil and Arab friends in the area. To the north-west, Bulgaria and Romania had been reduced to satellite status by Germany, compelled to supply half a million men for the Eastern Front, fully equipped and politically neutered. To the north the Germans reigned supreme over the rich arable plains of the Ukraine now basking in autumn sunshine and with a record wheat harvest to be transported back to Germany. To the south British reverses in the North African deserts had left Egypt twitching helplessly while to the west Italy was still in aggressive mode.

This was the situation when DIR/C came on stream and Churchill was able to give his full attention to Turkey. The diplomatic decrypts which follow reveal that the Southern Department knew well that the Turks would reject all attempts to bring them into the war unless one or other combatant invaded their territory. They knew there existed some differences of emphasis on this point among the leadership in Ankara. They also knew how both neutral and Axis diplomats appraised Turkish foreign policy, because they read the reports of foreign ambassadors, German, Italian, Japanese, Russian, Iberian, South American and Balkan, conveying to their home governments the Turkish attitude to the belligerents, while they could also study the occasional updates circulated by the Turkish foreign ministry to their embassies abroad. To Ankara came reports from Turkish ambassadors in the same capitals reporting secret conversations with others on the international diplomatic network. Many of these reports read by the Southern Department referred to the possibility of a Balkan front, and some, even at this early stage, glanced at the dreaded possibility of separate peacemaking, first between the western Allies and Italy, next between Germany and the Soviet Union. A separate peace would leave at least one major combatant on both sides with sufficient strength and energy to continue and extend the world war, perhaps drawing in the neutrals. The Southern Department also read of the fear, particularly in Spain and Portugal, of the possible Bolshevisation of Europe if Soviet successes were to be fully exploited. The FO knew from other sources that Stalin had no interest in the Comintern or in Trotskyism, but memories of the International Brigade in Spain five years earlier were still strong enough to keep this dire threat alive. The neutrals hoped for some sort of balance of power in Europe. As first Italy and then Germany declined as a power in the Mediterranean, these fears were transferred, first to the 'Anglo-Saxons', and then, irretrievably, to the Soviets.

The Anglo-Turkish Conference at Adana in southern Turkey took place on 31 January 1943 and is the subject of Chapter Six. It came as the climax of Churchill's efforts to get Turkey into the war on the Allied side. This and the next chapter set out to trace the origins of the idea of a direct approach to the Turks, using the DIR/C files. By connecting the diplomatic and Enigma intercepts of the period with the events leading up to the conference itself, it concludes that Churchill's minute study of the intercepts, and the decisions and events which followed, failed to alter the course of events. But this conclusion does not imply that the intercepts did not provide important and timely information on which action plans were drawn up and discussed. They were valuable to and valued by British foreign policy makers. Of these, Churchill saw both service and diplomatic traffic; the FO saw diplomatic traffic only; the COS saw Enigma but not diplomatic; and the rest of the War Cabinet saw arbitrary selections of both sources on a 'need to know' basis. Churchill found more cause for believing Turkey could be seduced into the war than anyone else. Though the Southern Department 'handled' Turkey, a passive or reactive view was taken there of Churchill's attempts to 'get her in', partly because it had no remit to instigate such a policy, and 'getting her in' would have entailed handing her over to Combined Allied Headquarters, Middle East, in Cairo. It was also very conscious of the danger of arousing Russian suspicions of a postwar Turco-British deal involving the Straits, and knew from the intercepts that Turkey remained fearful of a sudden Luftwaffe assault on Istanbul as late as autumn 1943.

Thus the Southern Department wanted to keep Turkey neutral, while the COS, largely under the growing influence of the Americans, were against any Balkan front or offensive action in the eastern Mediterranean which would divert Allied forces from Italy and western Europe, and probably alarm the Soviet Union. For the rest of the War Cabinet Turkish involvement was relatively unimportant. So Churchill concluded that he could and should make Turkish participation in the war on the Allied side a high personal priority.

Can his reading of diplomatic intercepts be seen to have direct influence on that policy? Or were there occasions when his determination to get Turkey into the war made him blind to what he read in the DIR/Cs? The message coming from the intercepts was unequivocal about Turkey, so no recipient of BJs would have been in any doubt that Churchill had an impossible job on his hands. Conversely it is quite possible that both Eden at the FO and the COS might have ignored evidence from the DIR/Cs which suggested that Turkey might be persuaded to enter the war because they had decided that her assistance was not worth the price. The Southern Department, the COS and the War Cabinet had differing views on the advantage of a change in Turkish neutrality, and these governed the attitudes, recommendations and actions of the department, but none shared Churchill's conviction that his personal intervention would change the Turkish mindset. So the Prime Minister went to Turkey without Eden, though with Alexander Cadogan, his permanent under-secretary. Despite the apparent failure of the Adana Conference, Churchill remained determined to create, if not a Balkan front, then certainly a lot of trouble for the enemy, by risking an attack on the Italian-held Dodecanese later in 1943. The disastrous though short-lived results of this campaign are the subject of a later chapter.

Diplomatic interception, decryption, translation, evaluation and distribution had continued through the 1938 war scare, when 'Station X' was set up in August at Bletchley simulating war conditions, to the establishment of Bletchley Park as a going concern by September 1939. This part of GCCS's workload was not part of the main cryptographic thrust which the arrival of the Enigma machine in Britain in September 1939 and the consequential breaking of the Luftwaffe high-grade ciphers generated. 'Dedip' was derived from both interception and cable scrutiny, and continued to be supplied to the FO and other Whitehall departments, alongside Enigma/Ultra. How this joint/parallel operation was managed does not emerge from the disclosed files in the PRO, but it must have been an uneasy marriage, brought to the point of separation (though never divorce) by the decision to hive off diplomatic and commercial traffic to Blitz-torn London from Bletchley in February 1942. From Berkeley Street the FO and Ministry of Economic Warfare (MEW or 'Mousetrap') continued to receive an uninterrupted flow of Dedip as part of its task to monitor the economic blockade. In Whitehall the usefulness of the diplomatic and commercial intercepts grew to a climax in 1943, when the interception and distribution of commercial messages was hived off from GCCS's diplomatic work in Berkeley Street and set up in nearby Aldford House, Park Lane, where careful monitoring of Spanish exports of wolfram, tungsten and manganese to Germany gave the Ministry of Economic Warfare all the information it needed to maintain the economic blockade. The FO rather than the MEW (which started the war as a department of the FO) looked after Turkish supply of chromite and other minerals to Britain, the USA and Germany, as part of its responsibility for Turkey. It failed to stop the supply to the Germans until 1944 by which time they had all they needed anyway. Through the British ambassador in Ankara the Southern Department sought to influence Turkey away from Germany by vague threats the ambassador found very difficult to make convincing, substituting a sort of offended withdrawal of interest which in the end may have played some part in President İnönü's revised anti-German policy in early 1944. But this is doubtful. İnönü on his home territory was never greatly influenced by anyone else's ambassador.

To conclude, a provisional answer to the question what actions were taken by which organs of British government on the conclusions they were drawing from a reading of Turkish diplomatic telegrams: the War Cabinet took instant and effective action to prevent any possibility of Churchill being murdered on his way back from Adana in February 1943 by Algerian extremists. This is recounted in Chapter Six. The War Office kept a military mission going in Ankara, extended runways on western Turkish airfields, and trained Turkish soldiers in the new weaponry and Turkish pilots in Britain alongside those of countries allied to Britain. The Air Ministry contributed by training Turkish pilots alongside those of several European allies, and keeping in touch with the Turkish military establishment in Ankara.

The results in the short term were modest. Churchill's visit to Turkey in January 1943 produced nothing tangible. The Southern Department admitted, to itself but to no one else, that its Turkish policy had failed, withdrew the ambassador, largely for security reasons, and may have consistently underestimated Turkish usefulness as a full ally. This would have been less due to reading BJs and perhaps more due to an inherent philhellenism (most FO officials were former classical scholars) which may have made them anti-Turk. The culture of the pre-war FO was conditioned by the pursuits of classical scholarship. Pierson Dixon was, in this respect, *primus inter pares* (first among equals). But when Greece was overrun by the Germans in 1940, and Italy firmly in the Axis camp, this love of Greece and Rome had little outlet. Classical archaeology in Asia Minor was still in its infancy, and understanding within the Southern Department of what Atatürk had achieved for Turkey between the wars was limited. Despite Loraine, FO views on modern Turkey were still conditioned by her Ottoman past and Islamic culture. The War Office, and the visiting generals, admirals and air marshals failed to make much impact on the Turkish military mindset.

This section has sought to set the stage for Churchill's use of Turkish diplomatic messages starting in the autumn of 1941.

DIR/C on Stream: September 1941

Governmental thinking and decision-making grew to rely on regular information from Boniface, for the COS, and diplomatic messages, for the FO, as soon as the likelihood of a German victory had receded – in fact by the spring of 1942. To appreciate the growing importance to government of sigint it is necessary to revert to its source at Bletchley Park (BP), where both Ultra and diplomatic decrypts were handled from 3 September 1939 until February 1942.

BP had grown considerably by September 1941. Two years after its establishment there, with the number of Enigma solutions growing exponentially, with complex new procedures improvised out of necessity, and with the beginnings of an Anglo-American sigint co-operative, the complexity of its activities outstripped the experience of those who administered it. Reflecting the pre-war constitution and priorities of GCCS, these were FO civilians and ex-service officers who had been trained for cryptanalysis and who still coupled their new administrative responsibilities, as the head of GCCS or as the heads of its sections, with the role of cryptanalyst.[3]

A management crisis, highlighted by a now famous letter asking Churchill for more manpower resources, and delivered to him personally by Stewart Milner-Barry, on behalf of Alan Turing, Gordon Welchman and Hugh Alexander in October 1941, beset Bletchley Park during that autumn,[4] by which time Churchill had been receiving a certain amount of signals intelligence. The supply was intermittent and limited in those early days – though Churchill may have expected a flood. Arrangements for reporting and handling the intelligence were distinctly informal and some reports may not have been retained (with no record of disposal). Moreover, in those days of invasion scares, an effort was made to minimise holdings of sensitive documents.[5]

Research into the provision of diplomatic decrypts to the FO, the MEW and Churchill in June 1942 suggests strongly that they were all receiving many diplomatic decrypts to and from Ankara from the very early days of the war, and before.[6] Government ministers, including Churchill, had been reading Turkey-based diplomatic intercepts since 1922.[7] Further, one should not overlook the 'because it is there' factor in assessing the importance of Turkish diplomatic messages to Churchill. A list of GCCS's diplomatic interception facilities dated 6 June 1942 is remarkable not only for its comprehensive coverage of diplomatic material but also for the indication that the material *from* Turkey was 'full cover', i.e. complete, and to be provided (alone of sending stations except France and Colonies to French Colonies[8]) not by wireless interception but, as has been shown, by clandestine scrutiny by Cable & Wireless Co Ltd.

All other targeted countries sent their messages by W/T, which were intercepted by some ten stations in Britain and abroad. These would be morse, enciphered, perhaps doubly enciphered, and in need not only of decrypting but of translating before assessment was possible. This in turn meant that recipients of BJs had unrestricted access to messages from Ankara. From there the ambassadors of France, Germany, Italy, Japan, Russia and Britain, as well as many Balkan and South American states and Iberia reported to their foreign ministries on Turkish reactions to 'Barbarossa', Pearl Harbor, Mussolini's misfortunes, Hitler's talks with Antonescu of Romania and the North African campaign.

However, many of the most valuable messages came *to* Ankara from neutral capitals where Turkish ambassadors were stationed. The list in Appendix 2 shows that Ankara-bound traffic from France and Germany was intercepted at Denmark Hill, from Persia and Italy at Sandridge, and from Switzerland at Brora, in north-east Scotland, and St Albans. This leaves unclear who intercepted Ankara-bound traffic from other leading suppliers of significant and reliable messages – neutral ambassadors in Tokyo, the Balkan capitals and Kuibyshev.[9] There is plenty of such material in DIR, but how and whence it arrived, usually in very good order with few 'garbled' or 'corrupt' groups, from these other originating centres is unclear. The point to stress is that the very quality and quantity of the Ankara-sourced material might have induced regular readers in the Southern Department, and Churchill, to take a particular interest in Turkish foreign policy – on a 'because it is there' basis.

Researching the history of Bletchley Park in those months, the reasons for the lack of DIR become clear. By September 1941 'Barbarossa' had come and gone. The FO had failed to predict Hitler's onslaught on the Soviet Union, despite the information the BJs carried. On the contrary, both the FO and the COS thought Hitler would mount a Balkan offensive through Romania, Bulgaria and Turkey to cut off Allied oil supplies, isolate Egypt and threaten the route to India and the Dominions. The British persisted in that view long after Enigma and the intercepts showed that Hitler would mount only a defensive campaign in the Balkans, to protect the southern flank of his great drive into the Ukraine, while maintaining his option to invade Britain, despite the bold determination of the German naval chiefs that the Balkan drive of 1940 should be consummated by a major thrust eastwards to join up with the Japanese in the Red Sea.[10] Evidence for pre-knowledge of 'Barbarossa' is harder to evaluate, and was probably more apparent to the War Office than the FO. It is equally difficult to guess how much the British learnt from signals intelligence about Turkey's plans to stay neutral in 1941 since few BJs have yet been released. But presuming the FO had access to them in roughly similar quantities and quality as in subsequent war years, Turkey would have continued to preoccupy the Southern Department.

Churchill, however, went further: it was he (as has been shown) who ordered Dill to order Gen James Marshall-Cornwall to leave his operational command, awaiting a German invasion of the British Isles, to persuade the Turks to join the war on the Allied side. And it was he who urged Eden to make his two fruitless visits to talk to the Turks in the spring of 1941.[11] The FO, in the person of Sir Alexander Cadogan, told Churchill on 6 April 1941 that Turkey had an obligation under the Balkan Pact to come to the assistance of Yugoslavia if she was attacked by Germany, but if Turkey did not look on this as a *casus belli* 'it was not worth trying further'.[12] Though the Southern Department and the War Office shared broadly similar attitudes towards Turkey, only Churchill saw that some activity – *any* activity – was better than nothing.

Across the Atlantic the Americans were furious that Turkey was still supplying chromite to Germany.[13] Their reaction was to cut down on Lease-Lend supplies to Turkey. The FO took a different view, because the British wanted to save their dwindling gold reserves by supplying Turkey with American *matériel*, and knew there was no way of playing the Turkey hand without also providing her with massive amounts of equipment and expertise in the use of the new weaponry. But the technicians supplied to Turkey by Allied firms were reluctant to go in case Turkey was invaded by Germany; and the home-based companies needed their services anyhow. Despite all this, the close Turco-British relationship was everywhere apparent. Turkish air officer cadets learnt to fly from British airfields, alongside Belgian, Polish, French and Dutch cadets. The British ran the Turkish air force and German spies regularly reported to von Papen on British officials organising the extension of Turkish runways.

In Ankara, Ambassador Hugessen was entrusted with the important and delicate task of keeping the Turks sweet. He had a hard act to follow in that his predecessor in the job, the popular and powerful Sir Percy Loraine, had been an intimate friend of Kemal Atatürk. Loraine's pre-war briefings to the FO on the importance to Britain of Turkey's friendship had been so influential in determining FO Southern Department policy that another British diplomat had fantasised in print that Atatürk would appoint Loraine as his successor in the presidency instead of his old protégé and companion in arms, Ismet İnönü.[14]

However, neither Loraine nor Hugessen nor anyone else at the British Embassy bothered to explore the hinterland of Anatolia to report on the actual socio-economic state of the country whose alliance they sought. Had they done so Churchill might well have followed Hitler in deciding against further pressure. Conditions remained primitive in the extreme. Though the Turks suspected Hitler of planning to cross their country to get to Egypt, they would keep out of the war unless and until they were actually invaded; and then they would fight the invader to the death. On 27 August Churchill wrote to Lt-Gen Sir Leslie Hollis of his defence staff – for the COS – about the staff conversations with the Turks: 'A good start has been made in recommending a rapprochement [between Turkey and the Soviets]. We do not mean to push the Turks into the war against their better judgment. Turkey will become a partner in the immense resources of the British empire and the USA.' But Ismay minuted that the Turks had taken fright.[15]

Warlike friendships were being offered to Turkey by all sides. On 1 September 1941 Churchill wrote to Roosevelt that the recent Russo-British invasion of Persia served the purpose of encouraging 'Turkey to stand as a solid block against German passage into Syria and Palestine'. Roosevelt disliked his allies' activities in Persia intensely, as did the Turks. Britain was going to make Persia a puppet 'and get all the wealth for nothing'.[16] 'Would a similar fate await Turkey?'[17] 'The genuineness of British friendship can always be measured by the degree to which their interest is involved.' The Turkish ambassador in London commented, 'neutrality no longer has any meaning . . . Britain will occupy Persia so we should be on the same side.'

Many Turkey-sourced diplomatic messages were also being read by Hitler from September 1941 onwards.[18] Hitler used them to pursue a moderate Turkish policy. As early as 1 March 1941 he had written to İnönü that the German move in Bulgaria should not alarm Turkey as he had ordered his troops to keep well back from the frontier.[19] His table talk showed him well briefed on domestic Balkan affairs.[20] He decided early on that Turkey should not be invaded or forced into the war: the country's benevolent neutrality suited him well, even when his egregious ambassador, Fritz von Papen, told him on 2 September that the Italians were expected to march through Turkey. But the Italians observed Turkish reactions to the Russo-British adventure in Persia: there would be revolts in former Turkish territories on the Persian borders, fomented to justify Russian intervention. Now that England was allied with Russia, the British-Turkish link was weakened, and the Turco-Axis link strengthened. Turkey would offer to mediate between Persia and the Allies.[21] On 5 September Churchill told Soviet Ambassador Ivan Maisky that 'some offensive action might be possible in the spring of 1942', perhaps in conjunction with Turkey, who 'would be encouraged to join with us as she saw our strength grow'. 'No Balkan front,' Churchill told Stalin, 'could be opened without the help of Turkey.'[22] A week later, Halder, the Wehrmacht Chief of Staff, noted that 'things in Turkey are going our way'.[23] Hitler told his dinner guests: 'The Danube is the link with Turkey. Gerede has been called to Ankara . . . The fall of Sebastopol has caused great jubilation . . . Gerede may be appointed [Turkish] Foreign Minister. He is not a militant diplomat like Oshima but he is absolutely convinced that Turkey and Germany must go forward hand-in-hand.'[24]

In Britain the question arose, who should handle Turkey? Combined Forces HQ in the Middle East or the FO? Both urged their cases to Churchill, but he and the FO were at one on this issue at least: it must continue to be handled by the Southern Department, from London. In late September 1941 the War Cabinet wrote to GHQ ME:

> Turkey occupies such an important position in our foreign policy that relations with that country must be directed from London . . . If Turkey came into the war the position would be radically different.[25]

The question recurred constantly, particularly when Churchill and Gen Sir Henry 'Jumbo' Maitland Wilson needed troops and equipment for the Dodecanese operation of autumn 1943. But since Turkey never passed from a political to a strategic relationship with the Allies, the Southern Department maintained its hold on Turkey, while in all material respects Churchill himself acted for them.

Following the invasion of Persia, the possibility of a move in Afghanistan presented itself to Churchill, when the influential Italian ambassador in Kabul reported that the government there was prepared 'to grant anything the British cared to ask'. The PM sidelined this BJ heavily and ordered it sent to the 'F Secy' (*sic*) 'to be returned to WSC'.[26] The PM wrote to Eden:

You have an open door which you should force at the earliest moment . . .
Let us get rid of [the ringleaders of the pro-Axis rebellion there] now
while all this part of the world is under the impression of our Persian
success.[27]

Eden then wrote to India about 'secret information from reliable sources . . .
the Afghans would grant any demand we might make . . . short of military
occupation'. Using the same words of Churchill and the intercept, Eden was
making little personal contribution to policy.

This accumulation of Turkish diplomatic messages culminated on
13 September[28] when the well-informed Japanese ambassador in Ankara,
Sho Kurihara, reported that the Allies 'were forcing Turkey to join up with
them'. British pressure had increased since the Allies went into Persia; but
'Turkey would resist such pressure as they are afraid of Germany'.[29]
Pressure from a different point came from British insistence that Turkey
should allow British ships through the Dardanelles so the Russian navy 'can
leave the Black Sea'.[30] Churchill minuted to the First Sea Lord
(Adm Sir Dudley Pound), 'What is the Admiralty view? Would you like [the
Russians] to get out or leave them to keep their command of the Black Sea
till the end of their tether? Better have this looked at.'[31]

This section has linked the Turkish diplomatic messages received by
Hitler as well as Churchill to the development of both Axis and Allied
policies towards Turkey from September 1941 till September 1942. The
next three months were to prove conclusive so far as Churchill's grasp of the
Turkish problem was concerned.

Churchill's Turkey Hand: October–December 1941

Churchill's advocacy of his Turkish policy was by now in full spate. On
17 September he wrote to Stalin, the very day British and Soviet troops
entered Tehran after the Shah's abdication: 'The great prize is Turkey; if
Turkey can be gained another powerful army will be available.'[32] And two
days later, on the 19th, he wrote to the COS on the 'effect produced upon
Turkey by our being able to add two divisions to the forces . . . thus
appreciably increasing the chances of influencing the Turkish action'.[33] The
most immediate prize would be getting Turkey to resist German demands
for passage of her troops through Anatolia. He added to Stalin on 21
September: 'Effective help would come if Turkey could be induced to resist
a German demand for the passage of troops, or, better still, if she should
enter the war.' The next day he was addressing the COS: 'It would be well
worth Great Britain and Russia revising their arrangements . . . in order to
induce Turkey to come in on our side.'[34] His reading of the Ankara material
coincided with his wish to make a personal and sensational contribution to
the war effort by a personal visit to Turkey.

But Turkey was pressing ahead with an agreement to supply chromite to

Germany, in order to raise much needed foreign currency and also to maintain the balance of neutrality. US Secretary of State Cordell Hull was outraged and sent for the Turkish ambassador in Washington for an explanation.[35] The demand was deftly passed to Ankara, but in London the Japanese chargé reported to Tokyo that 'Turkey had given in to Germany's vigorous demands. It seems that the British are not actually opposing this though it is against their wishes.'[36] Dr Carl Clodius, the German trade negotiator, upstaged von Papen and conducted his business directly with the Turkish government.[37] The Vichy French ambassador in Ankara (Massigli) learnt '. . . *d'une bonne source j'ai reçu connaissance des négociations avec le gouvernement turc . . . Les négociations se derouleront dans une atmosphère cordiale.*' Clodius first approached the French, to ask the Turks under *l'accord du 8 janvier 1940* to help Germany to get the chromite for steel refining.[38] But this astonishing piece of diplomacy foundered since the accord provided chrome only for Britain and France, and Vichy France was now almost *hors de combat*, not yet part of the Axis but scarcely neutral. Menemencioğlu himself left Istanbul for Ankara to lead the Turkish delegation:

> The Germans will buy oil, maize, agricultural produce, tobacco, cotton. They will demand manganese, chrome and *antimoine*. They will make available 75 million Turkish pounds.[39]

In Berlin, Hitler realised that one strategic option, which included the invasion of Asiatic Turkey, had been aborted by the Royal Navy. The Japanese chargé in Berlin reported on the modest size of the Russian Black Sea Fleet. The Wehrmacht was contemplating crossing from the Romanian and Bulgarian coasts:[40]

> So Turkey's position would be jeopardised . . . Britain would be compelled to thrust her fleet into the Black Sea and upset Germany's landing scheme . . . If the German army attacks Turkey the British fleet would force the Straits and enter the Black Sea. As Germany is aware of this, Germany will not at present attack Turkey.[41]

On the same date Hugessen wrote to his friend Emrys Evans:

> My main job is to diagnose how far the Turco-German treaty really represents a falling away from the previous stout-hearted policy. If one found oneself unexpectedly surrounded by Huns (as the Turks did in May) one would at least avoid all foolhardiness . . . they won't throw all away for our beaux yeux. Clodius and co. have been here for about a fortnight. We put a big spoke in their wheel over chrome. I hear the Hun delegate is sick as mud.[42]

On 2 October the Greek chargé in Cairo reported to London:

> The Turkish government is disquieted as German action appears imminent, whereas Turkey wishes to stay outside the ring and will . . . make many concessions, much more substantial than is generally supposed . . . The highest [Turkish army] officers exclude a [quarrel] with Germany . . . The Foreign Minister [Numan Menemencioğlu] anticipates a German attack . . . to justify non resistance he is putting forward various excuses, such as inadequacy of supplies of war material, and Britain failing to honour the Second Front in the West . . . He hopes that by the Spring Russia will be defeated and that the war will thus be brought to an end by negotiation before Turkey is compelled to take part in it.[43]

On the same day (2 October) De Peppo, the Italian ambassador at Ankara, reported his conversation with Clodius:

> My own impression is that he took some political soundings too, and that he is convinced that Turkey [garbled] to maintain her neutrality against everyone. In the matter of foreign trade, too, Turkey is trying to keep out of either camp, with leanings towards Britain who controls and regulates Turkish trade with herself and the US [Churchill to Eden: 'This is noteworthy'].[44]

The next day GCCS circulated an intercept from the German chargé in Stockholm noting that:

> . . . the whole world had its eyes on Turkey . . . Everyone wishes to win her to his own side. England naturally wishes to see the German and Turkish armies weaken themselves in fighting one another, but Turco-German friendship stands solid. Sweden has understood from this how great a danger Russia, with her desire for a corridor to the open sea, constitutes both for herself and for Europe.[45]

On the same day the Japanese ambassador in Ankara spelt out a twelve-point scenario for Turkey:

1) Germany will drive to the Caucasus.
2) Turkey will keep in step with Germany.
3) If Turkey's attitude is ambiguous Germany will exert pressure 'or even try conclusions with them once for all'.
4) Germany will [garbled] Turkey in the end so the outlook is not hopeful.
5) Britain attaches great importance to Turkey as 'centre of Near Eastern defence'.
6) Anglo-Soviet activity in Persia was a sideshow.

7) Popular sentiment in Turkey is expecting a breakaway from Britain.
8) Britain may demand passage of Soviet aid through Turkey.
9) British ships would go through the Straits.
10) There could be a joint (Allied) defence in the Caucasus, consisting of Russia, Britain and Turkey.
11) Turkey will lean neither way.
12) The British are becoming desperate.[46]

George Clutton in the Southern Department of the FO minuted forcefully during October: 'We can only reflect on our folly in refusing the Turkish proposals of 1939–40 that we should take the total chrome output for a period of twenty years.'[47]

On 10 October, the Japanese ambassador reported from Ankara to Tokyo that Gerede, the Turkish ambassador to Germany admired by Hitler, advised İnönü 'to disregard Anglo-Turkish relations and cooperate with Germany. The President is understood to have accepted his advice on the whole and to have decided to follow an opportunistic policy'. He also reported that two high-ranking Turkish generals had been invited by the Germans to inspect the fighting on the Eastern Front:

. . . taken in conjunction with the recent German-Turkish joint declaration and trade agreement, this is seen to indicate a tightening of relations between Germany and Turkey. Generally speaking Turkey sees that the outcome of the fighting on the Eastern front is already decided and the collapse of the Soviet is near at hand. Little by little, therefore, she appears to be trying to bring about a rapprochement with the Axis and I have the impression that the feeling is that this attitude has been decided upon earlier than expected.[48]

This message was repeated to Berlin and Rome. Berlin may have obtained it through the *Forschungsamt*, who may well have used similar arrangements to the British for reading Ankara-based diplomatic traffic.

On 14 October 'C' told Churchill that the Turks expected to be invaded by the Germans in the spring and on the 19th an intercept contained speculation about a German attack on Suez through Turkey.[49] The next day Churchill was writing to Roosevelt about Turkey:

She may be consolidated in her resistance to Hitler. We do not require Turkey to enter the war aggressively at the present moment, but only to maintain a stolid, unyielding front to German threats and blandishments.[50]

His language about Turkey strikingly mirrors that of the German diplomat in Sweden.[51] Churchill was well aware, through his intercept reading, of the true state of German global intentions in late 1941, as Oshima reported from Berlin to Tokyo the next day: 'German plans for an invasion of England were still in an active phase. The next step is the overthrow of Britain.'[52] He reported Hitler and Ribbentrop saying to him that 'Germany is firmly resolved to carry out an invasion of Britain'.

Both Hitler and Ribbentrop admired Oshima because he spoke as much for the Japanese Army as the Foreign Ministry. They were almost equally impressed by Gerede, the Turkish ambassador in Berlin, summoned to Ankara at the time, so they believed, in order to be appointed Minister for Foreign Affairs there. Hitler approved his pro-German stance but noted that Oshima had the more 'militant' mindset. In fact that key job went to Numan Menemencioğlu.[53] The report was sent to Ankara as well as Tokyo. On 18 October Hugessen asked the FO 'whether German boasts of victory in the East are bluff or not.' An anodyne reply was drafted which the FO sent to its main ambassadorial clients: Cadogan railed against Turkey's 'timorousness'.[54]

Hitler was still carrying all before him. On 11 November Oshima reported on German plans to shift their eastern offensive south, to pincer the British in the Mediterranean and enable Spain to take Gibraltar, while on the same day the new Japanese ambassador in Ankara, Kurihara, reported that Germany would continue south to the Caucasus and 'may send 15–20 divisions from the Balkans to proceed through Turkey and make Turkey the nucleus of their Near Eastern plans of operation'.[55]

The Mediterranean was, in fact, a sideshow for the Germans but mainstream for the Allies. The UK claimed to have fifteen divisions in the area but no one believed this, and the Turks, Iraqis, Persians and Syrians were all turning against Britain, looking for their independence with the whole of the Arab world, under German protection. 'So German troops in the Near East might mean a Moslem uprising and a mortal blow to the British Empire, India and the South Pacific.' The next day Kurihara was less specific about his Turkey-based information on German intentions in the area. If Germans crossed Turkey 'the consequences would be profound'.[56]

Diplomatic intercepts were providing not only valuable, if sometimes exaggerated, reports of German aggressive plans but equally important reports on the war plans of Britain's inscrutable new ally, Russia. Changes in the Soviet high command, reported by the Turkish ambassador in Kuibyshev, the temporary Soviet capital from 16 October, would not in any other way have been known to Churchill and the COS, since the latter acknowledged that diplomatic intercepts were not just their main but their *only* source of information on the Russian order of battle. And of more immediate urgency than the possibility of an invasion of Turkey was the apparently irresistible surge of Panzer troops through the Ukraine: it was here that the final outcome of hostilities would be determined, as Churchill knew well. On 30 November, his birthday, Churchill annotated a blue jacket: 'Fear. It does not prevent, it may provoke action. But it is a fact all the same.'[57] Who can blame Churchill for thinking of fear on his 67th birthday, with the invasion of Britain still on Hitler's agenda?

A fortnight later those fears were finally put to rest by Hitler, who declared war on the USA following the Japanese bombing of the American navy at Pearl Harbor on 7 December. The ring was closed. It was not enough for Japan to be fighting America in the Pacific, particularly as Russia saw no need to join in. It was not enough for Germany and Russia to be at each other's throats in the Ukraine, with the outcome in doubt and the possibility of a separate peace between them an ever-present nightmare. It was enough when Hitler finally overreached himself, and having forced war on both the superpowers, finally ensured that Churchill need no longer brood over his personal fears.

With Turkey now more likely to become a belligerent, the rest of the year saw little change in her position. On 5 December Churchill wrote to Eden:

> The attitude of Turkey becomes increasingly important, both to Russia and Great Britain. The Turkish army of 50 divisions requires air support. We have promised a minimum of 4 and a maximum of 12 fighter squadrons to Turkey in the event of Turkey being attacked.[58]

Kurihara, and hence Churchill, also knew of a German study of future operations including 'Plan Orient' – 'From Bulgaria, if Turkey were acquiescent, a force of 10 divisions . . . would traverse Anatolia into Syria' and 'Turkey will support the Axis in the Spring'.[59]

Kurihara was wrong. Before spring came many thousands of German and Russian troops had died of cold, as well as of combat. Singapore fell to the Japanese in February and Turkish neutrality was off the agenda. Warfare, even global warfare, is seasonal. If snow and ice make invasion impossible in deep winter, mud makes the passage of non-tracked vehicles impossible throughout most of the spring. The Caucasus and south Russia are among the muddiest places on earth and the spring mud thaw in Russia was in April. Hitler's ambitions were restrained by the weather. He realised the hard way a truth he passed on to Goebbels, that Russian soldiers fought best in winter and Germans in summer.

This section has traced Turkey's understanding of neutrality through the autumn of 1941, and has drawn on the early files of DIR/C (HW1) for the differences they indicate in Churchillian historiography between periods when a study of DIR/C can throw light on what he wrote, thought and did, and other periods (e.g. January to February 1942) when the DIR/C files are unavailable. What follows pursues this theme in the early months of 1942.

Turkish Neutrality and British Disasters: Spring 1942

Churchill's daily reading of diplomatic files and Enigma continued, and from the comparative safety and warmth of Whitehall, the FO developed its own plans for Turkey. Dixon of the Southern Department listened to the

Bulgarian diplomat Gavrilovitch, full of the advantages of a Balkan federation; full, too, 'of tiresome ideas about the future of Europe'.[60] George Rendel, formerly of the same department but by now minister plenipotentiary in Bucharest, commented with some foresight: 'we must prevent Russian encroachment into the Balkans postwar and at once consider what steps are necessary to forestall her.'[61] Dixon noted Turkish suspicions of Soviet intentions: 'We should pretend to dispel this. We want Turkey to stay wary of Russia.' Over both these diplomats loomed the presence of Permanent Under-Secretary Sir Orme Sargent, whose views of where Britain should be in world affairs came straight from the FO policy of about 1910. Looking for the re-establishment of British influence in the postwar Balkans at a time when peace was four years off, and Allied victory by no means certain, suggests a lurking *folie de grandeur* in the FO which contrasted with Churchill's instinctive grasping of the moment.[62]

Reality was different. The British were retreating before the numerically inferior Japanese down the Malay peninsula. Eden failed to charm the Turkish ambassador in London. Churchill ironically marked an intercept which told him that he was about to resign and the British cabinet would be reconstructed without him.[63] On 21 January Hugessen cabled the FO reporting his talk with President İnönü who was expecting a German attack through Thrace and had authorised many divisions of Turkish soldiers to bivouac there.[64] Churchill queried the COS: 'I thought Turkish forces were mainly in Anatolia, not Thrace?' But 40 per cent were manning the borders with Greece and Bulgaria.[65] On 9 February Numan Menemencioğlu was reckoned by the Southern Department to be the 'best bargainer the Turks ever had' and 'was reluctant to let slip any chance of extra arms'.[66] All this showed Churchill that the Turkish leadership was in an aggressive mode, with so many of their forces on the frontier with Greece and Bulgaria, prepared not only to defend Thrace, but if called upon, to invade Bulgaria – an action the officer class thought both desirable and inevitable.

HW1 is silent from 382 of 23 January to 385 of 23 February.[67] This particular lacuna may have been due to the reorganisation of GCCS which brought all work on diplomatic and commercial messages from Bletchley Park to Berkeley Street, and later Aldford House, serviced by the FO intercept station at Wavendon near Bletchley at the end of February 1942.[68] Cadogan, to whom the diplomatic traffic came directly rather than monitored through BP's 'Director', Menzies, wrote that 12 February was 'the blackest day of the war'. Allied and neutral shipping losses achieved staggering proportions, the British were on the run in Libya and Singapore was about to fall to the Japanese.[69] So we do not know from the DIR files of the period what the diplomatic community worldwide made of British disasters. It is noteworthy that Pacific affairs always commanded less attention than European affairs in the reports of the diplomats. An event like the dismissal of Mussolini echoed round European chancelleries for months;

but a major victory or defeat in the Pacific theatre rarely commanded similar attention, though Allied defeat and eventual success in nearby North Africa did.

In Ankara an attempt was made on von Papen's life while he and his wife were walking to work. Three Russians and a Turk were arrested on suspicion, and a Soviet plot was assumed, though indignantly denied. Lengthy legal proceedings failed to prove conclusive guilt of the Russians and Turk arrested. The Turkish prime minister died and Sukru Saraçoğlu, former foreign minister, and a man of calculated indiscretion on occasion, took office, retaining his existing role until the cleverest of all Turkish statesmen, Numan Menemencioğlu, was appointed foreign minister. Some suspected him of pro-German leanings, but he served the Turkish cause assiduously and his dismissal by the president in early 1944 was rightly resented by his family.

On 26 March Hugessen wrote again to the MP Emrys Evans: 'Things here are very calm . . . the Germans have more important things to think about than attack Turkey . . . We are not likely to become more than a factor in some general scheme.'[70] But the next day the Japanese ambassador in Sofia reported to Tokyo that 'Turkey was in a state of extreme anxiety. If Russia is defeated in the west, it can still have Siberia as a stronghold for communist doctrine.'[71] The Japanese should take over India while 'others are otherwise occupied' to prevent it falling, via international communism, to Russia. A day later 'C' sent a significant intercept to Churchill. The Chinese ambassador in Ankara, having reported the assassination attempt on von Papen added: 'Turkish territory will not be subdued by the Germans, but the Germans think that if all goes well Turkey will be surrounded, and will become a second Sweden.' He went on to say that Turkey was hemmed in by the Soviets, and might have to escape by the Dardanelles if Germany occupied the Crimea. Bulgaria would then join in. If British and Soviet troops invaded Turkey, Bulgaria and Germany would enter Turkey. 'German troops are already in Thrace and the Aegean islands. Bulgaria hopes in this way to stop Turkey yielding to the Allies.'[72] In fact Bulgarian troops were never sent beyond the borders of their own country, Hitler respecting the traditional historical and religious Slavic entente between Bulgaria and Russia.[73] An intercepted message from the Turkish ambassador in Kuibyshev (read by British and Germans as well as Turks) reported hostile Bulgarian reactions to German demands for Bulgarian troops to replace some of their own casualties on the Eastern Front: 'these troops would be needed to defend Bulgaria against the Turks'.[74] So fear of the Turk pinned valuable divisions, already equipped by the Germans, in Bulgaria when they might have fought the Russians at Stalingrad; and Churchill's instinct about Turkey's key role in Balkan affairs was justified. These contrasting accounts of the state of Turkish morale suggest Hugessen was too bland, and other ambassadors, Chinese, Japanese and Turkish, got closer to the truth.

At the end of March, Hitler told his dinner guests:

I prefer the Turks [to the Romanians] . . . I would conclude a trade treaty with her, supply her with arms and ammunitions, and guarantee the inviolability of the Straits and the integrity of her frontiers, if the Turks had any wish for an alliance with us.[75]

In early April Rommel began his offensive against the British in North Africa. And on 9 April Churchill read that Germany would attack Turkey as part of the spring offensive, either from the Caucasus or Serbia.[76] Five days later Alanbrooke was reflecting on the consequences of a successful Japanese incursion into the Indian Ocean: 'Germany would get all the oil she required, the Southern route to Russia would be cut, Turkey would be isolated and defenceless.'[77]

This chapter has been mainly concerned with the world's reactions to Turkish neutrality in 1941, the period before BJs came on stream. In the welter of conflicting information available to Churchill, the Foreign Office and the COS as to Turkish intentions and potential, insufficient attention was given to the country's geographical and socio-economic conditions, or to the effect there of British disasters in the spring of 1942. The next chapter shows Churchill's personal handling of Anglo-Turkish affairs in a new light through BJs.

CHAPTER FIVE

Churchill's Turkey Hand
1942

Ambassador Hiroshi confided to [Gœbbels] that Japan would capture Singapore shortly. 'He is already forging plans for a joint [Japanese-German] assault on India. But we're some way short of that.'
David Irving, *Goebbels: Mastermind of the Third Reich*, p. 646

Fear! It may not prevent, it may even provoke action. But it is there all the same.
WSC HW/1 261

Churchill's depression at the course of events culminating in the surrender at Singapore on 12 February 1942 is palpable all through this period. The Japanese rout of British arms signalled the end of Empire, and Churchill was an imperialist. A perceptive American historian of Churchillian war strategy noticed Churchill's frequent inexplicable bouts of pessimism at this time.[1] This pessimism could well have been brought on by his compulsive reading of BJs. Writing in 1959, nearly twenty years before the breaking of the Ultra secret, Higgins's analysis of Allied strategy in 1942 remarkably anticipates the release of the most secret source and shows that history and historical perceptions are not greatly changed by the discovery of new sources, however clandestine and exciting. The same can be said for the official historians' account of Churchillian strategic planning and activity in the eastern Mediterranean from 1941 to 1943. Both draw substantially on Churchill's own history.[2] Churchill's disingenuous claims for his history are prominently displayed in Volume 5 (*Closing the Ring*):

> I do not seek to do more than make a contribution to history from the standpoint of the British Prime Minister and Minister of Defence. *In this, my directives, telegrams and minutes, written at the time and not in the afterlight are my stepping stones.*[3]

With hindsight, he can be said to have underestimated the influence his history would exercise on the work of subsequent historians, both official and revisionist.

Due perhaps to the very scale of British disasters in the spring of 1942, Turkish friendship rose high once again on Churchill's agenda. On 17 April he invited the Turkish ambassador to accompany him to Washington, to facilitate the movement of American Lease-Lend *matériel* and equipment to Turkey.[4] DIR files came to him there from 'C' at the rate of two and sometimes three a day. Turkey was deeply impressed by German successes in the Balkans and south Russia and by 21 April the FO read with some scepticism that Turkey would offer to mediate between Britain and Germany if Germany won the spring offensive towards the Caucasus.[5] Military talks were going on between the Turks and British in Ankara. The British learnt that Marshal Chakmak's deputy was pro-Axis, but none the less the Turks would not want either Germany or Britain to invade the Dodecanese, though they would accept a Greek takeover from the Italians. On 21 April the FO explained why it was hanging on to Turkey:

Turkey's position is of extreme delicacy and complexity. A fundamental factor is Turco-Soviet relations, and the bearing thereof on Anglo-Soviet relations, a subject outside the sphere of the Minister of State [Harold Macmillan]. Turco-American relations become increasingly important, and the complete picture *is only visible in London.*[6]

Throughout April BJs track Turkish reactions to Axis successes and to counteract these a party of Turkish journalists, fresh from a visit to Germany, was invited to Britain in May. The project was Eden's, and Hugessen was hesitant. Dixon thought the idea 'excellent' if the prime minister would agree to be part of the programme. The Turkish party was impressed by the Minister of Food, Lord Woolton, and the RAF, as well as factory managers in Glasgow. The audience with Churchill, however, was a disappointment. He reminisced in his atrocious French about the First World War with a veteran Turkish journalist and failed to notice his audience, all of whom were fluent English speakers. But on their return they said they were sure the Allies would win and Menemencioğlu thought they came back too pro-British.[7]

Deringil observes that it was essential for Germany to neutralise Turkey when attacking Russia.[8] The main Axis offensive did not start until 28 June, when the Germans defeated the Russians in the Kharkov offensive, and the Anglo-Soviet 20-Year Mutual Assistance Treaty was signed in London by Eden and Molotov, so Turkey realised that if she had to fight Russia she would have to fight Britain too.[9] The Portuguese ambassador in Ankara, who thought that a Russian victory entailed the Bolshevisation of Europe, reported that 'to avoid the triumph of Russia Turkey would sacrifice everything, even the British alliance'.[10] But the Turkish Foreign Ministry the same day assured its diplomats abroad that 'everyone is friendly, despite the recent bomb trial. [The attempt on the Papens' lives]. Our country is completely calm, united round our national leader.'[11]

Churchill, now at odds with Eden and the FO, wanted to offer *matériel* – 'a large, simple offer'. He roundly attacked Eden's foreign policy.[12] Both the

Southern Department and Churchill were following Turkish sensitivities day by day, and the record showed he was wavering himself. Though he wrote to Eden, 'I have proposed a practical and hopeful policy towards Turkey and I should be grateful if you would address your mind to this', an intercept on 22 May bears Churchill's comment that he was 'not too sure of the Turks'.[13]

HW1/596–9 of 25 May all show diplomatic speculation on Britain and the USA planning the invasion of Turkey but whether this was based on hope, or fear, or disinformation, or a successful war of nerves by Germany or a combination of all is difficult to determine. Certainly there is no evidence that the COS ever developed even a feasability study of a full-scale invasion, which would have gone against all their instincts. And equally certainly the Turks themselves were not unduly alarmed: when the Turkish ambassador in Madrid was warned by his Italian colleague about British designs on Turkey with the words 'the British will start a military action against our country', his reply was 'propaganda'.[14]

British reverses remained top of the diplomatic agenda. On 21 June Tobruk fell, with a resonance throughout all the Mediterranean countries, not least Turkey, who had always admired German military success and now began to doubt the wisdom of unconditional friendship with the British. The Chinese ambassador in Ankara reported that 'Turkey's desire was to remain neutral and independent. The British lost control of the Mediterranean so the Axis powers could get to Suez without using Turkey.'[15] At the same time the Portuguese ambassador in Ankara reported on the problems facing Turkey if Germany conquered Egypt. 'The Turks are great realists.' The Axis had not decided about Turkey but 'Turkey must declare herself soon'.[16] On 3 July Rommel halted his 400-mile advance at El Alamein in the face of the Eighth Army's fierce resistance, but Turkey was by now feeling the full weight of German pressure. On 7 July the Japanese ambassador in Istanbul (Kurihara) reported on Turkish relations:

> Turkey is shilly-shallying and heading for friendlessness . . . Since the fall of Tobruk Turkey was dismayed at the sudden change in the war situation, and seemed to be considerably agitated, and it is generally thought that there would be some change shortly.[17]

Neither Churchill nor the FO would have been pleased to read Kurihara reporting that:

> I think we [the Japanese] should lean on Turkey because the PM and Chakmak [marshal of all Turkish armed forces] have for a long time advocated co-operation with Germany, so Turkey getting closer to the Axis may not be difficult.

He had spoken to von Papen who observed that Turkey reacted badly to pressure, but would give some pledge to Germany 'when a suitable opportunity arose'.[18] In Sofia the same diplomatic reactions were expressed, as also in Madrid and Vichy, where the German representative pressed both Turkish and Hungarian ambassadors about their countries' attitudes towards Axis Mediterranean successes.[19] On 17 July the Turkish military attaché in Washington reported:

> 1942 was the year of the Axis powers. The British have been heavily defeated. The Americans have no experience of a shooting war, and there is no unified Anglo-US command.

The German offensive in the east looked unstoppable. The Portuguese ambassador in Stockholm reported that the Germans, whose summer offensive had begun on 28 June, were close to reaching the Volga, thus threatening the Caucasus through Rostov-on-Don and cutting off Russia from her oil supply. The 'threatened people of Asia Minor (including the Turks) do not like this joining up of German armies in Russia with those in Egypt.'[20] Would Germany go for a separate peace with Russia? Germany would in any event retain the territories captured from Russia (Churchill marked this with an exclamation mark). On 26 July the Turkish ambassador in Cairo reported to Ankara that British failures against the Germans put Alexandria under threat.[21] The new 'generation of [British] tank commanders were not as good as the old ones.' In the event of defeat Britain would flood Egypt and withdraw to the Nile. On 30 July Kurihara reported the Turkish view of the Russian plight.[22] He reported that the Russian army was said to be near to collapse. Stalin had gone to the front to shoot generals. Stalin meanwhile sent Maisky to Churchill to demand a second front immediately. A week later the Turkish ambassador in Kuibyshev reported to Ankara that the Russians were at last consolidating their positions behind the Don.[23]

On 29 July the new Italian ambassador in Ankara reported his talk with Saraçoğlu. Turkey intended to remain neutral despite the propaganda efforts of British agents. Saraçoğlu said Turkey will:

> . . . defend her frontiers without asking for help from the Axis, if Britain decides to open up another front [on the coasts of Turkey]. Turkey could no longer be indifferent towards the Arab movement . . . Turkey would abandon the policy of absenteeism towards the Arabs, adopted by Atatürk . . . Turkey shared common origins with Muslim Arabs . . . This need not worry the Axis.

Saraçoğlu begged his visitor to use discretion in relaying these far-ranging thoughts: 'keep the whole conversation absolutely secret'.[24] That interview gave the FO, and Churchill, new insight into the mind of the Turkish leadership: not just the frankness or the indiscretion, but the possibility of a recrudescence of panturanism – the longing for the great days of Turkish power, through a new approach to the Arab world, already half seduced by Hitler's charm. Not surprisingly Cadogan noted something 'rotten in the state of Turkey'.[25]

The FO had no divisions to implement its policy. It could only listen, ruminate, squabble and recommend in balanced paragraphs of faultless prose which infuriated Churchill, himself no mean stylist. On 24 August the Turkish ambassador in Berlin reported a renewal of Turco-German friendship over lunch with Hitler.[26] Five days later Hugessen reported on the supply to Turkey of German war, industrial and railway *matériel* as bait for immediate attraction: 'These developments suggest Turkey is insuring herself with Germany . . . The Turks are a hard-headed race and are doubtless trying to get as much as possible out of both sides.'[27] On 28 August Churchill was told by his private secretary that 'Turkish ciphers are known to be broken' and Ismay was instructed to keep the COS on their toes about Turkey.[28] On 31 August Clutton minuted that Turkish neutrality meant having a foot in both camps but with *one* more firmly placed than the other. 'This is the policy which Bismarck called re-insurance and what Menemencioğlu calls active neutrality.'[29]

The Southern Department had known for at least five months that Turkey was being heavily bribed by Germany. As far back as 25 March the Chancery at Ankara had reported that the 'Axis have been offering neighbouring territories to Ankara . . . Aleppo and some of the Greek islands'. A German diplomat in Ankara expected the Turks would demand Syria, Aleppo and Mosul. On 22 June Clutton wrote: 'quite likely the Turks have territorial aspirations in the Aegean islands, but unless they play a more active part in the war they are unlikely to see them realised.'[30] On 9 September the same official summarised Turkish territorial ambitions:

> We may see Turkish claims to a rectification of the Turco-Persian frontier, and in Bulgaria similar adjustments south of Burgas. . . . The Turks undoubtedly expect to receive a major portion of the Dodecanese and would also like Mosul.[31]

They were, moreover, angry at British failure to deliver *matériel* as agreed, and Rauf Orbay, the controversial but long-serving Turkish ambassador in London, asked to see Churchill rather than Eden, since Churchill was seen to be the more emollient of the two. The ambassador expressed his worry that Turkey was not being treated as a full ally. There was straight talk of less than complete mutual confidence.[32] On 12 September Orbay reported that London was at last expediting the war deliveries. Russian Ambassador Ivan Maisky, sitting next to him in the House of Commons Visitors' Gallery, whispered, 'There are new dangers facing Turkey.'[33] This view was expressed more graphically by Oshima in Berlin cabling Tokyo that 'the link between Europe and Asia must be perfected, opening the road over which

Japan and Germany may mutually fulfil their economic duties'. The anti-British struggle in India was intensifying, as means to that end.[34]

On 14 September Berkeley Street intercepted, processed and circulated a brief report from the Turkish ambassador in Berlin to Ankara: 'According to a reliable source Rommel [?is] going to attack in a week's time. ARIKAN.'[35] The same day[36] the Greek chargé in Ankara talked with the former US presidential candidate Wendell Willkie and Erkin of the Turkish Foreign Ministry. Willkie made six points:

- Importance of Turco-US relations.
- Allied victory certain.
- USA will be involved in the postwar settlement of Europe.
- Turkish foreign policy is approved of by the president.
- Allies victory in Egypt assured, despite setbacks.
- More *matériel* is to come to Turkey direct from USA under the Lease-Lend agreement.

This important démarche by a leading US politician, who travelled at the express wish of the president, did not include the Soviet Union. Erkin (Secretary General) was pleased and this was 'a measure of Turkey's distrust of Soviet designs'. The next day the Turkish foreign ministry distributed its observations on the Willkie visit to all Turkish diplomatic representatives abroad. Willkie had praised Turkish foreign policy as 'straightforward and loyal' (English word used). In London the Turkish ambassador noted that Churchill in parliament had lost 'nothing of his influence and power'.[37] The day after that Arikan reported from Berlin that 'two persons, not German, said Germany may come to terms with Russia through Japanese mediation'.[38] The source would be Japanese colleagues of Oshima. On 28 September the FO hinted at Turkish-related BJs in their telegram to Hugessen (which, they reminded him, must not be quoted, and burnt after reading); the Turkish ciphers were not only compromised but being read, and the progress of the Turco-German armament negotiations and about chrome were routinely read by all parties.[39] On 30 September the Turco-German agreement, chrome for arms, was signed.

The tide of war was beginning to swing towards the Allies, yet German relations with Turkey remained friendlier than Churchill and the FO intended, or than the Americans and Russians understood. This was because the Hitler/von Papen axis put forward a simple and acceptable theorem to the Turkish leadership, and stuck to it:

1) Stay neutral.
2) If you allow the British to persuade you to allow them air bases to bomb the Romanian oil installations, you will no longer be a neutral.
3) In that event we will retaliate by destroying Istanbul and its environs, and for you the war will be over.

By 12 October Churchill pushed for his personal intervention in Turkish affairs. He continued his pressure on Eden: 'I am after the Turk: I am not after your chrome . . . I am much disappointed at the way the gift I got with so much trouble has been marred by this verbose ambassador [i.e. Hugessen].'[40]

Four days before, Churchill had written at length to his younger colleague about what he thought was Hugessen's inept handling of the Turkish matter. 'In the picture I make to myself of the Turk, comradeship and generosity, the impression of power and resources, are what will count.' The chromite affair, conducted by the FO via the embassy at Ankara, had obscured this simple vision of a strong Turco-British war comradeship. 'I took great pains to get the tanks etc . . . the gift of arms from Britain to Turkey is meant as a token of comradeship and comprehension.' Later, on 5 November, Churchill again wrote sarcastically to Eden:

Although the world war is proceeding with diverse episodes of interest cropping up from time to time, the entire politics of the Foreign Office with Turkey are expressed in the one word 'chrome'. I thought you told me you were going to wind this up but your pertinacious secretariat and your verbose ambassador continue to wear out the cipher staff and aggravate the paper shortage, to say nothing of wearing out my eyesight by endless disputation.[41]

He added in his own handwriting, 'Don't let the military get out of giving the 200 tanks on the score that the Turks can't [*sic*] digest them. You know how my mind is working.' He repeated his urgings to 'press on' and instructed: 'we should send off 300 instructors for delivered tanks as fast as the Turks can take them, Middle East must face up to this.'

In Ankara, Hugessen and his team sang 'chrome sweet chrome'.[42] He represented the policy of the FO, which was proving inadequate for the job Churchill had in mind. Hugessen wrote regularly to 'Moley' Sargent about Turkey.[43] He was having a difficult time, he was doing his best, he worked hard for Turkish trust and friendship, he liked, and was liked by, the Turks; but perhaps in a world of state presidents and large armies, of looming global disasters, of international operators like von Papen and Churchill, he was the weak Southern Department link in a chain drawing Turkey towards the Allied camp. Churchill's antipathy to Hugessen's handling of the chrome issue may have been more influential in differentiating Churchill's policy from that of the department than was outwardly apparent. But Hugessen was always on very good terms with his FO *confrères*, and many of his staff in Ankara had already served their time in the Southern Department, so Hugessen in Ankara was simply an extension of the FO's Turkey policy, but more directly exposed than the Southern Department to Churchillian tantrums and Turkish wiles.[44]

Churchill records his own efforts to play the Turkey hand in his war memoirs. His most recent conference with the other Big Two (in Moscow, 12 August 1942) established an order of priority in order to win the war:

1)   Knock Italy out of the war.
2)   Bring Turkey into the war.
3)   Give the Axis no respite for recuperation.

Since the first item was on-going and the third no more than a rallying cry, the high priority Turkey now assumed in Allied thinking confirms the thesis that Turkey was now playing a key role in Churchill's European war picture. He records 'a ceaseless flow of weapons and equipment to Turkey'. He informed Stalin he had told Roosevelt about Turkey and how he should play the Turkish hand, and Stalin responded appropriately, if unspecifically. 'Now,' he wrote, 'I wished to clinch the matter' by making a personal appearance on Turkish soil to force a Turkish *imbroglio*. Elisabeth Barker, that most sensitive of the Second World War diplomatic historians, said:

> The exact shape of the project varied a little according to circumstances. When in January 1943 [Churchill] made an impromptu dash to Turkey to persuade the Turkish leaders to think hard about entering the war, and wanted to overcome their fears of the Russians overrunning the Balkans, he was inspired to set down his 'Morning Thoughts' and to communicate them to the Turks.[45]

Before that, however, Attlee and Eden both tried to stop him, for different, and in Eden's case complex, reasons. Eden resented Churchill's forays into British foreign policy making, which robbed him of the chance of an appearance on the world stage while marginalising his own attempts to conduct an active anti-Axis foreign policy. But Churchill was in his persuasive child mode and cajoled them by saying, 'if the Turks were afraid to come I should not feel at all rebuffed'. For a while his cabinet colleagues withstood his charm offensive and Churchill:

> . . . got quite upset . . . as I lay on my luxurious bed in the Villa Taylor [at Casablanca] looking at the Atlas mountains over which I longed to leap in the 'Commando' aeroplane, which awaited me so patient and contented on the airfield.[46]

In Turkey there were internal as well as external pressures on the leadership. John Sterndale-Bennett reported in FO diplomatic cipher on Saraçoğlu's account of Turkey's economic conditions, and evidence of rising anti-Semitism there. The iniquitous wealth tax penalising foreigners and traders was introduced. The FO monitored the effects of the tax, which included forced labour for some evaders, and ancient foes – rich, vulnerable, non-Muslim, mainly Greek, particularly Greek orthodox churchmen – as the chief victims.[47] The cost of keeping a million men in training and under arms was growing prohibitive. Saraçoğlu rightly said they had ceased to be producers and had become consumers, by leaving their farms and joining the army. Oliver Harvey, by now Eden's private secretary, noted that:

[Churchill], Eden told me, is wildly in favour of roping Turkey in and of entering Europe from her end. He even mentioned this to Maisky yesterday . . . I told AE on thinking it over, whatever the military merits, to bring Turkey in would involve enormous political troubles. It would arouse the worst suspicions of Soviet Russia and it would be doubtful if she and Turkey could be prevented from fighting each other. Russia is always suspicious of Turkey and would think we intended by this means to counteract her influence in the Balkans. On the other hand, the Greeks would be upset because they would fear for their islands. The Turks would prove grasping Allies.[48]

Though Eden replied that 'though Greece must certainly get her islands [the Dodecanese] this time it was the PM's idea to give the Turks nothing at all'. But Harvey was right. He was losing the battle for Eden's soul.[49]

The next day, 17 November, the Portuguese ambassador in Ankara reported that the ruling classes there 'greatly fear a German defeat, Soviet predominance, and the Bolshevisation of Europe'. But the Japanese ambassador in Rome took a cooler view: 'Turkey's attitude is open to criticism . . . it is not thought that she, fearful as she is of the power of the USSR, will depart from her neutrality straightaway.'[50] Iberian diplomats regularly, if not religiously, shuddered about the coming Bolshevisation of Europe if Russia managed to defeat Germany in the east. They did not realise that Stalin had already abandoned the aims of the Comintern and would settle for national communist parties faithful to Moscow in power from then until the day of his death.

The tide of war had decisively turned, and on 18 November Churchill wrote at length to the COS about Turkey:

A supreme and prolonged effort must be made to bring Turkey into the war in the Spring . . . Turkey must be won if proper measures are taken. Turkey is an Ally . . . She has a great desire to be well armed. Her army is in good order, except for the specialised modern weapons in which the Bulgarians have been given so great an advantage by the Germans.[51]

Recent allied successes in Egypt, Cyrenaica and, above all, Soviet army triumphs in the Caucasus, had rendered pointless Turkey's successful dodging of her obligations hitherto. It was now possible 'to build up a powerful British land and air force to assist the Turks', who:

. . . all through the winter from now on must be equipped from Egypt and from the United States with tanks, AT [anti-tank] and AA [anti-aircraft] guns, and active construction of airfields must be undertaken . . . Experts must be provided to assist the Turks in learning to use and maintain this material.

He repeated, 'A ceaseless flow of weapons and equipment must go to Turkey.' He also wrote to Stalin: 'A new Allied effort to get Turkey in' would 'help Russia by opening the shipping routes on the Black Sea and bomb the Romanian oilfields at Ploesti.' Stalin agreed.[52]

Elsewhere threats to Spanish as well as Turkish neutrality were being expressed: 'The Axis will take Gibraltar or invade Turkey.'[53] In London these two possibilities were expressed by the Turkish ambassador: 'Turkey would resist with arms . . . Turkey believes the neutrals coming into the war depends at present more on the wishes and plans of the belligerents than on our respective governments.'[54] The Turkish stance on entering the war was further commented on by Yamaji, the Japanese ambassador in Sofia. Kurihara in Ankara reported that the Turkish administration knew 'territorial aggrandisement was more a burden than a benefit' and would not be tempted to enter the war by offers of this sort by either side. Turkey would 'be an ally of no one'.[55] But von Papen was reported as saying the Germans would not be rash enough to invade either Turkey or Spain. In Ankara the Japanese ambassador Kurihara reported no change in Turkey's attitude. 'The Allies would occupy Turkish airfields without warning; bomb the Balkan oilfields while Germany was concentrating on the Eastern Front.' He also reported a plot to oust İnönü from the Turkish presidency and install a pro-Allied administration. The İnönü government, he added, 'reckoned that if Turkey comes into the war the Axis will without delay carry out an advance from Bulgaria and Greece, and gain control of Western Turkey'.[56]

What became of this coup attempt is not known and İnönü himself never displayed any worry about his own position as virtual dictator of a country which he had defended and helped establish with his charismatic leader, Atatürk. On 1 December he was re-elected President. Hitler was among the first to congratulate him. At the FO Clutton doubted whether he deserved a similar message from King George VI, but eventually that too was despatched.[57] The next day Kurihara commented on Turkey's traditional self-esteem. Saraçoğlu had told Germany that Turkey was Britain's ally but now it was no one's ally. 'Turkey relies on herself.'[58] Oshima reported from Berlin that Germany saw no need to invade Turkey. This was confirmed to British decrypt readers by Yamaji in Sofia reporting on 11 December about Bulgarian preparations to defend herself should she be attacked from Turkey. 'It was not wise for Germany to seek out new enemies.'[59]

Despite all this Churchill had been persisting in his shotgun wedding approach to Turkey, by telling Stalin on 24 November that the Allies 'needed a new effort to have Turkey enter the war on our side'.[60] The prime minister considered that 'an Anglo-Soviet guarantee of territorial integrity should be offered Turkey, and much equipment. A large Allied army assembling in Syria could help Turkey if the Axis attacked her, and your operations in the Caucasus or north of it may also exercise a great influence.' The consequences would include more effective bombing of the Romanian oilfields.

Surprisingly in these evident half-truths, blandishments and hopes as yet unfulfilled, Stalin acquiesced. On 28 November he had replied that everything possible should be done to get Turkey in. 'This would be of great importance in order to accelerate the defeat of Hitler and his accomplices.'[61] There seem more politics than conviction in this exchange of views on Turkey and anyway the Soviets had too much else to worry about. By 20 December Kurihara reported from Ankara that:

> [German circles] here are considering a passage through Turkey by force but I understand that as a result of the most thorough investigations they have reached the conclusion that, owing to topographical conditions in Anatolia, inadequacy of communications and various other difficulties which they foresee, a move southward from the Caucasus would actually be a short cut [to Egypt] and an easier route.

Germany considered the western Allies had no intention of laying hands on Turkey for the time being:

> But it is impossible to ignore the infiltration of US/UK influence into the Turkish army, the construction of airfields and roads with the guidance and collaboration of British and American engineer officers already present all the appearance of preparation for joint operations.

Another BJ of the same date from Oshima shows Ribbentrop assuring him that 'this was not the time to go out of one's way to turn Turkey into an enemy'.[62]

John Sterndale-Bennett, formerly of the Southern Department and now in Ankara, wrote to Sargent on 18 December, giving his appreciation of Turkish public opinion towards what all felt to be the coming war. In the Kayseri area an aircraft factory manager told his informant that 'undoubtedly Turkey would be in the war by May 1943', and that this belief was general. 'Turkey would settle affairs with Bulgaria in the Spring, but reckoned there was no danger of an invasion of Thrace by Germany.' 'Coming into the war' was the main topic of mess talk. Aggressive gestures towards the inveterate enemy Bulgaria were soon to be superseded by more defensive and more fearful thoughts – about the newly successful bearlike neighbour to the north-east – the Soviet Union.[63]

The year 1942 was the one which might have seen Turkey enticed by Churchill out of the arms of Germany. Increasing Allied success on all fronts should have pointed the way. Yet curiously the Turks derived little comfort from the battering Germany was getting in the Caucasus and the Ukraine, while the eclipse of Italy in the Mediterranean signalled not just the departure of one menace but the arrival of another one – Britain. Germany, with one shrewd diplomatic move, paralysed Turkey's wish to join the eventual winner for another two years of war by pointing out that allowing Britain landing rights for her combat aircraft on Turkish soil would be construed in Berlin as an act of war that would bring immediate retribution on Istanbul. Eden's view of Turkey had deteriorated still further: 'The Turks seem to be playing pretty double even for them . . . Is it not time that we were a bit rough?' But Churchill had more precise plans for Turkey in his mind.

The winter of 1942/43 was a milder one than 1941/42 with more diplomatic activity. The build-up to Churchill's stay on Turkish soil produced a flood of diplomatic decrypts which dominate DIR through much of 1943. Differences again emerged between London and GHQ Cairo, who wanted to handle supplying Turkey and all Turkey-related military matters themselves, despite the PM's ruling that Turco-British relations, being political, were the responsibility of the FO. In London Churchill was at odds with both Eden and Attlee over the wisdom of his inspirational trip to Turkey, while in Washington the State Department sought to minimise the extent to which Britain should be the sole player of the Turkish hand, and distinguished political from military handling. They accepted the military arguments but were concerned about the political risks of Churchill's Turkey policy and had no interest in his eastern Mediterranean plans. William Strang, a senior FO official then in Washington pleaded ignorance of British assertiveness, though he conceded that recent conferences reflected that view, and had to beat a hasty retreat as the Southern Department grabbed the whole hand again, deploying the somewhat broadbrush division of responsibilities established by Roosevelt and Churchill recently at the Washington Conference with a quasi-legal authority which was at least open to challenge.

The Road to Adana

The reasons for the FO's possessiveness about Turkey lie at the heart of this book. For many years, under the aegis of Sargent, it had pursued interventionist policies in the Balkans, and Turkey was for Britain the key to the Balkans, so playing the Turkey hand was seen merely as a continuation of existing policy. But there was more to it than this. All through the 1930s friendship with Turkey, as has been shown, had been the cornerstone of FO policy in the eastern Mediterranean. But by 1939, despite Loraine's personal friendship with Atatürk, this policy had only generated the Mutual Assistance Pact and some fairly glutinous expressions of mutual esteem. It was never put to the test until 1942–43. When it emerged it was a failure. But the FO mandarins would not admit defeat and hand over to the military

The prime minister and the president: Churchill and Inönü in 1943.
All photographs from the Imperial War Museum, London, unless credited otherwise.

JAPANESE AMBASSADOR, BERLIN, REPORTS INTERVIEW

WITH RIBBENTROP.

L_o

No: 126184

Date: 16th December, 1943.

From: Japanese Ambassador, BERLIN.

To: Foreign Minister, TOKYO.

No: 1460.

Date: 12th December, 1943.

[W/T: I A].

Urgent and secret.

I called on Foreign Minister RIBBENTROP on the 11th and had a talk with him lasting more than an hour. The following is the gist of it.

(1) First of all I thanked him for his visit on the 8th and for GERMANY's entry into the war two years ago in pursuance of the spirit of friendship of the Three-Power Treaty, and I made a suitable greeting. The Minister in his turn expressed, in dignified tones, his congratulations on the victories won by the Imperial Japanese armed forces during the past two years, and affirmed his enthusiasm for cooperation with JAPAN in the prosecution of the war.

(2) I then told him that I had received from TOKYO a communication about which I should very much like to speak personally to Chancellor HITLER, and I informed him of the sense of your telegram No.985 [in unbroken cypher]. He listened attentively and, after expressing his thanks for the message in question, said that the war situation in EUROPE was just as he had told me the other day, and that in the east there was no great change, operations continuing to be limited to local fighting. On the Italian front the position fluctuated from day to day and there was nothing special for him to tell me.

(3)

Director (4).
F.O.(3).
Admiralty(2).
War Office(4).
Air Ministry.
M.I.5.
M.E.W.(2).
Sir E.Bridges.

Oshima intercepted: a typical BJ. *Via Author*

A classical cryptographer: A.G. Denniston, 1934. *Author*

Roosevelt, Inönü, Churchill, meeting in Cairo. Also in the photograph are Alexander, Cadogan and Eden.

Churchill in Cairo. Among the group are Killearn, Cadogan, Alanbrooke, Portal, Cunningham and Eden.

Churchill on Turkish soil: meeting soldiers of the Turkish Army at Adana, January 1943.

Hitler greets the Japanese ambassador to Berlin, Hiroshi Oshima, February 1939.

'Il Duce', Benito Mussolini, in conversation with Field Marshal Erwin Rommel, January 1944.

Hughe Knatchbull-Hugessen with Winston Churchill, 1943.

The Big Two of Anglo-Turkish friendship shake hands.

because that would have meant a serious loss of face and one of its main wartime areas of responsibility. They sought Churchill's support for continuing to handle Turkey and he gave it, albeit reluctantly, since Eden failed to follow through on his Turkish initiatives. The alternative for Churchill would have been even worse because he would have had even less direct access via GHQ Middle East, which wanted Turkey to be part of Macmillan's bailiwick. Playing office politics in wartime is a dangerous pursuit, where the people on the spot are the ones who win. And the spot, unquestionably, was London, while the person was Churchill.

Since the Southern Department had unlimited access to Turkish intercepts secretly provided to GCCS via its Istanbul office, it was always up to date on what the leadership in Ankara was thinking. Intelligent study of these, as we have seen, gave the department accurate information on the chief characters involved, their intentions, their prejudices, their trustworthiness, their hopes and fears. Since Turkey was run by oligarchs with only formal reference to the National Assembly, what the department knew on a daily basis was far more valuable than anything GHQ ME might glean from reports on British attachés in Ankara and neighbouring capitals. The intercepts were circulated widely within the department, and reports and minutes on them from quite junior officials would end up as British policy, signed off by the Secretary of State himself.

Churchill's access to the intercepts through Desmond Morton, and strengthened when he became prime minister and when the supply of DIR grew to a daily file, encouraged him to insist that the Southern Department should be responsible for Allied policy towards Turkey but that he, in this respect, was the department. This goes some way to explain his determination to fly to Turkey in January 1943. Reading Turkey-related BJs in the run-up period with something of the same care Churchill himself did enables the historian to study the subsequent months of negotiation with a new interest. And it was Churchill's refusal of gists and summaries, and insistence on the actual words in DIR that is the key to this new explanation of HMG's policy towards Turkey in the war. It was for this reason that in January 1943 he sought to explain to Menzies and the head of Hut 3 at Bletchley Park just why 'documents [decrypts] needed to be authentic. The whole force is destroyed in the paraphrase . . . As I have told you before you greatly weaken the value of your information by paraphrasing.' 'C' passed this to Gp Capt Eric Jones, in charge of Hut 3 at BP, who commented pacifically: 'It is generally felt that few men rival the Minister of Defence in this mastery of language . . . few of our recipients [of Ultra] would detect points raised by him . . .' But 'matters of major strategic importance are sent *ipsissima verba* [in the actual words].'[64]

Turkey seemed to be coming out of its shell. On 5 January the Portuguese ambassador in Bucharest reported to Lisbon 'that the Turkish ambassador drew me aside and said Turkey might join the Allies in attacking the Balkans from the Black Sea'.[65] Two days later Clutton minuted that 'the Turks are slowly coming out of their shell . . . The best means of drawing the Turks into the open is to make a combined plan of their fear of Russia and their inveterate hatred of Bulgaria in the hope of thereby embroiling Turkey and Bulgaria.'[66] But Oshima reported that 'Bulgaria was terribly frightened of Turkey . . . Turkey wanted Germany to retain her position as a great power . . . There would be no change in Turkey's attitude.'[67] On 9 January Cadogan noted that Eden was 'in his usual weekend flat spin about Turkey, but was convinced by Snatch's [Hugessen's] reports that it might be a disaster to get Turkey into the war'. He convinced Eden of this.[68] On 15 January Sargent commented that Hugessen had not produced a detailed report on Turkey's readiness for combat prepared by the military attachés in Ankara. He left it behind on a routine visit to Whitehall, where officials read it with interest and some surprise. It may have confirmed some in their view that his competence was not entirely sound.[69] Indeed, all through this period Hugessen seems to have been at odds with the FO and had to put up with some coldness from Whitehall, for reasons which are not clear. As has been shown, Dr Hugh Dalton observed that the FO had reservations about him. During an earlier tour of duty in Nanking he upset the Chinese authorities by driving through a war zone without asking permission. His views on recruitment to the diplomatic service did not reflect the slowly awakening wish of parliament to open up the service to non-Etonian, non-Wykehamist, non-Oxbridge entrants.

On 16 January Clutton drafted a situation report on Turkey. On 18 January the British Joint Planning Staff issued their policy document on Turkey. Turkey would not come into the war unless she could hold Thrace without Allied assistance and immediate air defence would be forthcoming. Turkey's value to the Allies was as an offensive base for air rather than for land operations. The invasion of the Dodecanese was being studied by GHQ ME: three divisions and 123 air squadrons would be needed. 'We should exploit Turkish fears that Turkey will lose allied support which is conditional on her entry into the war without delay.' Turkey would be used 'as a base to bomb Ploesti, to close the Dardanelles to the Axis, and to force increased dispersal of German troops by using Turkey as a threat to the Balkans, and to deny chrome to Germany'.[70]

On 21 January the German air attaché in Sofia told the Japanese minister there that Germany would require twenty divisions to attack Turkey, and therefore had no intention of doing so.[71] On 25 January, six days before the main Stalingrad pocket surrendered to the Russians, the Turkish ambassador in Washington reported: 'If it be true that the buffer states of central Europe have begun to try federation with Russia, this fact is of immense importance [to Turkey].'[72] The next day the foreign minister in Ankara reported to his colleague in Washington that 'the Bulgarians fear the Turkish army may one day attack them. The present Bulgarian regime relies entirely on King Boris. If Russia forces landings at Varna, Bulgaria will go over to the Soviet. A coup d'état in Sofia awaits only a German defeat.' It would be partly communist-inspired and partly a matter of Slav brotherhood and 'partly in reliance on Russia to escape punishment at the hands of England'. The same day, 'travellers to Budapest report fear that Turkey may enter the war on the allied side'.[73] Two days later Menemencioğlu reported on continuing Turkish neutrality, despite the weakness of Greece, and carried on playing chess with Vinogradov.[74] Hugessen told Sterndale-Bennett that the Turkish oligarchs 'thought the Balkans should be occupied by the Allies before the Russians got there'.

On 28 January Churchill, in Cairo, was at loggerheads with the FO, Eden and Cunningham over the fate of the French fleet, but mentally preparing for Turkey. The next day was spent in planning for his visit and considering:

> . . . how best we can help the Turks. During the meeting a long paper dictated by the P.M. arrived bit by bit, hot from the typewriter, for the Commanders-in-Chief to check. It proved to be a statement of the position for the Turks, from which the Prime Minister proposed to speak when he met President İnönü.[75]

On 19 January 1943 Churchill queried Eden about 'the leaky conditions' at the Ankara embassy, suggesting they reflected badly on Hugessen. Eden agreed cautiously.[76] As a communicator Hugessen was obviously first class. His intelligence and conscientiousness were never in doubt. But doubts were surfacing again. Further references to the 'leaky conditions' at the embassy occasionally appear, though when the 'Cicero' leaks became dangerous they appeared not at the embassy but in the ambassador's private residence, or possibly the chancery building. His eccentricities, such as his habit of practising on Soviet ambassador Vinogradov's Bechstein through the hot summer afternoons when others were either working or sleeping, would have been remarked on, but hardly called for censure. Possibly he found it difficult to delegate or share credit, a not uncommon phenomenon among those who know they are abler and more intelligent than most of their colleagues, as Hugessen certainly did and was. For instance, when his fifty-nine paragraph annual report on 1942 was only briefly acknowledged by the Southern Department, his colleagues, who were assumed to have 'helped the compilation', were officially thanked; it was some time later he pointed out that the report was in fact 100 per cent his own work.[77] In it Hugessen mentioned the Bulgarian threat to use its ancient ties with Russia to achieve frontier rectification in Thrace at the expense of Turkey. The Turks, according to Sterndale-Bennett, 'believed the Balkans [i.e. Bulgaria] should be occupied by the Allies before the Russians got there'. This was reported back by Hugessen. Eden knew the 'Bulgars' were better equipped, with the latest German weaponry, than the Turks. He also knew 'from other sources' [i.e. BJs] that von Papen knew in advance about Adana.[78]

So the run-up to Adana concluded. Hugessen and Cadogan represented FO Turkish policy, while Alanbrooke and other high ranking service officers represented the views of the COS. Unfortunately neither viewpoint was heard in the plenary sessions, which were totally dominated by Churchill and İnönü, so it is difficult to tease out the complex attitude the FO took of Turkish neutrality at this key moment when, having gained the right to play the Turkey hand, it found that hand whisked out of its grasp by the prime minister.

CHAPTER SIX

Adana and After

He had the feeling that the time had come to cash in on the Russian victories, and on the favourable turn of events in the Mediterranean, and to nail Turkey to the mast . . . He felt that a talk between him and the Turkish president would show the world clearly which way the wind was blowing.
Ian Jacob, December 1942 in JAC B1/16 p. 94 (in Churchill College, Cambridge)

Preparations

In the previous chapter the claim was made that by reading Turkish diplomatic intercepts on a careful and regular basis Churchill knew how and when to approach the Turkish leadership directly, what to say, and what not to say to them; in short, how to appeal to their hopes and fears. He now put his 'Morning Thoughts' in a document designed to bring the Turks closer to the Allies while allaying their fears of a powerful Soviet Union postwar. All this is clear from the previous chapter. But without the BJs he might never have gone to Turkey and a great opportunity would have been lost. Such a claim cannot, of course, be proved. Against it can be set the fact that the meetings at Adana were so chaotic that inspirational extemporisation was all that was needed. For this Churchill had great talent, which he fully exploited. Though he summoned a large staff of advisers, experts and spectators from Cairo, Ankara and London, including his egregious son Randolph, he spent most of the time talking himself, either at the plenary conference at the start of the proceedings or privately with President İnönü on political implications. That his BJ reading provided value backup for this improvised programme is not in doubt; that it was responsible for making a success of Adana is more than the section that follows claims.

Churchill himself did not go into details when compiling Volume 4 and 5 of his *Second World War* history,[1] preferring to select such documents as his 'Morning Thoughts' and his other communications with Eden, and the COS make his case for him, the case being that Adana was an important step towards beating the Germans. Other attendees, including Hugessen, Ismay, Cadogan and Alanbrooke left first-hand accounts. Hugessen's 1943 jottings and Brig Ian Jacob's journal, both in Churchill College, Cambridge, are the only circumstantial accounts still unpublished. It must be remembered that Jacob had access neither to Ultra nor Dedip. Also, since

Adana was a short conference with maximum security but also maximum propinquity, both of the high with the low and the Turkish team with the British, handling Most Secret Source material in the train outside Adana would have endangered its security; so no contemporaneous Turkish intercepts were available to the British party.

On 28 January Churchill had written to Eden from Casablanca: 'We play the hand in Turkey . . . Is not this the opportunity and the moment for me to get into direct touch with the Turks?' Two days later he joked about Adana, to Eden: 'You can imagine how much I wish I were going to be with you tomorrow on the Bench [in the House of Commons] but duty calls.'[2] In making his pitch for a direct conference with the Turkish leadership on Turkish soil, he drafted a cable for Roosevelt to send to İnönü, 'if approved by my colleagues':

To President İnönü: 'Churchill, who has been conferring with me, is going shortly to Cairo. He will in all probability wish to confer with you and with your Prime Minister at some convenient secret place. In case Prime Minister Churchill does seek a conference I earnestly hope you or your Prime Minister will find it possible to meet him.' ROOSEVELT.

The ensuing argument about whether to go, where to go and who should go, so historians of diplomacy agree, seriously weakened Eden's standing as foreign secretary.[3] Turkey was an important part of Eden's portfolio, and it was not only the fear of a Turkish rebuff but a simple dislike of Churchill hogging the limelight that made Eden so nervy.[4] A 'clear the line HUSH' telegram from Attlee and Eden to Churchill on 25 January had strongly opposed Ankara as the venue of choice.[5] It was 'full of German agents . . . there would be serious risks . . . Remember the Papen incident'. Adana, on the Mediterranean seaboard and many hours' train time from Ankara (then in deep snow), was preferred.[6] Churchill renewed his arguments a day later, despite the rebuff he received from the War Cabinet. Having consulted Roosevelt he got somewhat ambiguous backing for his venture which he used to overcome cabinet objections. On 24 January he had cabled İnönü suggesting 'a secret *rendezvous*'. He then blandly wrote to the War Cabinet: 'I am most grateful to you for allowing my[7] [*sic*] to try my plan, and even more triumphantly to the C.I.G.S. that the war cabinet were in entire accord with him and that 'the United Kingdom plays the hand in Turkey . . .' He even got Stalin to 'not deny the rumours that you have gone to Moscow'. Rarely has such a poor hand been played with such bravura.'[8] Churchill's account of the Adana Conference[9] starts with a lengthy quotation from his 'wooing letter containing an offer of platonic marriage both from me and the President' which was handed to İnönü.[10] İnönü had replied to the earlier invitation that he would prefer to meet Churchill, openly or secretly, in Ankara and could not leave Turkey for constitutional reasons. Churchill was delighted when he accepted, according to Jacob. He kept saying:

'This is big stuff.' He read and re-read the telegrams and was obviously not unhappy at the thought of how right he had been and how wrong the Cabinet and their advisers [the FO] had proved.[11]

The British party assembled in flying kit over civilian clothes on Landing Ground 224. It consisted of Gens Alexander, Wilson and Air Marshal Lindsell; AM Drummond, Air Cdre Dundas; Peter Loxley, 'Mr Kinna' and Jacob himself.[12] The generals occupied the flightdeck, Jacob had the bomb bay.[13] The PM travelled from Casablanca in another plane with his son Randolph, his doctor Sir Charles Wilson, his security guard, 'Tommy' Thompson, two police officers and Sir Alexander Cadogan.[14] The airport was close to the town of Adana in the centre of an alluvial plain between the Taurus mountains and the north-east coast of the Mediterranean. At this time of year the fields were all waterlogged, if not submerged.

> The villages we saw were extremely squalid. The houses were built of mud, the general practice being for the family to live in an upper storey reached by ladder, and built over the shed which is the home of the cattle, goats and poultry. The roads are atrocious, and the whole country is obviously primitive in the extreme.[15]

At the airport the two British parties met the embassy contingent, which outlined the manoeuvre to install Churchill on Turkish soil. He was to be taken to a nearby level crossing 'where he would be whisked on board' his special carriage which would pause for the purpose. The co-ordination of planes, cars and trains was complicated and extemporising was needed, particularly when Hugessen arrived with his team. 'However, all was well and at 12.50 p.m. cordial greetings were taking place, after Churchill had inspected the Hurricane aircraft supplied by the RAF to the Turkish air force and drank with the Turkish officials on the aerodrome.'[16]

The PM's party were to arrive in time for lunch on Saturday 30 January and stay for twenty-four hours. An advance party under Gp Capt Hudleston (an Air Staff officer) would set off earlier. From Ankara Ambassador Hugessen would be accompanied by his military and air attachés (Maj-Gen Arnold and AVM George). They were to accompany the Turkish party and bring interpreters. 'Our communications would be by our own W/T set to Cairo and thence to London.' Sir Alexander Cadogan and Peter Loxley of the FO arrived from England. The whole operation was shrouded in secrecy. In Ankara Hugessen pretended to be off on a shooting expedition, despite deep snow, and waved his guns at local journalists to prove it. He left Ankara for the eight-hour journey to Adana using a small station outside the capital. Unfortunately the president's party organisers had the same idea, and a small army of Turkish labourers, busily brushing away the snow to permit the presidential car to get through, witnessed the ambassador's arrival. The next day, according to

Numan Menemencioğlu, everyone knew that Churchill was coming to talk Turkey.[17]

On 31 January the day of the Adana Conference and the day Stalingrad fell to the Russians, the Southern Department read many Turkey-relevant BJs. The effect of Allied victory in North Africa dominated the BJs of this period, during which Hugessen's pressure on Menemencioğlu to come off the fence, on instructions from the Southern Department, took a new turn.[18] The Turkish foreign minister made only debating points in response, as Clutton's draft to Hugessen, approved by Sargent, noted. The head of the Southern Department from 1941 till 1945, Douglas Howard, noted that:

> . . . [our] veiled threat to keep them out of the Peace Conference amounts to nothing . . . The Turks are conceited enough to think they are indispensable to us. And I am not sure they are not right.

Cadogan and Eden both signed off this memorandum, indicating their view that this should become policy. Hugessen in Ankara told the FO: 'The Turks above all want to conserve their strength against Russia.' A reply drafted in the Southern Department contained the suggestion that the British might occupy the Dodecanese, but this was struck out by Eden who no doubt thought the FO was exceeding its brief. Steinhardt, the politically ambitious American ambassador in Ankara, was thought to be overactive, though he had recently assured Hugessen that it was his rule (as instructed by the president through a junior embassy official in Ankara) to follow Hugessen's lead on Turkish neutrality; but 'He cannot keep still or quiet' and Hugessen's wish to keep his American colleague in the picture over this new Turkish development received a cautionary note from Cadogan.

In the Train

The whole party came aboard the train at the designated level crossing and settled down for lunch (eating and drinking took up a great deal of the time). Hugessen, who had brought the embassy party from Ankara through thick snow by train, told the party that the Germans knew all about the meeting and von Papen had rung the foreign ministry to ask 'whether this meant that the Turks had come down on our side of the fence'.[19] Jacob described the Turkish leadership as:

> . . . rather nondescript people, obviously very delighted with the whole affair, and having none of the pomposity of Ministers in some countries . . . They put on no airs, and the whole arrival was more like a family welcoming a relation than an official reception.[20]

The bigwigs had a special saloon for their lunch where Churchill met İnönü, both with their ministers and Churchill with Hugessen. 'Gradually more and more people squeezed in, including Marshal Chakmak [*sic*].'[21] Churchill conducted the preliminaries in his franglais. He and İnönü decided on a formal meeting of the two delegations (one political, one military) forthwith, but continued their tête-a-tête before joining the political session.[22] Churchill produced the paper he had been working on in Cairo and held forth for over an hour – having dispensed with the services of Paul Falla, the British Embassy junior official listed as secretary and seconded to act as interpreter. Falla had not been properly briefed or given a sight of Churchill's document; and when he translated Churchill's 'miles' into 'kilometres' for the benefit of his French-speaking Turkish hosts, Churchill waved him away on the quite wrong assumption that he was not following the exact words – instructions so close (as we have seen) to his heart.[23]

Most of the British were fluent French speakers, and the Turks might have got down to business more quickly had Falla been allowed to proceed. Jacob wrote:

> The result was completely intelligible to all the English present . . . but the Turks could only have formed a very hazy idea of what the whole thing was about . . . Peculiar though it all was, I do not think anyone felt like laughing. They couldn't help admiring his determination and self-possession. The Turks were much too polite to express any surprise or amusement.[24]

Hugessen later wrote: 'Practically all the talking [in French] was between the PM and Ismet [İnönü] . . . The PM played all the right cards at the right time.'[25] Later Peter Loxley, Knox Helm, Paul Falla and Mrs Sterndale-Bennett translated Churchill's document into real French for the Turks.

İnönü then proposed the conference should separate off into the political study of the circumstances in which Turkey might become involved in a war and a military question of how to prepare for that situation. He and Churchill and their advisers should attend the first group, Alanbrooke and Marshal Fevkik Chakmak, the Turkish military supremo, the second. Meanwhile Hugessen's diplomatic message revealing German knowledge of Churchill's whereabouts was not seriously regarded.[26]

Churchill's whole demeanour bowled over his Turkish hosts, who found it quite easy, nevertheless, to resist his blandishments. And İnönü charmed Churchill who later wrote: 'I find him a very agreeable man and made friends [with him] at once.'[27] There were not two but three items on the agenda: encouraging Turkey off the fence with carrots in the form of modern war equipment, and sticks in the form of the need to come to terms with the imminent possibility of a major Russian success in the Caucasus or at Stalingrad; possible joint operations in the eastern Mediterranean involving the capture of the Dodecanese and the recapture of Crete; and bombing raids by British or American aircraft from Turkish bases on Romanian oilfields.

The Turks were worried about the outcome of Russian successes to their

north and less about the Bolshevisation of Europe which so panicked the
Iberians, more about Russia's likely demands for the rectification of the Straits
settlement at Montreux in 1936, as a prelude to a more aggressive stance in
the eastern Mediterranean. The military men discussed the *matériel* the British
could supply the Turks, whose 'oriental behaviour showed in the keenness
with which they entered into this aspect of the business, which was the only
thing they were really interested in . . . They asked no questions about the
progress of the war' nor what had been decided at Casablanca. They agreed
to the meeting because of their fear of Russia's intentions postwar, and the
state of Europe following a German collapse.

> They wanted to be sure of our support if Russia turns nasty. They were a
> bit apprehensive that the P.M. would come with proposals for their
> immediate entry into the war. When they found he had no intention of
> trying to push them along, they heaved a sigh of relief and entered whole-
> heartedly into the fun.[28]

Alanbrooke pressed his opposite number with what the Turks could do,
since Lindsell had been having a hard time establishing meaningful dialogue
in Ankara. He and his staff could now:

> . . . really get down to the Turkish problem which they had never been
> able to do before. The Turks have always tried to exclude foreign
> influence, remembering as they do the domineering attitudes of the
> Germans in the last war.[29]

The political group had made good progress too, and both parties
reassembled for a huge dinner, 'tottering off to our sleeping cars' at
1.00 a.m.[30]

Churchill had been working on his 'Morning Thoughts' for some days, as
we have seen; he finished them in the saloon-car of his train at Adana on
31 January.[31] They gave a vision of postwar Europe, with three or more
blocs. Turkey's highest security lay in becoming a 'victorious belligerent'.
Churchill remained 'in love with his idea'.[32]

The conference was due to conclude that same day. Drafts were prepared
and approved, but the proceedings were by no means over, and it could well
be said that Churchill may have overstayed his welcome: he certainly said he
was in no hurry to go while the soldiers were still talking to each other. He
thought he would return to Cairo via Cyprus to see some of his old
comrades in arms there, but changed his mind after lunch and said he must
get to Cairo to telegraph Roosevelt, Stalin and the War Cabinet in London.

Hurried goodbyes were exchanged at the level crossing, and the large and
well-fed party proceeded by car from the train to the aerodrome where one
of the aircraft failed to take off and slewed off the runway into the mud.
Getting it out took hours of manoeuvring supervised in part by Churchill

himself. By 17.40 hours the party was in the air, but whither? That was the next question. It was too late to get to Cairo in daylight so Jacob's proposal that they stay another night on Turkish soil was accepted, and back they went to the level crossing and the train. İnönü left at 20.00 hours having better things to do than prolong the goodbyes: 'He was most charming and might have been saying goodbye to his dearest friends.' At dinner that night the politicians changed places with the soldiers and Chakmak was with Cadogan and Hugessen while Sukru Saraçoğlu dined with the British generals. Eventually the Turkish train steamed off at 11.00. Numan Menemencioğlu, the foreign minister, was so exhausted that he sensibly went to bed before dinner.[33] The British party left Turkey the next morning, some members no doubt with a hangover. Churchill reported to Deputy Prime Minister Attlee from Cyprus.[34]

This description of the Adana Conference has used eyewitness accounts. Access to contemporaneous BJs was denied to Churchill in this, as in other, foreign trips. Their inadvertent disclosure to the Turkish leadership on the train would not only have undermined Churchill's protestations of friendship but might have seriously affected İnönü's commitment to join the Allies at some time in the future.

The PM in Danger

Lacking BJs, this account of the Adana Conference, as already stated, is based on first-hand reports. But it is only right to quote the official historian, whose paragraph on Adana requires little change in the light of recent releases of documents:

> From Cairo the Prime Minister flew to Adana on 30 January 1943 accompanied by the C.I.G.S and by Sir Alexander Cadogan from the Foreign Office. Friendly meetings took place with the Turkish President, Mr. İnönü, the Prime Minister, Mr. Saraçoğlu and Marshal Chakmak. Arrangements were made to increase supplies of British and American equipment to Turkey and Mr. Churchill was able to assure the authorities of the readiness of anti-aircraft and anti-tank units and of divisions of the 9th Army to come to Turkey's help, particularly now that the German threat from the North was much less. But the Turks, conscious that Russian and British successes might lead to a desperate venture by the Germans to reach oil by the middle road through Turkey, were not prepared to risk encouraging such action by granting them the use of airfields from which to attack the Romanian oilfields.[35]

What exactly had been achieved? According to Cadogan there never were men so resolutely disinclined to be drawn into a war as the Turkish leaders:

> When the conversation began to veer towards anything like practical

action on their part it seemed that they found more than usual difficulty in hearing what was said. The Turks had already showed themselves to be co-operative in allowing the British to build up stores on Turkish soil . . . It became plain that [the Turks] looked upon Russia as the principal threat. Perhaps Mr. Churchill, in his heart of hearts, did not disagree . . . Saraçoğlu was evidently not convinced by the Prime Minister's evocation of the international organisation which was to restrain aggression, or by his assertion that he had never known the Soviet Union to break an engagement. Turkey, said Saraçoğlu, was looking for something more 'real'. All the defeated countries would become Bolshevik or Slav if Germany was beaten. The *Pensées Matinales* claimed that the new world organisation would embody the spirit, but lack the weaknesses of the League . . . The military men agreed on increased supplies of modern weapons to Turkey. This was the only practical result of the Adana Conference . . . Turkey's determination to cling to her neutral position and keep her forces intact against Russia was well known to the Germans from the intercepts.[36]

Cadogan was referring here to Goebbels' notes on the diplomatic intercepts passed to him by the *Forschungsamt* in 1942–43. One such note reads:

Other intercepted diplomatic reports from Ankara proved that Turkey intended to hang grimly on to her neutral position until the war is over if possible. The main reason given is that Turkish statesmen realise the necessity of maintaining their armed forces intact at the end of the war, in order to be able to ward off possible encroachments by the Soviet Union.

Goebbels later learnt from his intercepts that at Adana Churchill proposed a three-way partition of Europe – into Southern, Northern and Central blocs: 'Churchill has put it to the Turks that he has no intention of destroying the Third Reich. But of course one knows just how much to believe of these Churchillian protestations.'[37]

Churchill himself came away from the discussions believing that 'the Turks have come a long way towards us'.[38] But Deringil quotes Erkin as saying: 'At Adana and in the months that followed the Turks and British had not spoken the same language.'[39] At the FO Turkish *politesse* was taken at face value as a 'change of heart' and it took months of mutual exasperation before officials there acknowledged that their policy had failed. But Eden minuted to his officials, 'As the department know I never liked the Adana meeting or the Adana policy.'[40]

The immediate aftermath was suffused with vague noises of camaraderie. Stalin sent a message from the Kremlin via ambassador Ivan Maisky:

I received your message of the impending meeting with the President of Turkey. I will be very grateful to you for information on the results of the conversation. The importance of this meeting is clear to me. Of course your wish will be respected and we will not deny the rumours that you have gone to Moscow.[41]

Churchill's doctor, Sir Charles Wilson, recorded his patient's delight at the results he had achieved at Adana: 'He will bring Turkey into the war and is in great heart.' Churchill told him this was 'about the best day's work I have ever done'.[42] Jacob's diary shows Churchill revelling in the thought that he had outmanoeuvred the rest of the War Cabinet, displaying a pettiness that his subsequent detractors seem to have overlooked. Alanbrooke was later to note in his diary:

The PM was a great success, and the day ended on the whole successfully . . . On our arrival at Adana the Turkish foreign minister . . . told me how delighted the whole of Turkey was at this visit by the PM. I asked him how this could be, since the visit was being kept as a matter of first-class secrecy and nobody could know that he had arrived. To this he replied: 'How could you keep an event of that kind secret? Of course everybody knows about it.'[43]

Hugessen noted that Churchill and İnönü did practically all the talking. Churchill:

. . . played all the right cards at the right time . . . His conduct of the business was brilliant . . . All the cards which had been put into his hands were played at exactly the right moment and with the fullest effect . . . Really a triumph.

Hugessen wrote this on 3 February, adding that, 'I hear the Germans are flabbergasted and really frightened that Turkey was coming in on our side at once.'[44]

Until DIR was released to the public in 1994 historians of the war were unaware of the dangers the British Prime Minister was in. The day after the conference closed, on 1 February, Charles Wilson, Churchill's doctor companion, noticed inexplicable arguments about whether the party should fly home immediately, and by a new route, or whether to continue as planned via Cairo. By that time Churchill may have known that plans to assassinate him had been intercepted in London.[45] On the same day a Tangier to Berlin message was intercepted by Bletchley Park of which the gist is as follows:

Parsifal. According to reports here Churchill went from Ankara direct to Cyprus and then on to Egypt. From there he will probably go by airline direct to Gibraltar via Algiers and on to England, probably breaking his journey at Lisbon. MUH will try through TONI to get people to Algiers and Casablanca in time. As it takes at least five days to get people across the frontier, it appears doubtful whether Churchill can still be reached.

This message was sent by the Sicherheitsdienst (SD). TONI is identified as an Islamic militant whose organisation had already attempted to assassinate Giraud, French General Officer Commanding Mediterranean. MUH (abbreviation for Muhamet) is alias for Peter Schulze, the 28-year-old second press attaché at the German Legation in Tangier. The timing of Churchill's intended assassination shows the attempt would certainly fail but Attlee, the Deputy Prime Minister, took immediate action on being shown an intercepted telegram of which the text is as follows:

> Hans Peter Schulze, head of German S.D. repeat S.D. in Tangier is trying to arrange attack on Churchill repeat Churchill probably at Algiers and/or Casablanca. Attempt if any would be made through agents of Sidi Abdelhalek Torres repeat Sidi Abdelhalek Torres leader of native nationalist reform party in Tangier. Also through agents of Sherif Ibrahim El Wasani repeat Sherif Ibrahim El Wasani, founder of Oficina [sic] nationalista in Tangier. Arrange inform governor immediately as Chiefs of Staff here are also wiring him. Informed. Extinguish.[46]

He reported to Churchill as follows:

CLEAR THE LINE
1) C reports a communication from Germans in Tangier to Berlin which show that your itinerary, i.e. Algiers, Gibraltar, England, has been accurately forecasted and that attempts are going to be made to bump you off.
2) We have studied possibilities very carefully and I and my colleagues, supported by the Chiefs of Staff, consider that it would be unwise for you to adhere to your present programme.
3) We regard it as essential in the national interest ['we strongly recommend' crossed out] that you cut out visits to both Algiers and Gibraltar and proceed to England, stopping only at Marrakesh.
4) We have taken following action:–
   (i) warned Gibraltar that present plan may be changed, but that in case you adhere to it special precautions are to be instituted;
   (ii) requested Eisenhower to make arrangements for your reception and safety at Marrakesh early tomorrow and lay on communications. At the same time, all possible security measures are to be instituted at Algiers in case present plan is adhered to.

This section has shown how the War Cabinet reacted effectively to intercepted signals intelligence. The actual danger to Churchill was more apparent than real, and his pneumonia on return to London provided a more cogent reason for the sense of anticlimax which followed the Adana Conference.

Aftermath

Churchill telegraphed Stalin to ask him to state that he had been kept fully informed of events at Adana, and said, 'the Turks have come a long way towards us', to which Stalin replied chillingly: 'Of course I have no objection to you making a statement that I was kept informed on the Anglo-Turkish meeting, although I cannot say that the information was very full.'[47] Adm Howard Kelly in Ankara earned grudging praise from the Southern Department's Pierson Dixon when he commented that 'an Imperialist Russia is much more frightening to the Turks than a thoroughgoing Communist Russia'. And the PM wrote tersely 'Yes' to a request that the Turkish officers and NCOs in training with the British should be fully subsidised by their hosts.

The FO circulated a 'Most Secret' memorandum early in February[48] summarising the Adana conversation under three headings: A) present, B) war future, C) postwar future.

Under A) there was 'the underlying suggestion that Turkey might come into the war either through being attacked or on her own initiative and in her own interests, or at least stretch her neutrality to a very wide extent in our interests.' On B) Turkey might be attacked by Germany to obtain oil or as part of a *Drang nach Osten* [push to the east] effort. 'It was on this basis that our proposals for completing Turkey's defences were based.' The prime minister is then credited with three hypotheses: 1)The destruction of Italy and the capture of Tunis would lead to action in the 'western Balkans' and therefore the need for Turkish security was paramount. Coupled with these was the Russian advance, precipitating a crisis in the summer. 2) Turkey might allow Britain to use her airfields to bomb Romanian oil installations; 3) Turkey might invade Bulgaria. But Churchill asked 'for no engagement. Turkey must decide for herself. She should not act until it was in her interests and those of the Grand Coalition to do so.' Menemencioğlu remarked that this 'was extremely reasonable'.

Under C) postwar Russia was the most important factor. Churchill urged an international agreement but added: 'If Russia attacked Turkey, we should arrange the best possible coalition against her and he would not hesitate to say so to Stalin.' He also told the Turks of Roosevelt's wish that Turkey should emerge from the war free and strong and independent. Finally the gist of Churchill's 'Morning Thoughts' highlighted the various possibilities in the Balkans which might induce Turkey 'to win her place in the Council of the Victors'.[49]

In Ankara Saraçoğlu reported to the National Assembly on the outcome of Adana in what Clutton called 'a very pretty speech. Never before, not even in the safe and palmy days of 1939 has the "Alliance" been so amorously intimate.'[50] A week later Churchill spoke about Turkey in the House of Commons:

> Turkey is our ally. Turkey is our friend. We wish her well, and we wish to see her territory, rights and interests effectively preserved. We wish to see, in particular, warm and friendly relations established between Turkey and her great Russian Ally to the North-West, to whom we are bound by the 20 years Anglo-Russian Treaty. Whereas a little while ago it looked to superficial observers as if Turkey might be isolated by a German advance through the Caucasus on one side and by a German-Italian attack on Egypt on the other, a transformation has occurred. Turkey now finds on each side of her victorious Powers who are her friends. It will be interesting to see how the story unfolds chapter by chapter, and it would be very foolish to try to skip on too fast.

These fine words were sent back in diplomatic cipher to many of the world's capital cities, including Ankara, so Churchill found himself re-reading them in the BJ from Rustu Aras that Cable & Wireless had routinely intercepted and transmitted to Berkeley Street for processing, the day after they had been spoken.[51]

The BJs were full of Adana from neutral diplomats in Berlin, Ankara, Rome, Lisbon, Madrid and Buenos Aires to their respective foreign ministries:

> une nouvelle offensive diplomatique et une de pousser les derniers neutres a entré dans la guerre . . . mais, a-t-il ajouté, je suis absolument sûr que les Turcs reprouvront en justifiant leur politique par le danger russe et la nécessité de faire la paîx en Europe.[52]

The Japanese ambassador in Sofia reported that many Russians were entering Turkey, which would suggest joint Allied pressure.[53] Two days later Kurihara reported to Tokyo the comments of the Polish commander, Gen Anders, that 'there was strong anti-British but equally strong pro-American feeling throughout Russia'.[54] He added that there was 'serious tactical bankruptcy' in Anglo-American war planning, which relied on saturation bombing and being no match militarily with the Axis and suffering heavy losses at sea; while the Portuguese ambassador in Ankara reported that the Adana meeting was to urge Turkey into the war – and it failed. The plan was to polish off Tunisia, occupy Crete and the Dodecanese, attack the Balkans, occupy Thrace. Neutrality was a word to be avoided. It was likely that Turkey would gain time by pleading lack of armaments (PM marked this 'important' for Alanbrooke to read).[55] Mussolini commented to his son-in-law Galeazzo Ciano that the weakness of Britain was proved, if Churchill must go to the trouble of begging for

Turkish help. He added: 'Turkey is too important not to be exploited . . . I do not think Turkey has been neutralised as Berlin says.'[56]

On 20 February the Japanese ambassador in Ankara noted that the many Allied spies in Turkey looked like a preparation for joint operations.[57] From Berlin Oshima told Tokyo that 'this was not the time to go out of one's way to turn [Turkey] into an enemy'.[58] The Turkish foreign ministry put out an anodyne account of Adana, talking of complete friendship and cordiality. 'Churchill had observed the lack of mechanisation of the Turkish army. Churchill would put this right. Churchill praised Turkish foreign policy, and asked for no change in it.'[59] Reports of Adana continued in the intercepts to and from the neutral capitals.

Neutral diplomats were less aware of the continuing problems to Turkey of its determination to sell its chrome to both Axis and Allies. This remained an issue which continued before, during and after Adana.[60] The Germans had failed to expedite sendings and the Americans sent 'wild men', in Clutton's phrase, to 'ginger up the chrome business' by contacting the mine owners direct, and sabotaging Germany-bound chrome convoys.[61] Clutton minuted that the Turkish mineowners hated the Germans like poison:

. . . provided they received adequate compensation they wouldn't mind if production suddenly ceased and wagons became derailed. The best way to stop the Germans getting chrome is to let the Turks do it.[62]

But the mineowners were also on the losing end of the wealth tax: profits were down 60 per cent.

Through the Adana period Maisky delivered notes to and from Churchill and Stalin. Churchill noted on 3 February in his own handwriting that:

I feel most strongly that this is a fine opportunity . . . I cannot conceal my desire for a warm renewal of friendship between Russia and Turkey similar to that achieved by Mustapha Kemal. Thus Turkey, while increasing her own defences will stand between two victorious friends . . . In all this I am thinking not only of the war but of the postwar period. Tell me if there is anything I can do.

Dixon minuted: 'We want Turkey strong and ready to play her part' and Clutton commented:

It would be moonshine to imagine that in a couple of months distrust that goes back centuries can be dispelled. It will probably always remain. But there is no reason why this distrust should not be kept in control and indeed so exploited that the Turks come to realise that their best means of protection is collaboration and participation in the war.[63]

He also minuted that:

Turkey has a strictly controlled democracy, and the way it performs its functions are both mysterious and Gilbertian. The system, however, works, and that is the important thing.[64]

On the diplomatic front the Southern Department read from intercepts that Menemencioğlu told Vinogradov to say to Moscow that the Turkish government was willing to improve Turco-Russian relations, and cautious steps towards a rapprochement were instituted.

On 17 February Churchill, back with his BJs after his pneumonia, told Eden to get Hugessen 'to impress upon the Turks that they miss their opportunity altogether with Russia and that now is the time to reach favourable agreement'. Cadogan expressed caution about bombing the oil installations at Ploesti, refuelling at Turkish bases: 'Wouldn't it be rather dangerous to tell the Turks that we and the Yanks want use of bases but that we don't ask for them for the Russians?' Hugessen replied about Turkish views on Russia. Distrust 'remains as great as ever, not through fear of communism but of imperialism.' Clutton commented that 'we seem to have steered the Turks successfully off the Balkans', and Dixon noted that we knew from other sources [BJs] that 'the Turkish government had sent very reasonable instructions' to the Turkish ambassador in Moscow.[65] The Turkish consul in Moscow observed to Ankara, 'I respectfully submit my opinion that this year the lands which the Germans have destined for their living space will become their dying space.' On 20 February the Portuguese ambassador in Stockholm reported that the only way into Europe for the Allies was via Turkey.

Consequences: The Foreign Office and the Record

What has been attempted in the foregoing pages is to use the FO intercepts, which the Southern Department and Churchill read, to trace the cause, course and consequence of Churchill's Turkey visit in January, to answer questions raised by the differing perceptions both within the FO and between that body and the prime minister as to the advantages or otherwise of playing an aggressive Turkey hand. While this enterprising move produced no immediate consequences of any significance, it revealed a lack both of vigour and rigour in the Southern Department's policy recommendations in regard to its prize client, Turkey, at a time when a bold reassertion of traditional British involvement in Balkan affairs might possibly have materially affected the timing and the outcome of the Italian campaign and the early preparations of D-Day, as well as the rise and fall of the South of France option ('Husky') for a second front in the west.

Churchill's concentrated study of diplomatic messages during the period autumn 1941 to spring 1943 guided him towards a view of Turkish neutrality which, while at odds with the Americans, the COS and often the Southern Department, shows him to have been still an instinctively imperialist maker of British foreign policy, capable of maintaining valuable if precarious relationships with both the real power brokers, Roosevelt and Stalin, and with new potentially useful friends like İnönü.

In Ankara Ambassador Sho Kurihara reported 'tactical bankruptcy' in Allied war planning, with most action concentrated on the Eastern Front and with German and Italian U-boats taking a dreadful and growing toll on neutral as well as Allied shipping. Kurihara continued that there were eighty divisions of Asiatics [non-Russian communists] in the Russian army:

> . . . they have forgotten [their aim of] making the world red, and are burning with desire to defend their fatherland . . . The Allies' talk of a second front may be via Turkey and the Balkans. The Anglo-Saxons relied on saturation bombing and were no match militarily for the Axis.[66]

But no one seriously expected the Anglo-Saxons to invade the Balkan heartlands and beat the large and well-equipped armies who would then be defending their fatherland. Something short of this, and something involving Turkey.[67] But what? Hugessen suggested on 1 March a three-phased de-neutralising of Turkey:

1) Defensive – make Turkey strong.
2) Turkey lends US/UK air bases.
3) Turkey joins the war.[68]

But The Times argued for postwar planning which would exclude Turkey – Russia would keep the peace in eastern Europe. The New York Times disagreed, as did Ankara. British foreign policy, led at different speeds by Churchill and Eden, now involved a strongly pro-Soviet stance while German forces were still strong, but others were beginning to anticipate the Cold War. On 15 March the Portuguese ambassador in Bucharest reported on Churchill's demands on the Turks at Adana, while from Ankara Kurihara reported to Tokyo that after their North African successes the Allies would begin operations in the Balkans.[69] Churchill had pressed for a new Balkan entente, and for Turkey to have a strong and well-equipped army. İnönü's comment that Churchill was not making up to Turkey 'pour nos beaux yeux' was given wide circulation.

In Whitehall it was unclear who had offered what to whom at Adana. Lord Leathers, the Minister of Supply and one of the few Labour politicians Churchill liked, on 27 March told Churchill that he 'asked the WO and COS what Turkish commitments amounted to but could get no answer.' Ralph Assheton of the Treasury supplied Churchill with fortnightly reports of what was going to Turkey but the whole subject remained a bone of contention throughout the next nine months. Churchill was grateful to Ted Leathers for offering to sort out the mess he had himself created, and added: 'I will telegraph İnönü so as to market our wares as effectively as possible.'[70] Churchill did not join the anti-Bolshevik chorus because of the Anglo-Russian alliance and because to be anti-Bolshevik could imply Fascist leanings, but the Turkish ambassador assumed that the proposed new Balkan entente would be anti-communist. The next day Kurihara reported: 'Not only is the outcome of the fighting on the Eastern front important to Turkey but it will decide the fate of the war. So Turkey is watching very carefully.' The next day his daily telegram reported Britain's failure post-Adana to deliver aid as promised: 'Since Feb 10 no more weapons had arrived as Turkey will not let Britons train Turks on Turkish soil' – this being an infringement of sovereignty and a continual cause of mutual irritation.[71]

The rest of the war in the eastern Mediterranean can be seen as the aftermath to Adana. But the war itself moved into another gear by the spring of 1943, and even in the eastern Mediterranean, for Russia and America something of a backwater, if not for Germany, Italy and Great Britain, Adana faded into the British disaster in the Dodecanese that autumn – the subject of the next chapter.

After Adana, Turkey was temporarily on the back burner at Berkeley Street. During April the BJ telegrams Churchill read concerned alleged separate peace proposals between Russia and Germany, a perennial nightmare quite enough to drive Turkish involvement out of his mind. The Japanese ambassador in Sofia reported fictitious Axis confidence and Churchill annotated to 'C': 'I presume the President is kept informed of all this rubbish, which none the less [sic] tells its tale of despair.' The next diplomatic intercepts to be circulated came from Kabul where the Italian ambassador reported to Rome that 'nationalist and imperialistic sentiments are completely replacing the communist idea'; and the Japanese ambassador there 'watches with pleasure while the European powers break each other's heads'.[72] On 15 April listeners learnt that a deterioration in his condition had made Mussolini become temporarily incontinent. The Bulgarian army was good and well-equipped and would strike back at any US/UK offensive in the Balkans. Hungary was fearful of an Allied offensive in the Balkans according to the Turkish ambassador in Budapest, while the Afghan minister in Rome reported there would be no separate peace for Italy.

The neutrals began to wonder what the Allies would do next, when they realised that the initiative had passed from the Wehrmacht to the Allied high command. But the second front in the Balkans which was so widely canvassed was never a real starter, because Russia would suspect a postwar agenda in any such Anglo-American initiatives while the Americans had no wish to divert any more forces away from North Africa and the beginning of the build-up to the invasion of Sicily and D-Day.[73]

Turkey had been temporarily sidelined by a spasm of massive indecision by all the belligerents, but the FO continued to play what was left of the Turkey hand. Eden thanked Hugessen for his 'admirable summary' of current negotiations: Orme Sargent minuted: 'great importance attached to chrome not only from the point of view of Anglo-Turkish relations but because it is also a touchstone of German/Turkish relations.' Fortnightly reports on the supply situation were requested using the unbreakable OTP procedure. A chrome control officer was appointed at the Ministry of Economic Warfare, which was a regular customer for the commercial as well as the diplomatic section of Berkeley Street BJs. The commercial counsellor in Ankara was given discretion to agree the price which Turkey would propose to demand from the Germans in their contract. Price was 'not to be the determining factor . . . but we and the Germans are going to pay heavily for the chrome because it will be the Turks who will fix the price.'[74] The non-arrival of the equipment promised by Churchill at Adana exacerbated relations. The doyen of Turkish journalism wrote about the 'bad Briton', who 'adopts all sorts of disguises, resorts to all sorts of intrigues . . . Nazism and Fascism have merely become jealous of the English imperialist'. Referring to the non-arrival of war supplies the journalist asserted that Britain was 'now asking the Turks to throw themselves into the fire'.[75]

A British military mission arrived in Ankara under Gen Sir Henry Maitland Wilson in April but achieved none of its set objectives – permission for British officers and troops to train the Turkish soldiery in the weapons, and to develop the runways and harbours. Kurihara reported Wilson's huge, alarming presence, and added Wilson was openly critical of İnönü and would cut short his visit to Turkey.[76] The Brazilian ambassador also reported Wilson's visit: 'finishing touches were being put to the Allies' offensive against Greece and the Balkans.' Kurihara reported Wilson was too boastful and, wrongly, that İnönü had been taken in by Allied propaganda.[77]

In London the Southern Department was concerned that control over Turkish affairs was being wrested from it. For a start Adm Kelly would not report through the correct channels (the ambassador to the FO) though none could deny that he had the ear of the senior Turkish military and served a useful purpose. Besides he was the PM's personal appointee. But when GHQ ME sent Wilson, and later ACM Sir Sholto Douglas, Chief of the Air Staff, ME, on ill-defined and open-ended quasi-military missions to Ankara the FO tried to put its collective foot down, though Dixon observed: 'if it is a fact that [all the visitors from Cairo] are frightening the Germans and even leading them to pull their punches on the Eastern front, that is an argument in favour of maintaining such visits.' Sargent, Cadogan and Eden concurred. In fact Wilson's visit concluded with his agreement with Wavell's remark in 1941 that the Turkish army on the Allied side 'would be more a liability than an asset'. Wilson's view of Turkey was perhaps influenced by his having presided over the disastrous 1941 Greek campaign.[78]

And any diplomat who could seriously think that the titanic battles being then waged between the Russians and Germans in south Russia would be affected by the presence of British military missions in Ankara were seriously out of touch with reality. This is illustrated by Cadogan's draft for a Turkish policy to Hugessen, amended by Eden, who rightly deleted a sublime statement of the obvious: 'it is a problem of steering a course between being too pressing and not being pressing enough.' GHQ ME, reproved by Eden for the presence of its representatives on Turkish territory, said it 'had no intention of short-circuiting the Ambassador'.[79] Cadogan wrote again on 15 April:

> The Turks want to eat their cake and have it – to keep out of the war and to have a hand in arranging the peace. We hinted enough to them at Adana that if they wanted a place at the conference table they must book it (and earn it) in good time. I think we ought to let them see that they are not in the inner circle until they have established the right to be there.[80]

But the truth was it was not part of Turkish foreign policy to accept Allied *matériel*, codenamed 'Hardihood', if this entailed alienating not only Germany but Russia as well. Clutton fumed in London that 'the Turks will be taught the lesson which exists in the Christian bible and doubtless in the Koran – that you cannot serve two masters'. In June Hugessen reported, 'I have pretty well given these people up'. Eden felt the FO's implementation of Churchill's Turkey policy should be reviewed. Churchill thought the FO were spoiling his Turkish plans and suspected that not all the foot-dragging was Turkish – some might be British diplomatic and military incompetence. The FO had the same doubts and instructed Sterndale-Bennett in Ankara to insist to Numan Menemencioğlu that 'maximum cooperation with the Turkish government was required'. Menemencioğlu replied 'we were in effect asking for Turkey to abandon her neutrality. Such a request could not be reconciled with what Churchill said at Adana. There were more than one ways of killing a dog than hanging it.' He was not prepared to provoke German antagonism 'before we are ready to', so the proposed new policy would be difficult.[81] Sargent commented that 'Numan, like every Turk, is convinced the Russians will pour over the Balkans and Persia postwar and envelop Turkey.'[82]

The unstoppable Kurihara submitted:

> . . . the following observations, prolix though they be . . . Turkey unflinchingly and unchangingly leaned towards none of the belligerents, but after Adana leaned towards the Allies . . . This does not mean that it is to be feared that Turkey will enter the war . . . no change in radical policy of continuing to preserve neutrality to the last.

Turkey doubted the possibility of a German victory in the east (Churchill sidelined). But the western Allies would not beat the Germans. Turkish neutrality was based on a possible threat from Soviet Russia. Turkey was merely borrowing the power of Britain, using it as a cat's-paw to guard against the danger of Bolshevism after the war. British talk of occupying

Turkish air bases to attack the Balkans was propaganda. The British failed to get Turkey in and settled 'for second best'. The Axis think the Turks may offer nominal resistance and may be drawn in by the enemy. If Germany is defeated on the Eastern front 'Russo/Japanese relations will be important.'[83]

Kurihara may have been prolix but he had got close to the heart of the Turkish leadership. His colleague the Japanese ambassador in London was less reliable when he reported: 'Churchill will be driven out by leftwing elements, legally or illegally'. This 'C' forwarded to Churchill commenting, 'This is an amusing example of the nonsense which the Japanese forward to Tokyo.' Churchill ticked the comment.[84]

On 12 May, the day of the main Axis surrender in Tunisia, Churchill realised that Italy had ceased to be a potential danger to Turkey and played the Turkey hand, commenting that 'Turkey . . . had always measured herself with Italy in the Mediterranean' and should now 'enter the war . . . The moment had come when a . . . request might be made to Turkey for permission to use bases in her territory' which 'could hardly fail to be successful if Italy was out of the war'. What had Churchill in mind? Controversy has continued: what is clear is that Turkey loomed as large as Italy in his war strategy. On 17 May *The Times* made sweeping postwar plans for the total emasculation of Germany which the Turks found offensive; even the pro-Soviet Turkish paper *Van* wrote on 20 May describing the proposals as 'another Versailles'. However the Americans declined to join the pressurising of Turkey, and thought their bombers were better used in Italy than in Turkey. The British were left to play their hand without American support. This led later in the year to the debacle in the Dodecanese and extended Turkish suspicions of the Allies when apparently acting in concert. The fall of Mussolini, then Russian ambitions in the Balkans and Aegean, together with American withdrawal of interest in that part of the world, led Turkey in 1943 to hope for the defeat of the Allied powers with particular vehemence and she strengthened her ties with Germany. Other neutrals reflected on 'how small a guarantee British protection can give and that in general it cannot be trusted'.[85]

BJs had now become Churchill's most important source of information. Some seventeen of them were sent to Washington for him, as well as daily summaries of their content.[86] In the intercepts of early May, Balkan leaders showed themselves restlessly waiting for the invasion of Turkey. Antonescu thought there was no alternative.[87] The Japanese foreign ministry thought Germany should withdraw from the east and go for the western Allies; otherwise these would build their strength to defeat Japan. The Greek ambassador in Ankara reported more of Saraçoğlu's indiscretion. The Japanese ambassador in Rome reported that Turkey was preparing for a joint assault on the Dodecanese with the British and told his colleague in Kuibyshev of Saraçoğlu's latest indiscretions.[88]

The Japanese ambassador in Rome reported a talk with a Turkish colleague: 'Turkey had no territorial ambition and would maintain neutrality.' But the Turkish general staff was gearing up towards a joint landing with the British on 'two or three of the Dodecanese . . . sufficient to safeguard navigation in the Mediterranean'. On 10 June the Japanese foreign ministry circulated a directive reporting 'efforts made to get Turkey into the war by the Anglo-Saxons'. The next day Raphael, the long-serving Greek ambassador in Turkey, reported to London that Berlin thought the Allies would push towards the Balkans through Turkey, while in Moscow (whither he had returned from Kuibyshev, now the Soviets were winning) the Turkish ambassador, Acikalin, reported that the Germans were profiting by the time they had 'before the opening of the European front by the Turks, British and Americans. The Russians were expecting the opening of the Second Front by the Turks; the Germans would cope with the Eastern Front first, by peace overtures or victory.'[89]

In mid-June Kurihara summed up his view of Turkish policy towards both Axis and Allies. The Turkish press was worried about German defensiveness: 'There was a tendency towards friendship for England manifest after Adana, but this was thought to be less marked. The press were instructed to be less anti-Axis. Turkey was becoming politer towards Germany again.' However an Oshima despatch on the war situation reported the view of 'the contact you know of' that possibly the main allied offensive will be in the Eastern Mediterranean through the Dardanelles, the coercion of Turkey, to threaten Romania and Bulgaria through the Black Sea. [Churchill sidelined.] All Axis powers retain respect for the British navy – as friend or enemy.[90]

This was a very productive period for Berkeley Street. The overwhelming interest of the neutral diplomatic world in events in the Mediterranean ensured that Turkey would continue to dominate the BJs. Churchill annotated many of them, and sent some to Eden for comment. But earlier in this chapter the question was raised whether our new knowledge of BJs in mid-1943 would require the rewriting of the history of Turco-British relations. BJs, as is clear from the foregoing pages, acted as a spur to Churchill, the FO and the COS. Their recent reappearance as HW1 in the PRO enables the historian to focus on the different ways in which neutral diplomats reacted to events in the Mediterranean, but requires little rewriting of the record. The official military historian's account of Adana, already quoted, admirably sums up the situation and requires no revision.

The love/hate affair between Turkey and Churchill with his intercepts and Eden with his secretariat at the FO can now be seen to be the main feature in the months after Adana. It persisted, but this time instead of the FO it would be the services ministries and Eisenhower who would effectively block Churchill's private war against Hitler, to be waged off Turkish waters, and possibly even on Turkish soil, with the object of bringing Turkey into the war. The Dodecanese debacle coupled with the arrival of Cicero at Hugessen's residence in the early autumn of 1943, provide the flavour of the next chapter.

CHAPTER SEVEN

Churchill's 'Island Prizes Lost' Revisited

The inhabitants [of Bodrum] took part in the evacuation of British forces from Cos. They all remembered the pellmell retreat and the awe inspired by German power.

Selim Deringil, *Turkish Foreign Policy during World War Two, p. 215.*

Preparations for the Dodecanese Assault

This chapter relates both Allied and Axis preparations for the fighting in the Aegean in October 1943, to the cause, course and consequences of the Dodecanese campaign and the manner in which British policy in the eastern Mediterranean reflected the differing understanding of both service and diplomatic intercepts shown by the COS, the FO and the PM.

For Churchill this phase of the war was unbearably distressing, as he reveals in 'Island Prizes Lost' in volume 5 (*Closing the Ring*) of his history of the war. All other historians of the Dodecanese disaster have used this chapter as a prime source.

Churchill knew from reading BJs that the surrender of Italy gave the Allies 'the chance of gaining important prizes in the Aegean at very small cost and effort'. His determination to pick up these treasures was thwarted mainly by the United States' Chiefs of Staff who redirected the landing craft needed in the Dodecanese to India, insisted on withholding both troops and ships for the eastern Mediterranean, and saw any resurgent Balkan initiative sponsored by Churchill as yet another attempt to postpone or avoid Operation 'Overlord'. Gen Wilson's handling of the situation from faraway Cairo was also criticised. In all this Eisenhower's reluctance to back Churchill's initiative was compounded by Tedder's unwillingness to send air support to the islands while the invasion of mainland Italy was in full swing, and by a change of command in the British navy (John Cunningham taking on the Mediterranean from his cousin Andrew) which resulted in poor naval co-ordination and support of British invading troops already outmanoeuvred by the Germans who rediscovered their earlier skills at combined operations at the personal insistence of Hitler. The Führer believed the Allies planned, and had the resources, to mount a successful

Balkan Front from Turkey, giving the Anglo-Saxons credit for an invasion scheme which never existed except in the mind of Churchill. The Dodecanese can thus be presented as something of a personal contest between the two warlords, won by Hitler, which disrupted Churchill's immediate plans to involve Turkey in the war. By the summer of 1943, he wrote:

> . . . the command of the Aegean by air and by sea was within our reach. The effect of this might be decisive upon Turkey, at the time deeply moved by the Italian collapse. My parleys with the Turks were intended to prepare the way for her entry into the war in Autumn 1943 . . . This did not happen because of unfortunate events in the Aegean.[1]

This chapter uses Churchill's own anguished account of what happened in the Dodecanese, as does the official military historian's chapter on the same subject.[2] It remains definitive, despite the recent access to Boniface enjoyed by more recent war historians, one of whom, Prof Hinsley, draws on Enigma/Fish intercepts substantially when retelling the story of the campaign.[3] At the start of his exposition of the Dodecanese imbroglio Molony quotes Churchill's brief to the COS of 2 August 1943:

> Here is a business of great consequence to be thrust forward by every means . . . I hope the Staffs will be able to stimulate action which may gain immense prizes at little cost though not at little risk.

Churchill's archaic rhetoric may have been a subconscious smokescreen to conceal his lurking conviction that the risks were unquantifiable and the chances of success, given the other Mediterranean priorities, extremely doubtful. Molony adds that the Germans 'largely through war's extraordinary chance . . . won a resounding tactical success but no long-term advantage'.

Prof Hinsley's account is based, as already noted, on his exclusive access to the DIR/C archive. The influence of Enigma messages when delivered in time for appropriate reactions, is compellingly demonstrated: British success against enemy shipping, for instance, was directly derived from timely Ultra. But growing delays in W/T communications, doubtful interpretations of enemy intentions and the non-availability of combat-worthy aircraft led to inadequate (or 'unsatisfactory' in the word used by the Enigma translator in Hut 4 and also by Churchill) British resistance to well-mounted enemy combined operations. Hinsley's account of the Dodecanese echoes that of Molony, Howard and Roskill and is a classic statement not just of the usefulness of sigint to the Allies at the time, but of the smallness of the changes needed to the historical record already in place.[4]

> The intelligence historians were faced with two problems common to all the official histories dealing with the last years of the war: the massive volume of data available; and the difficulty of avoiding duplication with the *Grand Strategy* and *Theatre* series.[5]

A major miscalculation by the C-in-C ME as to German strength and intentions in the area was caused by the very success of the Allied deception operation codenamed 'Mincemeat' in persuading the enemy that the Allied plan for Operation 'Husky' was a project for a major landing in the Aegean. The Germans thereby believed in an Allied invasion of the Balkans in the summer of 1943 and transferred extra troops, ships, aircraft and guns and ammunition to this front thus making it more hazardous and ultimately impossible for Wilson's pared-down operation against the Dodecanese to succeed.

Churchill's plan for Turkey was to get her into the war that autumn. Operations in the Dodecanese were planned in late November 1942 as a preliminary step. But skilled Turkish delaying tactics as well as British reverses off the Turkish coast aborted the plan. As far back as 7 February 1941 the War Office had speculated on Hitler's intentions in south-east Europe, noting that 'his object in attacking Turkey would be to advance ultimately through Anatolia to Egypt', adding that if Great Britain 'is defeated by invasion this will prove unnecessary'.[6]

By 27 November 1942 the tide had turned and the Joint Intelligence Committee now considered opportunities for Allied action in the Balkans from Turkey.[7] At Casablanca in January 1943 an Allied strategy that promoted action in the Mediterranean at the expense of the war in the Far East was accepted and Wilson was directed by the COS to prepare for amphibious operations in the eastern Mediterranean on 12 February 1943. The next month the Joint Planners considered what should follow the projected invasion of Sicily and the plan to bring Turkey into the war, codenamed 'Hardihood', was discussed on 20 April. By 7 July Kurihara reported the Ankara view that, because a second front in the west would involve heavy casualties, there would be no second front, either in the Balkans or in France that year, and therefore no change in Turkish neutrality. The Anglo-Saxons 'cannot lay hands on Europe' and '. . . in a state of semi-paralysis have set about exerting themselves to win over Turkey . . .'[8] A visit by King George VI was offered as a carrot; İnönü's answer was 'no'.

On 20 July Wilson developed three versions of the planned operation in the eastern Mediterranean, to be known as 'Accolade' and in early August opted for an opportunist 'quick' assault in the wake of the Italian collapse. Throughout August Wilson's quick plan was thwarted by Gen Dwight D. Eisenhower and ACM Sir Arthur Tedder, neither of whom had access to Dedip.[9] On the 12th Eisenhower, Alexander and Tedder revised their recent commitment to 'Accolade' and a week later the 'Quadrant' Conference (14–24 August) limited Churchill's freedom of action in the Dodecanese. Despite this Wilson signalled on 23 August that he was loading the 'Accolade' task force (the 26th Indian Brigade at Suez) and on the 31st Wilson was forced to tell the Supreme Commander that, 'Any enterprise against Rhodes or Crete except as unopposed walk-in is now impossible.'[10]

Hitler was challenged by the Italian collapse to save the situation in the eastern Mediterranean. He had not lost all the initiative after the battle of Stalingrad, because thanks to Manstein's spring 1943 victories, he was able to launch the Kursk initiative on 5 July, disastrous though it proved.[11] He had been waiting (as had the neutrals) ever since for a combined Allied war strategy to emerge, to exploit the fall of Italy. Alanbrooke blamed himself for failing to convince the Americans to exploit the Mediterranean. Churchill, who had always backed this project, pressurised him remorselessly. If only Alanbrooke had done so, perhaps Crete and Rhodes would have been taken and the gateway to the Danube opened.[12] The Balkan Front never happened, partly because there was no agreed Allied policy in the Mediterranean, or any other area, except the unconditional surrender of Germany, and how that was to be achieved depended on the when and how of the second front in the west. Stalin knew this, and so did Churchill and Roosevelt, though the former exercised his ingenuity and persuasiveness over the months to postpone D-Day until the chances of victory were significantly increased. Playing the Turkey card, therefore, was his main offering to the strategic debates of 1943. The aftermath of Adana had left Turco-Allied relations in disarray, although protestations of friendship alternated with mutual criticism.

The British ambassador Hugessen was entrusted with the thankless task of mitigating Turkish resentment at the non-arrival of the promised *matériel*, of neutralising the effect on diplomatic opinion of the British failure to stop Turkey selling chrome to Germany, and of keeping a watchful eye, through intercepts, through agents via SOE and SIS and via some good service attachés stationed in Ankara, on the progress of the war on the Eastern Front and its effect on Turkish views about whether and who to join. It was a bad day for him when on 13 July he interviewed Eleysa Basna for the job of being his personal *kavass*, or valet. Basna was nicknamed 'Cicero' by von Papen.[13] Cicero joined the staff at the British Residency sometime in August, by which time the success of the Allied landings in Sicily was alarming the Turks.[14] Kurihara reported to Tokyo from Ankara that Turkey respected the power of the Axis and had refused to let the Allies set up repair shops and store goods in Turkey. Churchill marked this intercept for the FS (foreign secretary) to see. Eden commented on the FO view:

> We too read our Tunis victories as discouraging the Turks, because their previous attitude may have deterred Germany from attacking Russia . . . . Now they have no such excuse.

Churchill optimistically expected the invasion of Sicily would speedily lead to the collapse of Italy, and 'this should fix the moment for putting the strongest pressure on Turkey to act in accordance with the spirit of the alliance.'[15] The view in Kuibyshev was rather different. There the Turkish military attaché reported a second front was vital, with 'various parts of

Europe, especially France, being the optimum points; thus Germany would withdraw forces from the Eastern Front and so Germany would be defeated by Russia'. He was right, but it was to take nearly two more years.[16]

Diplomatic intercepts played a key role in Churchill's handling, or mishandling, of the Dodecanese campaign. October and November saw the British defeated by German troops in the Aegean in a disaster regarded by the press at the time as of the same order as the Dieppe raid and the Cretan campaign of 1941.[17] It was a smallish sideshow, so far as the Americans, who gave no help, were concerned. But it was an important strand not only in Churchill's personal war strategy but also in Hitler's, who insisted his forces retain Rhodes whatever the cost, partly to pin down a number of non-existent British divisions which he had been deceived into locating in the area, and partly because it was generally expected that the Allies would build on their North African success by invading Italy and establishing a Balkan Front to the east.

Initially it was not Churchill but Wilson who sponsored the Dodecanese debacle. What use Wilson made of Boniface is not known but Churchill would have learnt not only of the build-up of enemy forces but the reason for the success of the British deception operation referred to earlier. So why did he press it? The clearest answer comes from his own directive to the COS: 'at no little risk'. That, he certainly knew, was an understatement. Thirty years before he had flung imperial troops through the Dardanelles where they were mown down by Turkish bullets there.[18] It might be thought that he was trying again, because an aggressive mode had to be sustained: victory would have brought substantial benefit to the Allies, including the possible acquisition of Turkey as an ally. Like Queen Victoria he was not interested in the possibilities of defeat: they did not exist. So he pressed on with the operation disregarding the intercepts which all pointed to Hitler's determination to retain the islands, despite inferiority in numbers and the pessimism of his local commanders.

Since 1940 Churchill's instinct had played with a second front in the Balkans. In June 1941 'Barbarossa' had put this on a back burner. But Turkey always hoped for an Allied invasion, from the Dodecanese and the Straits. The Turks did not realise that the Americans had no intention of deflecting their war effort to these remote regions and away from their primary areas of concern – the Far East, North Africa, Sicily and Italy, and, eventually, 'Overlord'; while the British had neither the troops, the organisation nor the psychological energy to plan realistically for a Balkan thrust along the Danube to Vienna. The Balkan project withered at source from 1941 till D-Day when it died. But in September 1943 it bore bitter fruit in Wilson's attempt to take over the islands from the Italians only to lose them to the Germans. Behind Wilson loomed both Alanbrooke and Churchill who maintained daily telegraphic contact with the C-in-C from 10 September to the end of November.[19]

Hitler for his part insisted on his local commanders and in particular

Lt-Gen Friedrich Müller maintaining the initiative despite poor weather, lack of back-up and the overwhelming demand for all resources, especially aircraft, on the Eastern Front. Müller's island-hopping in the Dodecanese, first to rid them of the Italians, next to expel or kill British troops and terrorise the islanders, impress the neutrals and strengthen Hitler's Eastern Front at its southernmost point, can be partly explained by two factors which the release of DIR newly establish.

One, as has been shown, was the success of Dudley Clarke's deception campaign in the eastern Mediterranean, which had established some ten (non-existent) Allied divisions in the Mediterranean, ostensibly in preparation for an invasion of the Balkans.[20] Hitler believed that he needed to maintain aggressive pressure in the area to deflect a full-scale British invasion of the Balkans. The other was the reinstatement of Mussolini as German puppet. Hitler clung to his friendship with the Italian dictator – as much in bad times as in good – and this led him to believe in an Italian *resorgimento* which never happened. The ups and downs of Mussolini's later career path were carefully monitored by neutral diplomats for whom he remained a pivotal figure in Mediterranean politics. Both factors influenced Hitler's determined stance in the Aegean that autumn.

Mussolini had been toppled from power on 25 July, replaced by Badoglio, who tried – from 3 August to 3 September – to conclude a separate peace with the Allies and remove Italy from the war. The BJs of the period comment on his failure to put together a credible administration. Italy's surrender seemed imminent and the COS therefore decided to concentrate all resources on polishing off one third of the Axis. At the 'Quadrant' Conference the Americans recognised the psychological frailty of British military thinking. (The US Secretary of State Henry L. Stimson told Roosevelt just before 'Quadrant': 'The shadows of Passchendaele and Dunkirk still hang too heavily over the imagination of the leaders of the [British] government.'[21]) The Americans saw in Churchill's interest in recapturing the Dodecanese – particularly Rhodes – no more than an attempt to evade or postpone 'Overlord', while the COS knew that unless many German divisions were pinned down in Italy, 'Overlord' might prove a costly and terrible disaster – so neither group was keen to divert forces needed elsewhere to support Churchill, who saw in a Dodecanese venture an ideal opportunity to get Turkey in.

Speculation on the opening of a Balkan Front continued throughout August, a month which also saw preparations for the campaign.[22] On 1 August Wilson opted for a scaled down, improvisatory 'Accolade'. The next day Churchill wrote to him: 'Here is a business of great consequence to be thrust forward by every means. Should the Italians in Crete and Rhodes resist the Germans and a deadlock ensue, we must help the Italians at the earliest moment, encouraging thereby also the support of the populations.' On 3 August he ordered the COS to stop supplying Turkey and to work up an action plan for the Dodecanese. On 5 August Wilson asked Eisenhower for eight ships, four squadrons of P-38 Lightnings, transport aircraft and troops, to arrive in the Middle East by 14–15 August. On the 7th Eisenhower agreed to some but not all of these requests but five days later he and Tedder reconsidered the commitment and urged the abandonment of 'Accolade'. The 'Quadrant' Conference set limits to operations in the Aegean but despite this drastic change in Allied Mediterranean priorities Wilson signalled Eisenhower on 23 August that he was loading the task force for 'Accolade'.

Operations in the Aegean – September to November 1943: the Limitations of 'Boniface'

'Improvise and dare,' Churchill wrote to the COS on 9 September, the day of the Allied landings at Salerno south of Naples and the day after Italy's surrender: 'This is the time to play high.'[23] The Salerno landings coincided with Badoglio joining the Allies, despite his knowledge that the Germans knew through intercepts what he was up to. And on 13 September he telegraphed Wilson: 'The capture of Rhodes by you at this time with Italian aid would be a fine contribution to the general war.' On 25 September he telegraphed Eisenhower: 'Rhodes is the key both to the eastern Mediterranean and the Aegean. It will [*sic*] be a great disaster if the Germans are able to consolidate there.' On the same day[24] 'an unknown naval convoy was due at Milos at 04.00 hours, due to sail again at 17.00 hours for Candia [Crete]'. Operational instructions were issued the same day. First Rhodes, then Cos, then Leros had become the target for a British assault and a successful German counter-assault.

Wilson was to undertake the long-planned capture of Rhodes largely by bluff, since Eisenhower by now refused support. He had to be content to try and occupy the lesser Dodecanese islands, Kastellorizo, Leros, Cos and Samos, while sending an Inter-Service Mission to Rhodes to treat with Gen Scarioni and Adm Campioni and attempt to destroy the 7,000 strong German Assault Group based on Rhodes. If this was successful he planned to land the 234th Infantry Brigade in three merchant ships, not assault loaded; success would depend on the use of the harbour at Rhodes and the airfields on which one or two squadrons of Spitfires would be ready to land. But Müller managed to catch him off balance. On 9 September Hitler ordered Müller to resist all attacks on Rhodes from any source, and when on 9–10 September Maj the Earl Jellicoe led the Inter-Service Mission to Scarioni and Campioni, the German Gen Klemann seized the former while on 11 September the latter ordered the Italian garrison on Rhodes to capitulate to the Germans. The Germans had adjusted to the possible loss of Italy following the Axis collapse in North Africa in May 1943, by training Gen Klemann's mobile division on Rhodes to be able, in the event, both to accept the surrender of far more numerous Italian troops there, and then also repel the British assault of Rhodes.

Churchill continued to exchange signals with Wilson, pointing out on 13 September that 'the capture of Rhodes by you at this time would be a fine contribution to the general war', while Wilson kept Churchill in touch with his scaled down assault on the smaller islands in a signal the following day.[25] On 17 September a substantial force of imperial troops invaded Cos.[26] On 21 September Wilson submitted similar plans to the COS for Leros and two days later 2nd Battalion, Royal West Kent Regt (minus B Company) invaded Samos. But the next day the German Assault Group was assembled to retake Cos and plan the retaking of Leros under the codename 'Leopard'. On 27 September[27] a TOO intelligence report on the Aegean situation noted that (German) landing craft left for Piraeus with all the Italians on Kythera.[28]

Drache was attacked off Syros; *Polone* was blown up and an unspecified operation by Bulgaria was postponed for twenty-four hours owing to lack of air escort. The Greek ship *Elleni Coliorio* sailed from Pegadia but was set on fire by the Luftwaffe south of Skarpanto.[29] BJ 137725 reported two landing craft and 200 troops on Mytilene were to 'operate against the island of Chios'. Cephallonia was occupied by the Germans on 26 September after a heroic ten-day Italian resistance and nearly 100 Italian officers were murdered. Churchill, learning of this from an Enigma decrypt exploited the German atrocity for all it was worth, stirring the Turks, Italians and French with the news of German callousness. On Kythera the Italians joined the Greek partisans and offered stout resistance on Andros.

On 2 October the Italians were being disarmed by the Germans on Andros, and operations were in progress against Naxos, Paros and Antiparos.[30] Reinforcements were requested for the garrison on Syra. The next day Cos fell to a German group of 2,000 troops, 17 ships and 130 bombers after what Churchill (picking up the phrase from its opposite in a Fish intercept) described as 'unsatisfactory resistance'. The day after, he was heavily marking an intercept which contained the following German signal:

> The aim of the enemy [in the Aegean] is clearly apparent. It is to obtain possession of the Dodecanese islands and to create there sea and air bases from which to cripple shipping in the Aegean which will serve for a base from which to launch an operation against Northern Greece – Salonika – from the Aegean, if it should be undertaken. Daily recces are requested and if possible a survey twice a day of the naval base of Leros which dominates the Aegean, is necessary in order to obtain a picture of the further intentions of the enemy.[31]

Despite German successes among some of the islands, by the end of September the British had established themselves on Cos, Leros, Samos, Simi, Stampalia, and Icaria. By 3 October Churchill was telegraphing ACM Sir Arthur Tedder, C-in-C Allied Air Forces in the Mediterranean: 'Cos is highly important and a reverse there would be most vexatious. I am sure I can rely on you to turn on all your heat from every quarter, especially during this lull in Italy'; and to Eisenhower on the same date: 'We are much concerned about Cos, and are sure you will do all in your power to prevent a vexatious injury to future plans occurring through the loss of Cos.' Eisenhower and Tedder strengthened their view that the Italian campaign – however it developed – would need all available Allied resources. They were right about this in the long run, but Churchill knew from Dedip (and they might therefore have not known that he knew, not being privy to this source) that sparing some men and equipment for the eastern Mediterranean would have paid off handsomely. Their reading of Boniface and consequential appreciation of the war throughout the Mediterranean led them to a cautious and negative response. Dedip also told him the von Papen threat to Turkey – that the Germans would bomb Istanbul if they allowed the Allies to use air bases on Turkish soil – was no longer a realistic option for Germany, and it was most unlikely that Hitler would have sanctioned such a move anyhow.

By 5 October 600 British troops had been taken prisoner on Cos, and much booty captured. Churchill circled 'an Italian colonel shot'.[32] Two and a half thousand other Italians, with guns, cutters and 'one luxury yacht for the use of Oc Battle Gruppe' were also captured. German losses were reported as 15 killed, 70 wounded. Mopping up continued.[33] On 5 October the German Army Assault Division was assigned to Rhodes; a three-page intercept set out who was occupying which island; 'about 700 Italians went to the bottom in the SS *Ardena*'.[34] Good results were reported on Antimachia (Cos). There were indications, too, of impending operations against Naxos 'compiled from a document seen by source'.[35] The Luftwaffe reported Germany was in complete possession of Cos. Churchill circled German 'losses small in the face of tough English resistance', indicating his concern that German losses were not serious, and possibly contrary to what was being reported to him from Cairo. The Cos situation was still fluid and 'it is not certain whether Müller was in Crete or somewhere in the Dodecanese (e.g. Rhodes) when he sent his report'.[36] The same day the Germans were ordered to occupy Amorgis (in the Cyclades) and then go on to assist their fellows on Cos. Landing craft laden with prisoners were heading from Cos to the Piraeus.

Roosevelt was, as we have seen, more inclined to respect Turkish sensitivities than the other Big Two, and less interested in the eastern Mediterranean. So his 'final negative quenched [Churchill's] last hopes'.[37] He told Wilson: 'I am doing all I can', and on 7 October telegraphed Wilson: 'I'll back you through thick and thin even if things go wrong provided everything in human power is done.' Wilson's reply the next day referred to 'intelligence from all sources, including most secret sources', indicating that Enigma decrypts to GHQ ME were being read. How it was thought possible to co-ordinate resistance to the Germans in the Aegean from 700 miles away in Cairo remains a question to which military historians have no clear answer. They tend to pin blame for the Dodecanese disaster not on Wilson but Tedder, who refused to supply air cover except tokenly even when Allied superiority in the Mediterranean was massive – 4,000 Allied aircraft to 800 Axis.[38] On 10 October Churchill pursued the chimera of island prizes by telegraphing Wilson: 'If you are left to take a setback it will be bad. Do not therefore undertake this on the cheap. Demand what is necessary and consult with Alexander. I am doing all I can.' And the following day:

> Cling on if you possibly can. It will be a splendid achievement. Talk it over with Eden, and see what help you can get from the Turk. If after everything has been done you are forced to quit, I will support you, but victory is the prize.

Later, on 1 November, Alanbrooke blamed himself:

> If only I had had sufficient force of character to swing [the Americans] how different the war might be. We should have had the whole Balkans ablaze by now and the war might have finished in 1943.[39]

The irreconcilable positions of Churchill, backing Wilson, and Roosevelt, backing Eisenhower, were to leave marks on Anglo-American relations of which the slowing of the Allied advance up Italy may have been a partial cause. But not all the British commanders, quite apart from Tedder, shared Churchill's determination to win back the Dodecanese and force Turkey into the war. For instance on 6 October the new First Sea Lord and former naval C-in-C in the Mediterranean, Sir Andrew Cunningham, warned:

> The use of Turkish airstrips, while enabling us to provide a valuable support for offensive operations against the islands, would not help us a great deal to defend Leros and Cos on account of the distances involved and the absence of an adequate warning system.[40]

This may explain Tedder's reluctance to send aircraft. The next day Churchill begged Roosevelt for nine landing craft, standing idle because it would be six months before they would be needed for 'Overlord'. But Roosevelt answered two days later: 'Strategically, if we get the Aegean islands, I ask myself where do we go from here, and vice versa, where would the Germans go if for sometime they retained possession of the islands?' It was a good question: in the event they went nowhere.

On 7 November Menemencioğlu rejected Eden's demands for the use of Turkish airfields since this would constitute a commitment to enter the war, and would be so regarded by the Germans. Churchill turned to the FO, which had hitherto contributed little to the Aegean disaster except to warn Churchill not to upset the Turks. He wrote to Eden, then in Ankara on another attempt to get the Turks in – 'Is there no hope? If nothing can be done you should consult with Wilson whether Leros garrison should not be evacuated to Turkey'; and to Alexander, 'You should now try to save what we can from the wreck.' On the same day Tedder signalled that he 'must concentrate on the Italian campaign. "Accolade" must be postponed.'

Two days later, on 12 October, Eden met Wilson and the Middle East commanders in Cairo, where it was agreed that Cos could not be recaptured but Leros should be retained and everything depended on 'Handcuff' – the assault on Rhodes, now known by commanders on the spot to be impossible. Kalymnos was captured and garrisoned by the Germans on 7 October. Müller postponed 'Leopard' (the operation for Cos) 'for naval technical reasons'.[41] On 16 October HW1/2118 confirmed the enemy knew that 'Accolade' could not now be staged. Tedder's view had prevailed. Bad weather was feared. Churchill minuted to Portal, 'is all this to stop altogether? It seems very profitable.' Cos was being used as a base for German attacks on other islands. Churchill minuted to the COS via Ismay (his usual route): 'What actually is being left to ME? Are they getting any bombing help from Tedder?' and reminded them of Tedder's responsibility for the eastern as well as the central Mediterranean war zone.

By 22 October Churchill had become extremely upset about the Dodecanese, especially Cos and Tedder. From Boniface he knew of Müller's postponement of 'Leopard'.[42] From the same source he was aware the Germans knew that a mine-laying operation between Cos and Leros was impossible without MTB protection. He knew SS troops were involved, to oversee the disembarkation of troops on landing craft. This meant crack Nazi troops were engaged, causing still higher risks for the troops on the ground and even less chance of island prizes being won. He knew the Germans thought onward passage from Syros, in the Cyclades, to Cos was too dangerous 'unless Allied cruisers and destroyers were first eliminated'. He knew the German plan to get Amorgos and 'break through at dawn to Cos'. He knew the German reaction to the British commando raid on Levitia (an island of the Dodecanese west of Kalymnos) the day before. He knew that the local German commander sought permission 'to seize Italian uniforms for Brandenburg unit for use as a disguise.'[43] All this and much more he learnt from timely daily supplies of Boniface and Dedip.

But none of this knowledge averted disaster. All he could do was to congratulate Wilson on 'the way you used such poor bits and pieces as were left to you' and urged him to 'keep Leros safely. Nil desperandum.'[44] He did not need Boniface to tell him that on 22 October 4th Battalion of the Buffs (4th Battalion, Royal East Kent Regt) embarked for Leros in two ships, one of which, HMS *Eclipse*, hit a mine two days later, with the loss of 135 officers and men plus over 125 of the ship's crew. On 24 October Churchill telegraphed Wilson: 'I'm sorry you had bad luck over the destroyers and getting the Buffs into Leros yesterday.'[45] The next day Boniface revealed that the Germans had been ordered to occupy Amorgis (in the Cyclades) and go for Cos.[46]

British failure to retain control of the islands was an example of where the best intelligence is useless without the military means to take advantage of it. Hinsley's account emphasises the importance and yet the impotence of Boniface throughout the campaign. Yet Molony wondered why the British admirals 'could not have deduced from perplexing intelligence that German warships were about to go into action' – reflecting the lack of any local inter-service co-ordinating machinery or any of the infrastructure necessary for a successful combined operation. Tedder pronounced the Aegean situation fundamentally unsound but Churchill telegraphed Eden, now in Moscow, on 1 November to try and grip the Leros-Samos situation. 'This is in a most hazardous plight but the prize is well worth struggling for.' On 7 November Menemencioğlu rejected Eden's demands for the use of Turkish airfields and a commitment to enter the war. The same day Boniface reported that the Leros operation was imminent. 'Convoy to proceed as planned.'[47] There followed a German appreciation of British forces on Leros. Churchill circled strength of British navy and land batteries, He was telephoned by 'C' later in the day that the landing convoy was at Leros.[48] 'C' told him the next day that three German landing craft were aground there.[49]

HW1/ 2221, 2222, 2226 and 2234 carry more Enigma tactical details. The date 11 November was D-Day for 'Tragic'.[50] The Allied bombardment of Cos early on that day caused some German naval casualties.[51] 'Two British destroyers came out of Turkish waters and will fire on Cos.' Hinsley observes:

> Sigint made it clear that Hitler, though he increased the risks and prolonged the postponement by vetoing attacks on Allied warships as they lay up in Turkish territorial waters nevertheless remained determined that 'Leopard' should be carried out, as a surprise move, at the first opportunity.[52]

Hitler still believed that six or seven British divisions were standing by in Egypt to attack Rhodes, Crete, the Greek mainland and the Peloponnese.[53]

As for Turkey, Kurihara reported from Ankara to Tokyo on new Anglo–American–Russian pressure on Turkey to join the war . . . but 'it will be a considerable time before Turkey joins. Papen says Russia strongly attacks Turkish neutrality.'[54] There was pressure from both sides. 'An advance by the Soviet army is what Turkey fears most of all.' On the 9th (as already reported) Müller postponed 'Leopard' for twenty-four hours; Churchill marked the Boniface intercept. The Battle Group M (Cos) had been ordered to carry out Operation 'Leopard' on 9/11 by the latest, despite the loss of the Olympos convoy. 'It is of decisive importance for the whole operation.'

On 10 November the War Cabinet telegraphed the Joint Staff Mission in Washington as follows:

> Turkish government is now considering the proposal put to them by Foreign Secretary in Cairo last week that they should enter the war before the end of the year. In regard to Rhodes and the Dodecanese, although *not* operationally essential, it would clearly be desirable to clean up the islands as soon as possible and the idea should appeal to the Turks: (a) The Turks should be asked to say whether they are prepared to undertake the early capture of these islands; and (b) If they say they are unable to do this we should starve out the islands and occupy them later at our leisure.

On 16 November Leros fell to the Germans, after what Churchill described as 'unexpectedly strong resistance', another phrase he copied from an Enigma decrypt (he had marked approvingly a phrase used by the local German commander reporting back in identical terms). Not for the first time the Germans had put their own gloss on 'enemy' intentions, reasoning that if they were in the other's shoes, this is what they would be doing or at least thinking. No wonder Churchill found their reports so stimulating, yet so discouraging. The Turks, without access to Boniface[55] were also impressed. Aware that both Britain and Russia were by now agreed on a policy of forcing them into the war, they found the discomfiture of the British in the Aegean a convenient way of postponing their decision from the autumn of 1943 until the spring of 1944. Even then only a token support was forthcoming, and it was another year before they actually joined the Allies.

Under intense diplomatic pressure from both sides İnönü allowed Germany as well as Britain to infringe Turkish territorial integrity under certain conditions well understood by both adversaries.[56] One of the many Oshima reports told Churchill and the FO how things were between Germany and Turkey that autumn. The full paragraph is quoted in a note at the end of this chapter, but a summary of it dated 18 December 1943 was passed from 'C' to Robertson, to Martin for 'Colonel Warden' (Churchill):

> Churchill and Roosevelt carried out Tehran decision by pressing strongly for Turkish entry into the war, which USSR also desired urgently. Churchill threatened to suspend supplies to Turkey and Eden also took a menacing stand but Roosevelt adopted no such attitude. Turkish Foreign Minister told Papen that he was firmly convinced that even England was not strong enough to risk Turkish enmity by applying sanctions and that USA would in any case refuse to participate: Turkey had given absolutely no promise of entry into the war.

Ribbentrop's comment was that Germany made it clear that Turkey would be considered to have entered the war if land and air bases were granted even without direct participation.[57] The American High Command continued to refuse pressurising Turkey, or to allocate troops, landing craft or fighter aircraft to the eastern Mediterranean, accepting as a *fait accompli* that Russian successes in eastern Europe would leave the whole area open to Soviet aggression at some point in the future. Smolensk had fallen to the Russians on 25 September and on the 22nd the Red Army had crossed the Dneiper, the 'Eastern Rampart' south of Kiev, hailed nervously by the Turkish oligarchs in Ankara. The great Russian counter-offensive was about to unbalance still further the international politics of the eastern Mediterranean.

Turkey and the Dodecanese

While these stirring events were taking place by land and sea, diplomatic moves regarding Turkey and the Aegean were high on Churchill's agenda. On 10 October Eden was able to report to Churchill that:

> . . . the Turks have shown themselves unexpectedly co-operative in the matter [of Cos and Leros: the Turks were also unexpectedly co-operating with the Germans]. They have certainly strained their neutrality and their action [in offering protection to British warships off their western coast] is the subject of German protest.

On the same day Eden was to meet Wilson to see if 'there is any help we can give him with the Turks.' Churchill's Turkey hand had depended crucially on British success in the Dodecanese. Wilson's failure there not only depressed the Turks but signalled the end of Churchill's unilateral Turkey policy. His own account of the Dodecanese debacle is full of suppressed fury but free of hindsight.[58] He quotes his own speeches to Stalin at Tehran about Turkey. He prevaricated when Stalin asked what he would expect from the Soviet 'in case Turkey declares war on Germany, as a result of which Bulgaria attacks Turkey and the Soviet Union declares war on Bulgaria.' Poor Mr Eden had to ask for enlightenment: what exactly had Churchill in mind in getting Turkey into the war? Churchill recalls:

> Although I felt how deeply Turkish minds had been affected by the loss of Cos and Leros, and the consequent German command of the air in the Aegean, I left the subject, having got all I had thought it right to ask, and with fair hopes that it would not be insufficient.

This, perhaps, is his own epitaph on his Turkey policy.

On 19 October the opening of the Foreign Ministers' Conference in Moscow saw the beginnings of a new and unwelcome Russian phase of aggressive interest in Turkey. By the end of it the Red Army had cut off the German-held Crimea and recaptured Kiev on 6 November. Eden played up to Russian demands and confirmed 'there was no disagreement between the Allies as to the desirability of bringing Turkey into the war'. On 2 November a joint protocol was signed whereby Turkey would be asked to come in before the end of 1943. Roosevelt was reluctant and the Turks furious.[59]

It was against this background that Menemencioğlu met Eden in Cairo on 5–7 November. The meeting was not a success.[60] Eden offered Turkey a phased entry, beginning with the offer of bases and a movement from pure neutrality, but the Turkish foreign minister saw no advantage to his country in such a concession. The phased entry, which both Russia and Turkey thought pointless and counterproductive, was propounded nevertheless by the British because they realised that their successful Turkey-based deception plan would be exposed if Turkey immediately entered the war – and the great flow of seasoned Allied troops into Turkey failed to take place. Eden told Churchill, 'My persuasions were the less effective as both [Menemencioğlu and Açikalin] seemed to be particularly deaf.'[61] Deafness proved a useful device, and a report circulated in Cairo:

. . . that all the Turks were wearing hearing devices so imperfectly attuned to one another that they all went out of order at the same time whenever mention was made of the possibility of Turkey's coming into the war.[62]

Eden commented that German sources (by which he was presumably referring to Boniface) reported their successful brush-off of British forces from the Dodecanese.[63] The next day Churchill noted 'the nadir of Turco/British relations'.[64]

On the same day the *Forschungsamt* in Berlin intercepted reports of the Moscow Conference and showed them to Hitler, who read a German version of:

At Menemencioğlu's request Eden had had talks with him in Cairo. While there he advised him of the Soviet demand for military bases in Turkey . . . Eden represented the Soviet case only half-heartedly, and did not make it at all difficult for Turkey to reject them.[65]

He, or Ribbentrop or Kaltenbrunner, would also have been reading the British FO's correspondence to Ambassador Hugessen, as November was a productive month in Cicero's career as an international spy.[66]

Turkish neutrality remained even-handed, and despite the arguments and quarrels Turkey declared on 17 November that she would come into the war, but the Turkish press and public considered they had been bounced into action of which they did not approve. One journalist told Deringil that Britain was suspected of intending to face Turkey with a *fait accompli* by giving her just enough aircraft to provoke a German attack. Molotov's keenness at Moscow to have Turkey in quickly reverted to a more detached attitude, on the basis that he hoped thereby to separate Turkey from Britain, thus laying the ground for the Soviet postwar policy towards Turkey.[67] At Tehran later that month (28 November) Churchill offered to lay before İnönü 'the ugly case which would result from the failure of Turkey to accept the invitation to join the war, and the appetising picture of what help could be offered her if she did'.[68] He tried to go on playing the Turkey hand long after British intervention in the affairs of the Black Sea and eastern Mediterranean countries had ceased to be of consequence to the countries concerned.

The Dodecanese debacle rankled in Whitehall. Had Churchill agreed at this stage to anticipate Turkey's joining the Allies by putting the politics of the area under Macmillan, a different outcome to the state of affairs in the eastern Mediterranean might have resulted, with considerable after-effects stretching through to the postwar period. But after Adana Churchill was not in the mood to give Turkey to anyone, not even, indeed, to the FO. For he could study Turkey through BJs, but Wilson and Macmillan could not. Nor could Eisenhower, who only received briefing political analyses compiled from them; and recipients such as the FO and MEW lacked the authority to act on their authenticity and immediacy.

To sum up the Dodecanese operation: those without access to BJs lacked the power or knowledge to enforce decisions, and this led to the debacle and an unresolved conflict between Churchill and the other Allied war planners as to the priority rating of the eastern Mediterranean in the context of victory in the west and on the Eastern Front.

Churchill and Turkey: November 1943

This section analyses the complex causes which led to German victory in the eastern Mediterranean in November 1943.

The Dodecanese debacle had robbed Churchill of his credibility in the eastern Mediterranean. After mid-September when Rhodes was entirely in German hands, one island after another saw the weak invading forces of Britain capitulating, and drastic losses suffered by the British navy. The Turks took full advantage, and Churchill noted: 'Turkey, witnessing the extraordinary inertia of the Allies near her shores, became much less forthcoming and denied us her airfields.'[69] The FO expected the loss of Cos and Leros similarly to affect the Turks. Clutton wrote on 20 October that:

. . . we have no chance whatsoever of getting anything serious from the Turks until we have got the Dodecanese . . . in fact we missed the bus when we allowed 30,000 Italians on Rhodes to capitulate to 7,000 Germans.

Deringil met many eyewitnesses of the British disaster at Bodrum, opposite Cos, who all remembered the pell-mell retreat and the awe inspired by German aggressiveness.[70]

The official British military historian's account draws as heavily on Churchill's war history as almost every subsequent historian has done. He opens his account of 'the star-crossed British operation in the Aegean during the period September to the end of November 1943' by citing the occupation of Cos in mid-September:

[It] then fell to the German attack on 3 and 4 October. The island of Leros was garrisoned by a battalion in mid-September, was reinforced at intervals up to 11 November and was lost between 12 and 16 November . . . The forces employed during the whole period were not great but the losses were grievous. The land forces amounted to five battalions and some supporting arms and were lost. The naval forces, never all engaged at once, were 6 cruisers and 33 destroyers including 7 Greek, a few submarines, some lesser ships and craft. 4 cruisers were damaged, 6 destroyers were sunk and 4 were damaged, two submarines and coastal craft and minesweepers were sunk . . . 282 aircraft flew 3,746 sorties. 113 Allied aircraft were lost, including 50% of the Beaufighter strength.[71]

Who was responsible? Captain Stephen Roskill was in no doubt. The British chain of command was faulty, and Churchill, as Minister of Defence, as well as the COS, should have clarified it before encouraging operations in the eastern theatre on a considerable scale. The three C-in-Cs in the Middle East (Admiral A.U. Willis from 14 October, General Maitland Wilson and ACM Sholto Douglas) were a theoretically equal triumirate. But Churchill, with his special relationship to Wilson from whom he liked to hear direct, sent his Dodecanese messages only to Wilson. Moreover, while Wilson and Willis were independent C-in-Cs, Douglas was subordinate to Tedder, and relations between them were bad, as both made clear in their memoirs. Roskill also points to Churchill's 'illusion' about Turkish involvement 'for the Turks could not have defended themselves as long as the Germans held Greece and most of the Aegean islands. When in 1944 the Germans were forced to withdraw from Greece, the islands fell into our hands virtually uncontested.'

The Aegean campaign of late 1943 lasted from the Italian surrender in September to the Allied evacuation of Samos by caique into Turkey in late November.[72] Hitler's determination to hold on to Crete and Rhodes, it was acknowledged, resulted in a crushing local defeat for the British forces involved. Cos had fallen in two days (3–4 October) and Leros in five (12–16 November) to 'brilliantly improvised German and amphibious and airborne attacks launched from Athens and Crete'. What went wrong, particularly with the Royal Navy, given Allied naval superiority in the Mediterranean?

There was the mistimed change of command at the top. British destroyers laid up in Turkish waters by day – where Hitler forbade their being bombed by the Luftwaffe (as the Enigma decrypts of 12 October showed) – failed to protect or deliver British invading forces. There was American reluctance to commit troops on a scheme in which Roosevelt's military advisers had no interest. Boniface and BJs (as HW1 confirms) provided full intelligence of German moves, yet the Germans achieved an unintercepted tactical surprise landing of troops on Leros. The defenders of the island were not surprised as the invasion convoy was tracked, but it had also to be intercepted; this it was not. After land fighting as bitter as for Crete in 1941, the Allied garrison surrendered on 16 November. A recent war historian quotes from contemporary press reports and adds that:

> . . . they point to the twin problems of poor planning and equally poor execution resulting in the sacrifice of an entire infantry brigade, corps troops, and special forces, as well as frightful naval losses due to enemy air attack. The effort sustained did not achieve the primary objectives (Rhodes and Turkey) nor the secondary objectives (Cos and Leros).[73]

Jeremy Holland asks who in Whitehall was responsible? This book shows that the possession of vital signals intelligence about the enemy's plans and needs – which Churchill and Alanbrooke and Wilson all had – was not in itself sufficient to provide victory over Müller and his superiors, who, pressurised by Hitler, overcame all obstacles and won a brilliant if short-lived victory. Churchill very publicly accepted responsibility for defeat though continuing to criticise Eisenhower and Tedder – and by implication the US High Command – for failing to see the point of the operation and take the comparatively modest steps needed to bring off a surprise victory. Improvise and dare: neither option stood very high in the perceived priorities of the Combined Chiefs of Staff.

For the British all went wrong not only because there was no co-ordination of operations, but because the FO on the sidelines resisted a suggestion which seemed obvious – to bring Turkish forces in. The War Office also reasonably opposed the plan, arguing that Turkish forces lacked training in or experience of combined operations. None the less superiority in numbers and the closeness of Turkish air and naval bases to the Dodecanese should have helped Britain towards victory. The FO can be seen to be limited to preserving Turkey as its private possession, which she would remain so long as she did not take up arms against the Axis. But the official historian of the war at sea rightly concludes that most of the responsibility rests with Churchill 'whose addiction to the capture of islands which would prove difficult to supply' was well known.

> That he strongly resented Roosevelt's refusal to help is proved by the telegram about holding Leros . . . when he told him [misquoting St Matthew] that 'even the dogs under the table eat of the children's crumbs'. Furthermore his hope of bringing Turkey into the war, which was the principal plank on which he rested his case, was an illusion: for the Turks could not have defended themselves as long as the Germans held Greece and most of the Aegean Islands . . . Yet the Aegean fiasco

was a tragic, and one may feel a wholly unnecessary ending to a year which had brought important and long-awaited successes.

Molony's 1973 account of the Dodecanese requires neither alteration, emendation or supplementation, and Roskill's conclusion about Churchill's responsibility is one which no amount of intercept reading is likely to affect.[74]

On 18 November Adm Kelly, Churchill's special naval appointee in Ankara, arranged the withdrawal as well as evacuation of stragglers from Leros, and was now in Smyrna. The same day Churchill telegraphed Wilson: 'I approve your conduct . . . there was a serious loss and reverse but I feel I have been fighting with one hand tied behind my back.'[75] The next day sunset reports for Churchill told him the Germans were poised to beat the British and Italians. Churchill and Wilson were mortified.[76] But other tasks were to await them.

A comparison between Churchill's political performance off the Turkish coast in 1915 and 1943 is instructive. In the First World War, strategic objectives were set by the War Cabinet and carried out by the commanders of the armed forces. Churchill failed to produce a consensus on a viable operation at the Dardanelles that would have achieved his intended effect of neutralising Turkey, despite his enormous influence as First Lord of the Admiralty. In 1943 his powers were much greater, as the third of the Big Three. But even that, as we have seen, did not enable him to carry through his objective of retaking the islands. His powers were still limited, and his plans thwarted, by the Americans and the COS and the need to concentrate the western Allies' forces on the invasion of Italy. Hitler, on the other hand, with absolute power even after Stalingrad, simply overruled his generals and won the contest. Two failures off the Turkish coast, in 1915 and 1943, were both large, public and acknowledged by Churchill.

The Conferences

Churchill still persisted, writing to Eden in Moscow as late as 20 November:

> I remain convinced of the great importance of our getting a foothold in the Aegean by taking Rhodes, re-taking Cos, and holding Leros and building up an effective Air and naval superiority in these waters. Do the Russians . . . think this is a good idea, for its effect on Turkey?[77]

Eden replied on the 22nd: 'Stalin is keen to bring Turkey in, but thinks it can be done on the cheap'. On 15 November the FO expressed doubts about the likely consequences of interesting the Turks in the Dodecanese venture. Sargent minuted to Eden that Turkey should not come into the affair, but Churchill continued to pressurise Eden: 'Put the squeeze on Turkey. If they jib the Russians will get them.' On 24 November Eden and Ismay had met Numan at Cairo. Eden

. . . dwelt on the advantages that would be derived from Turkey's entry into the war . . . It may well hasten the process of disintegration in Germany and among her satellites . . . By all this argument the Turkish delegation was unmoved . . . considering what was happening under their eyes in the Aegean, the Turks can hardly be blamed for their caution . . .[78]

The prize was Turkey. 'If we could gain Turkey it would be possible . . . to dominate the Black Sea with submarines and light naval forces and to give a right hand to Russia.' Ismay observed that: '. . . recent events in the Aegean had evidently done nothing to erase their [Turkish] fears of the German power to take reprisals, or increase their confidence in our ability to protect them'.[79] On the same day Oshima distributed his nine-page overview updating not only his colleagues in Tokyo, Madrid, Lisbon, Ankara, Rome, Moscow and elsewhere but also Churchill and Eden, the British Foreign Office, and the Wilhelmstrasse and von Ribbentrop.

Later in November a key talk between Menemencioğlu and Vinogradov took place about the postwar settlement of the Straits.[80] At Tehran on 28 November Churchill asked:

How could we persuade Turkey to come into the war? . . . What would be the effect on Bulgaria who owed a profound debt to Russia for rescuing her in former days from the Turkish yoke?

Stalin asked:

How many Anglo-American troops would have to be allotted if Turkey came into the war? . . . [He thought] it would be a mistake to send part of our forces to Turkey and elsewhere and part to Southern France.

He added that 'the entry of Turkey into the war . . . was relatively unimportant'. Churchill reverted the discussion later to Turkey.[81] But Stalin was interested only in 'Overlord' and possibly the South of France.[82] Meanwhile Roosevelt was briefing his chiefs of staff about UK policy towards Turkey.[83] The president ended by saying 'he did not have the conscience to urge the Turks to go into the war'. Molotov reversed his policy and agreed.

From now on Turkey-related BJs continue to appear regularly till VJ-Day (as we shall see) and the FO and MOD continued to adjust their policies and practices in the eastern Mediterranean in the light of the intercepts from and to Ankara.

Turkey had been high on the agenda for the conferences at Moscow, Tehran and Cairo. Eden and the FO played the Turkey hand as energetically as they knew how, but failed to dislodge the Turks from their deeply held positions and their diplomatic deafness. The airwaves had little to say about what was going on at the conferences; but diplomatic comments on them followed shortly afterwards as Oshima's report to Tokyo of 4 February 1944 comprehensively attests.[84] The Tehran summit had been quickly followed by the two Cairo summits, at the first of which İnönü stalled. Hugessen told the FO on 3 December that İnönü was the key to the whole Turkish manoeuvre:

> He is taking some risk in coming to Cairo and it is surprising that he is able to carry a reluctant Parliament with him . . . I think he could bring the country along in a short time.

Menemencioğlu commented on the absence of the Russians from Cairo; his reconstruction was that 'the Soviets were pressing for a second front which the Americans could not yet provide, and the entry of Turkey into the war was to be their compensation'.[85] Although Roosevelt saw İnönü alone on 6 December to press Turkey to come in 'if she did not want to find herself alone after the war', İnönü may have known that Roosevelt did not have the conscience, as he said, to force her in. İnönü's achievement at Cairo was to postpone the date of Turkey's entry. Churchill was flattered to be kissed goodbye by İnönü but Eden remarked sulkily that 'that was not much for fifteen hours' argument'.[86]

Eden records that on 1 December, 'the question of inducing Turkey into the war was our first (Anglo-Russian) topic'. He then reported to the Big Three on his Cairo conversations with the Turks. Churchill said, 'I would be satisfied with a strained neutrality from Turkey . . . Turkey should come into the war on the side of the allies by the end of the year.'[87] The Turks had reluctantly assembled in Cairo, following their discussions with Eden of early November, and Churchill wrote to the COS on the action needed if Turkey 'came in on our side'. To Eden he wrote that:

> Angora must be left under no delusions that failure to comply when request is made on 15 February [1944] meant the virtual end of the alliance, and that making impossible demands is only another way of saying no.

He dismissed as nonsense the possibility that Germany would or could undertake a separate invasion of Turkey.[88]

On 13 December Churchill ordered Eden to instruct Hugessen to 'put the screw hard' on Ankara. He was to say that if the Turco-British military talks failed to produce results this time, Britain would not support Turkey after the war: 'The Turks must be made to see that with the development of aerial warfare the Dardanelles no longer held a crucial importance and that they were not indispensable.' The Turks took not a blind bit of notice.

On 15 December Churchill and the FO learnt that Menemencioğlu told the Turkish ambassador in Berlin the cabinet had decided not to accept the proposals made by the Allies in Cairo 'but this decision should be applied very leniently and everything possible should be done to preserve the Anglo/Turkish alliance intact'.[89] On the same day they read that Kurihara had learnt from von Papen that though Menemencioğlu had told him in spite of Allied requests for Turkey to enter the war, he'd refused because 'participation was not necessarily in the Allies' interests'.[90] Von Papen's telegram to Hitler was summarised.[91] Eden, Churchill and Roosevelt all spoke with different voices. Britain would not enforce sanctions against Turkey. 'C' sent this intercept via Gore-Brown to 'Spencer' (Churchill) to be destroyed after reading.[92]

On 16 December von Papen reported to Berlin on pressure on Turkey in Cairo, mainly Russian, therefore the Allies would send reinforcements through the Straits, so a Russian attack on the Southern Front would not begin until then (which was intelligent strategic thinking).[93] The same day Oshima reported that Churchill had threatened Turkey in Cairo, Roosevelt was placatory, and von Papen asked would the UK use sanctions against Turkey? 'Not even Britain was strong enough to make an enemy of Turkey, and USA would have no part of it.' Ribbentrop said if Turkey guaranteed air bases to Allies then 'Turkey had entered the war'.[94]

With so much open diplomacy the intercepts could throw little new light on matters. Oshima continued to report, including a twelve-page intercept describing his visit to the front. A copy of this was flown to Roosevelt. In Ankara the Turkish foreign ministry informed their ambassador in Berlin that 'Turkey will not accept the Cairo proposals' but they also wished to preserve the Turco-British alliance intact. Kurihara learned from von Papen that Turkey would not join the war, and that Roosevelt had extracted a promise from Stalin that the Soviet Union would fight Japan after victory in Europe. He also reported that government circles in Ankara believed the USSR would declare war against Japan when the second front took place in the west. The UK would not enforce sanctions against Turkey.[95] Months were to elapse before İnönü replaced Numan Menemencioğlu, stopped shipping chromite to Germany and eventually joined the Allies. On 21 December Oshima reported: 'at Cairo Turkey had to go to war, Turkey said no',[96] but on 23 December Churchill said he 'was resigned to Turkish neutrality'. Oshima remained in spate throughout the Christmas period.

The Dodecanese and the conferences passed from Churchill's priority list and he reluctantly confronted the greater demands of 'Overlord', for which Boniface and Dedip were to continue to provide vital information. But this belongs to a different phase of his war leadership than that which is the subject of this book. The year ended for Churchill's staff on 30 December with Ismay, Hollis and 'C' writing about 'master' (Churchill) now taking an interest in plans for 'Overlord'. 'Master rather buoyant at the moment but quite open to reason.' Churchill suggested a 'kind of reverse Dunkirk – small boats landing infantry then proper assault troops . . . I know this sounds impracticable but he is likely to harp on it until it is proved to him to be so.'[97]

This chapter shows the effect on Churchill's mind of signals intelligence, both Enigma/Fish and Dedip, in his final attempt to breach Turkish neutrality and create a diversion which would pin down German divisions in Greece rather than being seconded to the Western or Eastern Fronts. It also shows the limitations of signals intelligence unbacked by a strong coherent strategy, insufficiently flexible Allied leadership in Combined Operations, and growing rifts in the postwar goals of the USA, the USSR and the UK.

In Chapter 1 mention was made of two events – one disastrous and one ludicrous, on both of which new light could be thrown by Dedip. This chapter has given some account of the disaster, of Churchill's crucial part in it, as well as the use of Boniface and Dedip by all levels of British command in attempting to respond appropriately to the daring improvisation of the Germans. The ludicrous event is the subject of the chapter that follows.

CHAPTER EIGHT

Cicero, Dulles and Philby: 1943–44

It was a strange kind of colloquy with the great ones of the world, whose names turned up in the documents: Roosevelt, Hopkins, Churchill, Eden, Stalin, Molotov . . .

Eleysa Basna, *I Was Cicero*, p. 72.

Introduction

A sharp reminder of the importance of the Moscow, Cairo and Tehran Conferences to Turkey is provided by the care which the minutes recording them, or diplomatic reactions thereto, were studied not only in Ankara but also in Berlin. In Ankara the leadership relied as always on its ambassadorial reports – especially those from Moscow. But in Berlin supposedly vital documents, some bearing on the conferences, had arrived by a circuitous route which it is the aim of this chapter to unravel. The chapter also seeks to validate the claim that a study of wartime diplomatic intercepts from September 1943 till March 1944 can throw new light on what has universally been acknowledged to have been the most bizarre spy coup of the Second World War.

A new appreciation of FO attitudes and approach to neutrals – pre-eminently Turkey – is attainable from a study of what the Ankara-based BJs have to say about the course of the war; and this in turn opens up further diplomatic secrets when applied to the following attempt to chart the progress round Europe of the FO papers communicated to the British ambassador to Turkey, Sir Hughe Knatchbull-Hugessen. Since selections of these papers were routinely stolen from the ambassador's safe, photographed by his valet, sold to the Abwehr chief in Ankara, re-enciphered and transmitted to Berlin, a further dimension of diplomatic activity – this time German – can be added to the picture.

And finally, since a further selection of these were stolen from the German foreign ministry by one of its senior executives and presented to the American consulate in Berne (after having been turned down by the British) whence they were yet again re-enciphered (in the American diplomatic cipher) before transmission to both Washington and London, it is possible to complete the circle of excitement, mystification, horror, disgust and office politicking which ensued, after their final assessment by the department responsible for their original sourcing, in the offices of GCCS's diplomatic cryptographic department in Berkeley Street, MI6 in Ryder Street and Broadway Buildings, and the FO in Whitehall.

In reviewing the primary and voluminous secondary literature of what came to be called Operation 'Cicero' many questions arise. What was the valet (Basna) photographing? What did the Germans think of it and how did they use it? How did some of the material get to Allen Dulles in Washington; and to MI6, in the person of Kim Philby, in London? What did the Americans think of it? How did GCCS assess it? What was the real importance, if any, of the material to the conduct of the war by both sides, and in particular how did it affect Turkey's determination to stay neutral?

This chapter also looks at what would have happened had not the British ambassador in Ankara's valet done what he did in 1943 and 1944. In particular, what would have been the Russian, American and neutrals' view of such diplomatic ineptness? The answer put forward here is, 'very little'.

Historiography

The great spy coup was first revealed to the world as early as 1947 with the publication throughout the world of Ludwig Moyzisch's *Operation Cicero*. This achieved world fame and became the basis of a film, starring James Mason, called *Five Fingers*. But Moyzisch, who in 1943 was the head of the Ankara branch of the foreign intelligence branch of the German SD, itself a branch of the *Reichssicherheitshauptamt* – RSHA V1 – was not the only participant in the story to commit his part in it to paper. In the following years Walter Schellenberg, the charming young brigadier in charge of the whole SD foreign intelligence bureau in Berlin, published the results of his postwar interrogation, while in Ankara Hugessen's valet Eleysa Basna himself, as well as the German ambassador Franz von Papen and the British ambassador all published memoirs, though the latter failed to mention his problems with his valet.[1] 'A period of some difficulty followed' was how he described what his colleagues thought was the greatest breach of FO security prior to the Burgess and Maclean affair.[2]

Before the release of DIR the unpublished primary sources relating to Cicero were non-existent in the PRO, since the affair led to a comprehensive weeding of files containing any reference to this episode in FO history, though two files, FO371 44066 and 44067 carry references to the subsequent security mission to Ankara which failed to find anything amiss at the embassy, for the good reason that there was nothing amiss there, the theft of papers being perpetrated at the ambassadorial residence some way away.[3] There may still be files in the German and Turkish archives. But the BJs dated autumn 1943 and spring 1944 constitute a vital new primary source, which corroborate the descriptions by Moyzisch, Basna, and von Papen of the content of the documents photographed by Basna. Some of these DIR documents are identical with certain of those which were sold to Moyzisch in Ankara, and then transmitted to Berlin for evaluation and use by Kaltenbrunner, Hitler, Goebbels and Ribbentrop. Some of these were subsequently purloined from the Wilhelmstrasse by Fritz Kolbe, who took them in conditions of great secrecy and danger, to the American consulate in Berne. Here Allen Dulles, realising their importance to his masters in Washington, had them laboriously re-enciphered and sent in batches there as well as to London – to spread an encryptographic load which would otherwise have been insupportable. In London they were variously assessed by Philby and his superior Dansey in MI6. They were finally validated by GCCS (diplomatic) whence some of them may even have originated.

Fortunately, as we have seen, four leading participants and three minor players published memoirs. These have been derided in some official quarters as partial, lying, self-serving and based on no corroborative evidence. Though this is likely in the case of von Papen and Schellenberg, on trial for their lives, Basna's story which appeared in 1961, ten years after Moyzisch's, stands up well to renewed scrutiny in the light of the release of Churchill's BJs. Moyzisch's book ends with an epilogue by von Papen, the formidable and complex diplomat who at one stage of the war was widely thought to be a candidate to replace Ribbentrop as German foreign minister. Von Papen was later acquitted of war crimes but served a prison sentence for lesser offences under German law. Historians have labelled him a congenital liar and hate-figure, for no better reason, apparently, than that he was in no position to answer back. Actually the part he played in keeping Turkey out of the Allied camp was crucial to Hitler's strategy in the eastern Mediterranean, and his account of the Cicero period in Ankara is believable, and is corroborated by BJs. The intense mutual dislike between him and Ribbentrop is there for all to see. The three minor players were Allen Dulles, Kim Philby and Nicholas Elliott.[4]

There are many references to Cicero in the secondary literature, both popular and academic, of espionage in the Second World War. Of the former, Nigel West has probed the story most recently, and of the latter David Kahn has used German archives microfilmed after the war for National Archives in Washington. Anthony Cave Brown writes of Cicero in his monumental life of 'C' as well as in his *Bodyguard of Lies*.[5] The most widely respected academic historian of secret intelligence, apart from Prof Christopher Andrew and Sir Harry Hinsley himself, is Prof Bradley Smith, who wrote about Cicero in his *The Shadow Warriors*.[6] The official historian of British secret intelligence in the Second World War had to rely on a secretary with a good memory for the answer to the question what was Basna photographing? But it is now possible for researchers in DIR/C to identify secret documents, in some cases already correctly cited and reproduced by Basna in the early 1960s, as well as by Papen and Moyzisch. Though as an exercise in rehabilitating old sources this will be of some comfort to the descendants of Basna, von Papen and Moyzisch, for the historian of secret intelligence, little if anything is changed by the release of the BJs.[7]

This summary of the Cicero historiography in the light of BJs in 1943 and 1944 raises the question whether 'the greatest spy coup of the war' is a justifiable description of the tissue of muddle and mixed motives which surrounded the FO documents at the centre of the story.

What Basna was Photographing

Having reviewed the Cicero historiography it is now comparatively simple to answer the question posed at the beginning of this chapter: what was Basna photographing? Reference has been made earlier to the reliance of the official historian on the memory of a former secretary to answer this question. This was Maria Moltenkeller, the translator of Cicero's material in Berlin:

> From her interrogation and from the postwar capture of the telegrams to Berlin in which von Papen summarised some of the photographed pages, it appears that they consisted of briefing papers for, and reports on, the discussions in Cairo in November 1943 between Churchill, Roosevelt and İnönü and probably that in January 1944 between Churchill and the Turks, together with telegrams between the Ambassador and Whitehall about the subsequent negotiations, day to day business and reports from the Embassy about Turkey's trade relations with Germany . . . According to Maria Molkenteller there were between 130 and 150 telegrams and they included one in which the Foreign Office warned the Ambassador that Berlin had copies of important documents that had been taken from his Embassy.

Hinsley adds authoritatively that there is no foundation for the claim made by both Moyzisch and Basna that Cicero's material enabled the Germans to break the FO ciphers.[8] The converse, however, is reasonably certain: the translated, re-enciphered and re-translated and re-re-enciphered material enabled the British finally to break the German diplomatic cipher, as will be demonstrated later in this chapter.

The earliest claims about the content and importance of the material came from Moyzisch.[9] He reported they contained the signals passed between the FO in London and the British embassy in Ankara at a time at which German cryptographers were trying to break the British diplomatic code: 'The intercepts enabled the German SS to break an important British cipher.'[10] He also reported that the Japanese ambassador in Berlin, Oshima, knew about Cicero[11] and 'Turkey was the key place in global politics'. He confirmed that December 1943 was the crucial period for Cicero's work, and that the material was validated when the Allied air raid on Sofia on 14 January 1944 was correctly predicted. This intercept was not shown by

Moyzisch to von Papen, who thus knew some material was getting direct to Berlin and drew his own conclusions about the working of the SD.

Von Papen noted that Moyzisch did not know in any detail of the content and importance of the material. Von Papen himself assessed it very highly indeed, from the moment when he realised he was:

> . . . looking at a photograph of a telegram from the British Foreign Office to the Ambassador in Ankara. Form, content and phraseology left no doubt that this was the genuine article. It consisted of a series of answers from the Foreign Secretary, Mr. Eden, to questions which Sir Hughe Knatchbull-Hugessen had asked in another telegram, requesting guidance on certain aspects of his country's policy, particularly as regards Turkey. I realised I had come across a priceless source of information.

He then named Basna (whom he refers to as Diello in his book) as 'Cicero'. Von Papen adds: 'during the period of the Foreign Ministers' meetings in Moscow, of the Tehran and Cairo Conferences, and, indeed, right up to February 1944, the flow of Cicero's information was of priceless value.' He learnt of Moscow's decision to force Turkey to declare war against the Axis by the end of the year, communicated to Sir Hughe in FO telegram No. 1594 of 19 November and of Sir Hughe's reply (in telegram No. 875) which he proceeds to quote at length, and without permission. A footnote informs the cautious reader that von Papen's own files were lost during the war and the quotation is taken from 'an incomplete photostat copy of an article by Dr Paul Schwarz which he was given to understand appeared in the *New Yorker Staats-Zeitung*'.[12] Subsequent pages show von Papen fully apprised of the complex politics surrounding Turkey's continuing neutrality, the main political debate between the Big Three at Tehran concerning the unconditional surrender formula, the differences of opinion between the service chiefs at the same conference and the imminent launching of Operation 'Overlord'.[13]

Thanks to Basna the Turkish government's reply to the Allies about supplying the Turkish forces 'lay on my desk a few days after' 12 December when it was communicated to the Allies. As a result of reading Cicero's telegrams, von Papen concluded he should do all in his power to end the war, an ambitious project in which he failed. But he gave two reasons for his belief in the value of Cicero. One was the revelation of Allied intentions towards Germany postwar – intentions which differed sharply between each of the Big Three. The other 'of even greater and more immediate importance was the intimate knowledge it gave us of the enemy's operational plans.'[14]

Ten years later Basna, helped unspecifically by a German journalist, Hans Nogly, described what he had photographed nearly twenty years earlier. Despite Dashwood's statement that he was stupid and unable to understand English (a judgment of breathtaking ineptness) he knew, and describes in convincing detail, what it was he was looking at. Perhaps Herr Nogly had done some relevant research, because he quotes aptly from Churchill's war history. *I Was Cicero* gives evidence to the trained eye of care in research and narrative structure. Hindsight and subsequent editorialising may exaggerate Basna's feat in 1943, but the following passage could be endorsed by any reader of FO telegrams. On page 21 he writes: 'I put down the file beside me. It contained memoranda received at the British embassy. It gave me a clear picture of the little game in which Turkey, my country, was involved . . . I read what Churchill had to say . . .'[15]

He photographed everything he could lay his hands on. Telegram No. 1594 from the FO told Hugessen, 'You will recall our obligation under the protocol signed in Moscow to bring Turkey into the war before the end of the year' and directed him to tell the Turkish foreign minister the bad news. It was signed by Eden himself. Hugessen went to see Numan Menemencioğlu, the Turkish foreign minister, with a heavy heart, but later telegraphed the FO that 'M. Menemencioğlu assures me that the Turkish government will be prepared to take part as soon as it is clear that the allied landings in the west have been successful.'[16] Basna continued: 'The telegrams and memoranda deciphered for Sir Hughe passed through my room in the servants' quarters' and commented on his association with 'the great ones of the world': Churchill, Stalin, Roosevelt, Eden, Hopkins. He went on: 'The cover-name "Overlord" kept recurring in front of my camera . . . One telegram said, "if Turkey came in on our side it would free the escort vessels we need so urgently for 'Overlord'." A Hugessen memorandum recorded a conversation with the Turkish Foreign Minister. It said that the Turks were hesitating. If only they could be brought in, it would be a dreadful blow for Germany. This phrase echoes Churchill's signal to Stalin on the same subject and at the same time.'

The circumstantial description of what Basna was photographing contrasts with Hugessen's memories of the filched documents. Unfortunately Basna and Nogly provided verifiable references as well as descriptions of some of the documents, which are difficult to square with Hugessen's dismissive comments in two documents in the possession of the FO, and withheld from access, but which were provided to the present writer by Hugessen's daughter.[17] Hugessen's notes were compiled after the publication in August 1947 of Moyzisch's *Operation Cicero*. He emphasised that no British ambassador would have been privy to Operation 'Overlord':

My own connection with this consisted in receipting a telegram from the FO in which the word 'Overlord' occurred. No clue was given as to its meaning, of which I remained in complete ignorance . . . The main subject . . . related to schemes in the Balkans.

He added: 'I can categorically confirm that on no occasion whatsoever was a telegram sent by the FO announcing that the Western offensive was to take place on any given date.' Hugessen set down his observations 'based on a clear recollection of what took place'. He dismissed Moyzisch's list of filched documents as 'possible but doubtful'. He never learnt that 'Elias' (he did not know Basna's surname) spoke English, still less sang. He found it incredible, though he did not specifically deny, the suggestion that he was shown the first minutes of the Moscow Conference. The leakage of documents had been known to him and the FO in early November 1943 and a watch was kept on two likely sources. As to the minutes of the Tehran Conference, mentioned by Basna and Nogly, he had no recollection of ever having seen them or advance warning of the bombing of Sofia in mid-February 1944.

Who was right about the documents? Hugessen, the FO, or Basna/von Papen? Though no one can be positive, it is quite clear what Basna was photographing. The files of FO371 and FO195, and the BJs referring to Turkey in DIR/C between October 1943 and February 1944, contain many papers written or read by Hugessen, and some of these were undoubtedly photographed by Basna, and consequently read in Berlin, Berne, London and Washington. Reading *I Was Cicero* is like browsing through PREM3/446 at the PRO.

How He Did It

Before assessing German reactions to the material, it is necessary to answer some still unresolved questions about how he managed to do it.

Great ingenuity, courage, daring and expertise were required to copy the ambassador's safe key, purloin the documents, take them through the residence to the servants' quarters, insert them one by one on a makeshift tripod and photograph them with a hand-held camera before returning them undetected to their proper place. The chances of discovery were ever present, the likelihood of poor definitions of the negatives almost certain, and there was nothing in Basna's previous career or character to indicate such a combination of qualities. How did he do it? He was not even interviewed by Sir John Dashwood, head of the FO security team who investigated in the spring of 1944, and was told he must be stupid and ignorant. The Germans believed he must have a secret collaborator – the evidence of a pair of hands on one positive suggesting another conspirator – but this possibility is ruled out by Basna's own account of how he did it.

He had already removed the briefcase of his previous employer (a senior British diplomat also stationed in Ankara called Busk) and photographed secret documents page by page, climbing on to a kitchen stool to photograph them vertically from above, with an old camera previously only used to take snaps of his children: 'when I had finished I put the camera back in the saucepan, took the documents and the untouched brandy back to the study, and carefully put everything back exactly where I had found it.' So he was well able to handle the similar situation he found at the British ambassador's residence. The key in both cases was an intimate knowledge of his masters' habits, and in Knatchbull-Hugessen he had a man 'whose ways were so regular that you could have set your watch by them'.[18] Basna records that Hugessen always played the piano in the drawing room for an hour and a half after lunch. This is confirmed in Hugessen's manuscript diary for 1943 now in Churchill College, Cambridge. He was a keen musician, who provided a fortnightly concert for his wife, and was defeated only by the complexities of the last movement of Bach's Italian Concerto.[19] Basna built a home-made tripod and obtained impressions of the safe key. On 26 October 1943 he took 52 photos to the German embassy. His operation continued till February 1944. Even then, he was never found out, and later resigned more because he was bored and anxious and recently enriched by the Germans.[20]

So the answers to the two questions – how did he do it? And, how could he have done it on his own? – are that he was seriously underestimated by both his employers, and successfully exploited Hugessen's idiosyncracies. It could be argued that taking Basna at face value is somewhat ingenuous, particularly when he asserts it took him less than three minutes to process one day's documents. But possibly that day's haul was a small one, and Basna's English publisher got it right in his blurb: 'Nobody trained him, nobody briefed him. A piece of wax, a Leica camera and a 100 watt bulb was all his equipment. And with it he made himself free with the top secrets of World War Two.'[21]

The foregoing account of Basna's modus operandi makes no claim to be definitive for it is less important to establish how he did it than the evidence his photography provided that the FO – both in London and Berlin – highly regarded the Turkish diplomatic intercept traffic which supplied much of the raw material on which Turkish foreign policy was based.

Berlin Assessments

Further evidence of the significance of diplomatic eavesdropping by Britain is furnished by the excitement caused in Berlin by the arrival of Moyzisch's material. The first policy maker to see the documents was von Papen, and his view of them has already been noted. But Moyzisch reported not to von Papen but direct to the head of the SD in Berlin. He showed only some of the material to his local employer, who summarised and commented on what he was shown in telegrams to Berlin, while Basna's rolls of film travelled there from Moyzisch by diplomatic pouch.[22] There, no one was sure of their authenticity. Schellenberg, as has been noted earlier, exploited them to expand his flow of intelligence and was given credit for the success of the whole operation.[23] But Hitler and Ribbentrop used the telegrams to discuss Turkish neutrality with Hungarian and Bulgarian diplomats.

Hitler had known all along of the importance of Turkey and had been building up his forces in the eastern Mediterranean before Cicero appeared; as we have seen, he won back the Dodecanese by December 1943, just when Cicero was in full spate. Goebbels wrote enthusiastically about the Cicero material, shown by the fact that German archives contained files which included intelligence summaries derived from Cicero. Gen Jodl noted in his diary: 'Results from Cicero: "Overlord" = major invasion from Britain.'[24] Competition and discord among the different organs of the German government arose over Cicero, according to Allen Dulles. The intelligence community under Himmler and Kaltenbrunner, and the diplomatic service under Ribbentrop were at odds, 'as a result of which anything Kaltenbrunner thought was good, Ribbentrop thought was bad.'[25]

While all this was going on Eden cabled the substance of an MSS (most secret source – i.e. BJ) telegram that Ribbentrop read. Von Papen's telegram from Ankara to Oshima in Berlin contained the following:

(i)   Churchill and Roosevelt carried out Tehran decision by pressing strongly for Turkish entry into the war, which USSR also desired earnestly. Churchill threatened to suspend supplies to Turkey and Eden took a menacing stand but Roosevelt adopted no such attitude.

(ii) Turkish Foreign Minister told Papen that he was firmly convinced that even England was not strong enough to risk Turkish enmity by applying sanctions and that USA would in any case refuse to participate.

Turkey had given absolutely no promise of entry into the war. (Ribbentrop's comment was that Germany had made it clear that Turkey would be considered to have entered the war if land and air bases were granted even without direct participation.)[26] Eden's despatch could have made no difference to 'Colonel Warden' or to the course of the war, but Churchill relied on such summaries, and, as soon as possible thereafter, the actual Oshima BJs.

Washington Assessments

A number of Cicero telegrams were later removed, together with other secret documents, from the German Foreign Ministry in Wilhelmstrasse by Fritz Kolbe, a trusted senior civil servant there. Kolbe's motive for running this dangerous liaison remain obscure. He claimed to have hoped for a place in postwar diplomacy by revealing Nazi diplomatic secrets to the Allies. In fact his espionage was ill-rewarded.

In Washington the National Security Agency had by 1943 set up an effective interception operation targeting the secret diplomatic telegrams passing from the Soviet Vice-Consul in New York to Moscow Centre. Through this the Americans learned Soviet reactions to the Allied Conferences which formed the subject matter of the last part of Chapter 7. This material, codenamed 'Venona' later led to the unmasking of Donald Maclean – codenamed 'Homer' or 'Gomer' (a confusion arising from the

Russian Cyrillic alphabet). But the arrival twelve months previously, in 1943, of the Kolbe/Cicero material seems not to have alerted the NSA to the possibility of breaking the German diplomatic cipher, this being anyway a British assignment.

The material was brought by Kolbe to the American consulate in Berne. It is now possible to reassess what the Americans thought of the Cicero material. Their previous role, as related by Moyzisch and von Papen, was something of a cowboy exercise, involving spying on their British allies in Ankara and seducing a German employee of von Papen who happened also to be Ribbentrop's sister-in-law. But now Dulles was to introduce an American dimension to the Cicero material. According to OSS's war report, declassified in 1976, Kolbe went to Switzerland every few weeks.[27] Dulles, as we have seen, was in no doubt that he had a spy coup on his hands, and undertook the task of translating and encoding Kolbe's material which occupied the entire staff at Berne for weeks after each batch was received.[28] From it Dulles learnt of Basna's activities, and so did the British:

> As the Franco-Swiss frontier was not opened to Allied traffic until September 1944, no letters were sent or delivered before that date; instead all information for transmission abroad was enciphered and sent by wireless. In order to ensure their integrity during transmission from Geneva, the Kolbe/Cicero telegrams were divided equally between the British and Americans, half going to Washington and half to London.[29]

No extant files reveal American State Department reactions to Kolbe, but the recent release on the Internet of some early Venona intercepts, referred to above, dated autumn 1942 and extending to October 1943, show that the NSA at Arlington, Virginia took a lively interest, on behalf of the State Department, in foreign diplomatic intercepts and monitored the reports from the Russian consulate in New York to Moscow with something of the same zeal and expertise that the diplomatic and commercial departments of GCCS plied the FO and MEW in London with BJs.[30]

The Russians were running many agents supplying details of American war production and monitoring the communist activities of some of the British who worked in BSC (British Security Co-ordination) under Sir William Stephenson. One such intercept listed the NSA departments charged with intercepting and processing diplomatic material, indicating four departments, which:

> . . . encompass 14 sections: the first department consists of 3 German and 1 Italian section; the second department – French, Spanish, (C% Scandinavian) Arabian, Turkish, Russian and English sections; the remaining sections – Counter-Intelligence, photographic and officer [*sic*].

The American cryptographer Howard Gardner devoted himself to decrypting Venona on a daily basis, to show his masters that the Soviet Union had major reservations about their western Allies, and about the shape of the postwar world. Given these preoccupations it seems unlikely that, even had he been given the opportunity, he would have devoted much care and attention to what was arriving from Allen Dulles in Berne.[31]

Dulles later noted a connection with Cicero himself which led him to suspect a leak in British diplomatic security. He supplied a British diplomat in Berne with a Kolbe document which, he later suspected, brought about the Dashwood visitation to the embassy at Ankara, and a cessation of Basna's activities at the ambassadorial residence. From these two sources derived the American scepticism of the integrity and competence of the British secret intelligence services and foreign service, which was to last throughout the Cold War.

Given the traditional American caution with regard to European and especially Balkan affairs, and Roosevelt's own preference for open diplomacy, it is probable that diplomatic decrypts did not figure so crucially on the agenda of top American foreign policy makers as they did of the British. None the less, the answer to the question, what did the Americans make of their share of the Kolbe/Cicero material, apart from the memories of Allen Dulles and Kermit Roosevelt, must remain unanswered. But the half that went to London provoked an unlooked for bonus for the diplomatic cryptographers there.

London Assessments

This section reveals for the first time how important the chance arrival of some Cicero material was to the British diplomatic cryptographers in Berkeley Street, London. This office had been working on the German diplomatic cipher nicknamed 'Floradora'. This work had gone on since 1919. A partial breakthrough occurred in February 1942, helped by the American cryptographer Maj Solomon Kullback at Arlington.[32] The chief diplomatic cryptographer in London, Alastair Denniston, had coincidentally received the daily keys for Floradora from the British consul in Lourenco Marques. Although Floradora was diagnosed as unbreakable before the war, at least three factors led to its solution in early 1944. These were:

> The basic book fell into our hands. [This must be the Lourenco Marques bonanza.] The second – close co-operation with USA. The third was SS work by an able ally who obtained first hand information and one page of figures from a German cipher officer.[33]

By early 1944 some Floradora messages were being currently read, but a breakthrough occurred with the arrival of the Kolbe/Cicero material in Berkeley Street.[34] The London-bound portion of this came from Dulles in Berne, supposedly to the head of MI6, Gen Sir Stewart Menzies, but in fact straight to the offices of MI6 where, in the absence of the departmental head, Felix Cowgill, it came directly under the scrutiny of the then head of the Iberian section of MI6 and a Soviet spy, Kim Philby. A rarely cited passage in his controversial memoir *My Silent War*[35] details the moves he made to enhance his position within the secret service after spotting the value of the Kolbe/Cicero material. He went behind the back not only of his bosses, Felix Cowgill and Claude Dansey, but of the chief himself, 'C', to Denniston, who, he records, was extremely excited by what he was shown, and asked for more, which was duly forthcoming. He then confirmed to Philby that the telegrams 'exactly matched intercepted telegrams already deciphered, and others, proving of the utmost value to his cryptographers in their breakdown of the German diplomatic code.'[36]

HW1/2743 of 26 April 1944 contains a reference to these German diplomatic intercepts (including Cicero/Kolbe). A departmental note from Denniston to Menzies refers here to:

> . . . [a] special series called gunpowder . . . These contain what purport to be the close substance of German cipher telegrams relating to various countries, as obtained through a channel which has not yet been fully and finally tested. In a number of cases, however, it has been possible to exercise a definite check, and in these cases it has been found to be authentic.

If the assumptions made here are right the 'definite check' is the comparison of Philby's documents with those P.W. Filby and Denniston were working on a few hundred yards away. The 'close substance' or close paraphrase using the same key words 'with many words identical with the actual message' could be applied to the raw material which still eluded the cryptographers. It is noteworthy that HW1/2743 was given a particularly restricted distribution – in effect to 'C' (and so to Churchill) only, not even the FO, now revealed to Berkeley Street to be insecure, through Philby's Cicero material. Indeed the FO had no part in any of this: Dedip was dealing direct with the PM, using Menzies as a sorting office.[37]

It is unfortunate that the technical report supplied by Denniston at Philby's request validating the material is not to be found in any files yet released, but even without it, it is legitimate to conclude that the Cicero material, which was processed by Basna for Moyzisch, assessed by Kaltenbrunner and Ribbentrop for Hitler after translation and enciphering from the German diplomatic cipher, then brought to Dulles in Berne where it was re-enciphered in the American diplomatic cipher before being sent to Arlington and Berkeley Street, provided the coup de grace enabling Berkeley Street at long last to read the German diplomatic cipher, Floradora. This may have been one of the causes of the breaking of Floradora by the British. While at the time that cryptographic achievement was the subject of much jubilation, the actual messages proved of limited use to Churchill now that the war had moved into preparations for D-Day.

Thus in retrospect it can be seen that though Hugessen's insecurity may have ranked as the FO's greatest lapse before the defection of Burgess and Maclean and though the material his valet sold to Berlin was highly regarded there, the drama made no difference to the course of the war, as Kolbe hoped and Dulles claimed. The constantly re-ciphered FO telegrams, it is now clear led to the breaking of Floradora which was acknowledged as a great cryptographic success,[38] but since the outcome of the war was no longer in doubt, and D-Day was only four months off, the achievement made absolutely no difference whatever to the military or the diplomatic front. Nor indeed, as has become apparent during this chapter, did the Cicero and/or the Kolbe material.

This conclusion, similar to those reached in respect of the Adana Conference, the Dodecanese affair and the achievement of Turkish neutrality in 1942–43, together with questions of the second front and the possibility of a separate peace – between Italy and Britain, and between Russia and Germany – will be reviewed in Chapter 9. If the German diplomatic messages, broken in 1944, had been of real significance to Churchill's conduct of the war, they would have appeared in HW1 between 2743 and 3785, where the series ends. In fact they are few and far between.

CHAPTER NINE

Conclusions

There was no integration of the material except in [Churchill's] head.

Andrew Hodges

This book has set out to answer the question how Churchill, the FO and the British COS used their intercept information to formulate and implement policy in regard to Turkey from 1942 to 1944. It has been shown that behind this question lies the unknown territory of counterfactual history – principally, what would have happened had Churchill not become prime minister and minister of defence in May 1940 and/or had not been a lifelong student of intercepted messages from foreign governments. But subsidiary questions also arise: did the FO produce sufficient, well-informed advice on Turkey for the Secretary of State and the minister of defence following the French collapse of 1940? If not, why not? Did the entrenched attitudes of FO officials of the interwar period unduly influence the advice their counterparts in 1941 offered the government in formulating policy towards Turkey? What were the relations between the FO and the ambassador and his staff at Ankara? What sort of information was (and more crucially was not) given by these officials to guide Whitehall with a true view of Turkish capabilities and intentions? Did ambassadorial insecurity in Ankara seriously affect the course of the war? Was the FO's use of Dedip sufficiently sensitive and subtle given the volume of crucial information it was receiving from GCCS in Berkeley Street from 1942 onwards? Who in the FO was making real use of this valuable source, and why did it not lead to more positive proposals in regard to Turkey?

In attempting to answer these questions, the investigation has focused particularly on the work of the diplomatic and commercial sections of GCCS at Bletchley Park until February 1942 and thereafter at Berkeley Street and Park Lane in London. The BJs these offices produced for Churchill and the FO came as the climax of a 25-year-long task of reading the diplomatic telegrams of all the major powers. The developing relationship between GCCS and its client ministries, as well as with its prime user, Churchill, proved an inseparable part of the answer to the question about the value set upon its product, and the use made of it, by all concerned with it.

If these are some of the questions posed by the arrival of DIR/C at the PRO, a new range of counterfactual possibilities arise: what use, if any, was made not only by the FO of Dedip in 1941–44 in regard to Turkey but by the COS in 1943–44 regarding the feasibility of a second front in the Balkans launched from Turkish soil? Much is already known about how 'Boniface' was crucially employed by GHQ ME throughout the various Mediterranean campaigns of 1942–44, but a key operation in the Aegean in October 1943 has not hitherto received the attention it merits, and this is something this book has sought to rectify. In so doing the tactical importance of Boniface has been shown not to have been a decisive outcome of the Dodecanese assault, which was repelled by the Germans through superior skill. This is another example of the truism that battles, never mind wars, can never be won by superior intelligence alone. But had the Combined Chiefs of Staff really grasped the implications of what their intelligence advisers were telling them of the state of the German war effort would more attention have been given to the South of France landings and the Balkan Front, and less to 'Overlord'?

Such is the nature of historical speculation created by the appearance of Boniface and Dedip. It is clearly beyond the scope of this book which has concentrated on Churchill and on Turkey. This concentration has led to an analysis of Turkish diplomatic messages read by Churchill, and that in turn has led to the question what difference, if any, did this reading of those messages actually alter the course of the war?

It has been said by sigint historians that the history of the Second World War must be rewritten – and perhaps has been rewritten – in the light of Enigma and Ultra. Against this received wisdom, my book takes a revisionist standpoint: despite Enigma/Ultra and Dedip, there is almost nothing to add to or subtract from the official historians' account of the war, published in the early 1950s. These stand up well to renewed scrutiny, for their treatment of Turco-British relations without the benefit of Ultra.[1] They describe what happened giving due weight to the priorities and the surprises of war in the eastern Mediterranean, to the demands of other theatres, in the Mediterranean and beyond, to the concerns of Churchill, Hitler, İnönü; to the balance of advantages to both sides in having Turkey in or out of the war.

What might have happened had the War Cabinet not known what it did from sigint is little more than a frustrating counterfactual exercise. But we now know what Churchill and the generals, the admirals and air marshals knew of enemy intentions and potential. We may conjecture that had they not had vital secret information from the airwaves they might have assessed these intentions differently, and prepared counter-offensives differently – and these alternative plans might have been less effective for being constructed on less authentic intelligence. But the facts are that they did read and react to Enigma and Dedip, thus (among many other things) delaying Operation 'Overlord' until there was every chance of final victory – and this requires no rewriting of history, just some acknowledgement of the value of sigint to war planners on the Allied side – acknowledgement all concerned gave freely at the conclusion of hostilities.[2]

This book has shown how from diplomatic decrypts Churchill acquired valuable insight into why a conference on Turkish soil might be feasible in January 1943, and why later that year a successful offensive to retake the Dodecanese would have disproportionately large political implications for the whole Mediterranean sphere. These insights were based on secret knowledge acquired from intercepts of what neutrals, Turkey in particular, were thinking about the progress of the war, and how that thought could be usefully exploited. Diplomatic intercepts or reports – clandestinely obtained by Cable & Wireless in the case of messages originated in Ankara – did not provide instant tactical information but a broader context which was equally timely though not nearly so sensational. Churchill must have made direct use of it when the record is studied, but what did other readers make of it, and what might they have done differently had any of them something of Churchill's understanding of this source?

In the absence of any actual BJs in the FO files, and relying on the distribution lists in HW1, a definitive answer is impossible. The other readers were the Service Ministries, those in charge of political intelligence, the MEW, MI5, and so on. Possibly up to fifty people high in government would read them every day. They would also know who else read them and why. Those who derived some of the evident pleasure Churchill got from them would have found themselves remarkably, and indeed unnecessarily, well-informed about neutral hopes and fears in general, and Turkish neutrality in particular. To readers for whom Turkey was important – mainly at the Foreign Office – the BJs would have built up a consistent picture of how Turkish foreign policy was being conducted, which would have led them to doubt Churchill's hopes before and after Adana. Had they not been so well apprised of Turkish intentions they might have shared his enthusiasm for a Balkan initiative. But any intelligent student of the progress of the war would have known that Allied forces were at full stretch elsewhere, and man for man, officer for officer, the Anglo-Saxons were no match for the Germans until after D-Day. So Churchill's persuasive and sometimes hectoring conviction that he could personally get Turkey in on the Allied side in 1943 might still have fallen on deaf ears (as they did on the deaf Turkish leaders), in the Foreign Office, among the chairborne soldiery and in the rest of the Allied camp.

On the basis of the files available this book has attempted to establish that the Southern Department of the FO was instinctively opposed to Churchill's Turkish initiative. For over two decades it had been responsible for developing British friendship and trade with Turkey; it defended its right to look after Turkey partly because its restricted wartime role left little else on the agenda. The War Cabinet adopted the Eden line, and took the same view as the Southern Department, while after 1942 the COS had their minds on the western Mediterranean and never looked favourably on any Balkan initiative. The position of the Foreign Office at a time of total war was uncomfortable to say the least. All able-bodied men and women were being called up, or had already been; and working in a reserved occupation required justification to family, friends and neighbours. Several of the FO officials chiefly concerned with Turkish affairs had in fact served with distinction in the First World War 16 years before, as of course had Churchill and Eden. But a younger generation, George Clutton and Knox Helm outstanding among them, were too young to have borne arms. They would be distinguished from their older colleagues in one significant respect: they were not Old Etonians, or indeed former pupils of any of the leading public schools, and this despite the fact that none other than Sir Hughe Knatchbull-Hugessen opposed the merger of the diplomatic and commercial sections on the grounds that diplomats had 'to fraternize with the governing class in no matter what country'.[3] Such a merger would automatically have widened the social backgrounds of applicants. But the presence of such as Clutton and Helm in key positions in 1941 testifies to the changes in recruitment procedures which the FO had already put in place, despite Hugessen's doubts.

This book, it can thus be seen, has been about how Churchill, without much help from the FO, tried to bring Turkey into the war on the Allied side, first by sending emissaries, secondly by threats and promises, next by a personal visitation, and finally by starting up a personal war with Hitler in the Dodecanese in the autumn of 1943.

Before reaching any conclusions it is worth stressing the limits on Churchill's own powers, since in the early years of the war it was not Churchill but Hitler who made the running, just as in the latter years it was Stalin, not Hitler or Churchill. A book like this is, perforce, microcosmic. But standing in its shade are gigantic figures – Stalin, Roosevelt, Hitler, as well as Churchill – who actually created the situation in which Britain found herself in 1940, and again in 1943. Researching British diplomatic intercepts during 1943 powerfully reminds the scholar of the close connections between BJs and the great politicos of the world at war; one such reader was an obscure Turk of Albanian origin, Eleysa Basna, who while photographing BJs and other FO secret communications in Ankara, commented on the 'strange kind of nightly colloquy I had with the great ones of the world whose names turned up in the documents: Roosevelt, Hopkins, Churchill, Eden, Stalin, Molotov'.[4] This association over the airwaves of warlords, cipher clerks, bureaucrats and spies brings an unusual dimension to the study of diplomatic documents and prompts questions of the 'what if?' variety. The question posed throughout this book is, what if Churchill's daily reading and hourly attention had not been focused on those issues and battles presented to him in the DIR/C files which followed him everywhere? How would those issues and battles have been handled and fought differently, and how would other issues and battles, not so presented, have been handled and fought differently?

Coming to more specific events, what if Hitler had decided on Operation 'Marita', to invade Turkey and attack Egypt via Syria in 1940? All diplomats knew that the Luftwaffe could have destroyed Istanbul in fifteen minutes, the Wehrmacht would have marched through Anatolia at 30 miles a day, according to a War Office appreciation – a two-month job. There would have been casualties, but 60 per cent of the one million strong Turkish army would have been bypassed in Thrace, leaving the rest to defend their homeland against the so far all-conquering Germans. Ankara would have been blitzed and the Turkish government forced to retire to Erzerum or Kars. It could only have happened in 1940 and would have involved Hitler's early cancellation of 'Sealion' and a massive redeployment of Panzer army groups right across Europe from west to east. And even given these drawbacks Germany would almost certainly be putting her Soviet ally under intolerable pressure to defend her own southern borders. But at the time Hitler was being strongly advised by his successful generals to do just this, and the British knew it. The immediate gains would be the Persian oilfields and the cutting off of Britain from the Australasian Commonwealth, India and the Far East. Would that have been sufficient for Hitler? By 1941 he had decided not, particularly when he had every expectation that a successful combined operation against a weakened Britain would produce at worst a negotiated peace on French lines and at best German sovereignty of Europe. In 1940 Hitler did not overplay the hand his armies had dealt him with the conquest of Norway, the Low Countries, France, Greece and Yugoslavia. By the end of 1941 his supremacy over world affairs lapsed when he declared war on the Soviet Union and the USA.

In that mega game plan Britain was a minor player and Turkey even smaller. The war was to be won and lost by two factors. One was the tooling up of a vast North American war machine, able to supply its allies as well as itself, able to destroy Japan, able eventually (with Britain) to invade the German heartland and link with the Russians west of Berlin. The other, centred on the Battle of Stalingrad and the world's greatest tank battle on the Kersh peninsula, was the annihilation of German military supremacy by Soviet citizens defending their own country and dying in millions for it.

So 'what if?' yields little in considering Churchill's unavailing determination to play and win the Turkey hand in 1941–43. What if he had succeeded in persuading the Turkish leadership to abandon its policy of neutrality? Here counterfactual history itself encounters bedrock. It would not, could not, have happened. The reasons have emerged in the preceding chapters, they are clear from the record and the literature. They are further clarified by some understanding of Turkish self-identity in 1940.

The part Britain played in beating the Nazis was crucial and desperate in 1940–41, and became gradually less so as the USA and the USSR took up arms. The official British war historians, without acknowledged access to secret intelligence which enabled Churchill to hold his own as one of the Big Three well after the true facts of world supremacy had passed Britain by, worked from primary sources which incorporated intelligence reports and assessments based on the contribution Ultra made to the course of events but without acknowledging it. Ultra's immediate contribution is thus subsumed in the official record of the way the war developed. To assess its significance it has to be stripped out of existing accounts of the course of the war – in order to calculate how Britain would have fared had Ultra not existed. 'In the jargon of my trade,' writes Prof Sir Harry Hinsley, now the only surviving architect of the structures at Bletchley which actually turned Enigma into Ultra, 'We have to engage in counter-factual history', acknowledging this to be 'a dubious enterprise, only permissible if we are fully aware of what we are doing. But it is equally true that unless we attempt it, we shall not grasp the significance of Ultra's contribution.' What that was was best expressed in a 1945 report by the late Brig E.T. ('Bill') Williams: he concludes his report on the contribution of intelligence to tactical Allied victories by asserting that the whole intelligence apparatus 'was a hyphen between Bletchley Park and the soldier at war'. Had his report been made available to historians at any time between 1945 and 1973, a rather different history might have been written, though the actual narrative would not have differed more than marginally from what was published.

What Williams said of Ultra's part in Britain's contribution to the defeat of the Axis powers can be said even more of its diplomatic dealings with the neutrals and particularly with Turkey, because these were all part of the common aim which was to beat the Germans by all and every means possible. And they were both in large part conducted by the same person – the nearest thing Britain's constitution permitted to a warlord. While since 1973 the Ultra contribution to winning the war at sea and in the Mediterranean and North Africa has become a target for historical scholarship, the ambassadorial reports from European capitals which Churchill used to handle Turkey were released over twenty years later, as recently as 1994. This means that diplomatic historians have had no more than a few months to review the new material and undertake the dangerous counterfactual exercise which Hinsley both warned against and also showed had to be undertaken. This book has attempted to strip out the diplomatic messages from the general progress of Turco-British wartime relations to see whether, and how differently, Churchill would have played the Turkey hand on behalf of the Allies had this material not been available to him – in the actual words – in DIR/C. This attempt reveals that very little was to Churchill's hand apart from BJs and his own instinct about the importance of a strong Turco-British relationship, which may have been based on his experiences over the Dardanelles in 1915. The consequence of this is to take seriously his insistence on seeing the actual Turkey-based BJs, and that has been the thrust of the foregoing chapters.

Churchill, as has been shown, studied the Turkish BJs continuously from 1941 to 1944 and adjusted his policy in the light of that study. But it was not only the study itself which convinced him that he could persuade the Turkish leadership to attach their country to the Allied cause. His strong instinctive reaction to the German successes of 1940 had its roots in the First World War. So he might have pursued this will o' the wisp regardless of the BJs. Why, then, does their release in 1994 create a significant gap, requiring filling, in wartime diplomatic history? The answer to this fundamental question is that the BJs, however important at the time to Churchill and the Southern Department, did not of themselves develop in Churchill's mind a policy other than that to which he was already committed and which he consistently if unavailingly pursued.

DIR/C – HW1: Public Record Office

DIR/C first appeared at the PRO in spring 1994. The files date from 1940 to 1945 but there are significant gaps, particularly at the beginning. They are prefaced in the listings supplied by the PRO by a short summary of their content, which differs only marginally from what appears in Chapter 2. This summary draws attention not to five but to three items:

1) Items CX/FJ, CX/JQ and CX/MSS – Enigma.
2) Naval headlines.
3) BJs: selected translations of intercepted diplomatic telegrams.

They also mention 'certain original cover notes and actual documents passed to Churchill or in his absence the Lord Privy Seal and Deputy Prime Minister [Attlee], using Boniface, complete with annotations and minuting.'

All these documents are said by the PRO archivist to have been returned by Churchill to GCCS for safekeeping. This is doubtful. The BJ component was intended for immediate destruction after reading by each named recipient of each BJ; many of them had been reading and burning them for years before the start of DIR, and would never have lost the habit. In the FO wartime files there are no authentic BJs, though there are summaries, paraphrases, 'gists' and references to them as 'reliable sources' or sometimes 'our secret sources'. In WO106 and 208 there are clear indications of prewar BJs.

The only person who did not routinely burn them was Churchill himself, exercising his magpie instinct to throw nothing away. Strong efforts were made during his many absences from London not only to get the fullest possible amount of intercept material to him wherever he was, but also to safeguard security and ensure that the end-user, after Churchill, destroyed them himself. But Churchill must have somehow kept nearly 4,000 DIR files. Prof Hinsley tells me that they were discovered almost by chance at Chartwell after his death, and transferred immediately to GCHQ where they were used extensively in the history of British intelligence in the Second World War as 'Dir Archive'. The blue cover notes which accompany most of them emanated from 'C' and carry a serial number from 6112 (HW1/3) to 9995 (HW1/715). Thereafter the serial number ceases. For other Boniface messages the PRO archivist refers the researcher to ADM223/1–7 and 438–640, as well as to

DEFE, the main source used by previous researchers into the use of wartime high-grade sigint (see Anthony Best, *Britain, Japan and Pearl Harbor: Avoiding War in East Asia, 1936–41*; London, Routledge, 1995, p. 235).

Below are listed all those files containing Turkey-related BJs, many of them used in the chapters that precede this. Dates of decryption are also given: there are occasions on which the date of the file cover note may differ from that shown on an individual BJ. On the BJ, at the start of the series, two different dates sometimes appear, indicating the time difference between receipt of the intercept and its distribution in processed form. Churchill queried any undue delay indicated by these dates. Their usefulness derived largely from their immediacy.

HW1 (DIR/C) Diplomatic Intercepts Relevant to Turkish Neutrality in the Second World War from September 1941 till D-Day

1941

38	1 September BJ 095065: the Turkish ambassador in Moscow reported on British aims on Persia, and that the British believe the Germans will invade the Caucasus and get the Baku oil; the Russians will lose. Britain would pressurise Turkey to take the Suez canal: Turkey must take action before the Allies (Soviet Union and Britain) occupy Tehran. He also reported a discussion with the British ambassador – Sir Stafford Cripps.
44	4 September BJ 095168: Irish intercept, Berlin to Dublin; Turkey has grave cause for anxiety.
49	5 September BJ 095195: Italian intercept, Kabul to Rome (marked by Churchill: 'to be sent to the F Secy 6/9'); 'the Afghan government were prepared to grant whatever the British cared to ask'.
51	6 September BJ 095218: the Turkish ambassador in Madrid reported Axis demands on Turkey for the passage of the Italian fleet through the Straits to the Black Sea; the demand was 'not such that its rejection by you will involve our country in war'.
64	13 September BJ 095416: Italian intercept, Quaroni in Kabul to Rome; the Japanese ambassador in Ankara told him about increased Allied pressure on Turkey, which will be resisted by the Turks 'because they are afraid of Germany'.
67	15 September BJ 095417: Italian minister in Sofia to Rome: 'British would pressurise Turkey to allow British ships through the Dardanelles. Papen favoured gradualism, Ribbentrop a more radical approach. Papen may be sacked'. BJ 095432: the American ambassador in Turkey made clear to a Persian diplomat that Roosevelt disapproved of the Russo-British adventure in Persia (Ankara to Washington).
79	20 September BJ 095665/795 and 796: French intercept from

Vichy to Ankara. Dr Carl Clodius, in charge of German negotiations over chrome with Turkey wanted the French to help Germany but the Turco-Franco-British accord of 8 January 1940 only provided chrome for France as well as Britain. None the less '*les negotiations se derouleraient dans une atmosphere cordiale*.'

82   24 September BJ 095748: Japanese intercept, Berlin to Tokyo reported on Turkey's predicament: 'the German armies are contemplating crossing from the Romanian and Bulgarian coasts and landing in the Caucasus at one bound. So Turkey's position may well be jeopardized . . . Britain will be compelled to thrust her fleet into the Black Sea and upset Germany's landing scheme . . . if the German army attacks Turkey the British fleet would force the Straits and enter the Black Sea . . . As Germany is aware of this, Germany will not at present attack Turkey.'

86 (7629)   26 September: PM's query on distribution of Boniface.

93   27 September: the Japanese chargé in London reported to Tokyo that 'Turkey had given in to Germany's vigorous demands' for chrome. This was circulated to the MEW.

95 (7667)   26 September: 'C' and PM on 'dangerously large circulation of BJs'.

108 (7706)   2 October BJ 096091: Ankara to Tokyo reported that 'the Turkish government is disquieted as German action seems imminent . . . The foreign minister . . . hopes that by Spring Russia will be defeated and that the war will thus be brought to an end by negotiation before Turkey is compelled to take part in it.'

109   BJ 096081: Italian intercept (De Peppo), Ankara to Rome; reported his conversation with Clodius who 'took some political soundings too and is convinced Turkey [garbled] to maintain her neutrality'.

110 (7709)   3 October BJ 096132: German intercept, Stockholm to Berlin; reported that 'the whole world has its eyes on Turkey'.

112(7713)   3 October: Japanese, Ankara to Tokyo re Turco-German relations.

119   6 October: Enigma message that *Der Tag* was postponed until further notice.

159 (7858)   21 October: Japanese (Oshima), Berlin to Tokyo reported on German plans for an invasion of England.

206   11 November BJ 09756/326: Japanese, Berlin to Tokyo (Oshima).

207   12 November BJ 097604: Japanese, Ankara to Tokyo.

211   BJ 097641: Japanese, Washington to Tokyo.

255   20 November BJ 097939.

253   24 November BJs 098092, 098093, 098094: Turkish, Vichy to Ankara.

254   24 November BJ 098097: Japanese, Tokyo to Berlin (Oshima).

269 and 277   27 and 29 November: Turkish, Ankara to Tokyo, predicted an early start to the US-Japanese war.

281   30 November BJ 098360: Churchill on fear; also BJ 098373/219: Turkish intercept, Ankara to Berne, re Turkish unity.

288   2 December BJ 098452: Tokyo to Berlin (Oshima): 'We are about to be at war with the USA'.

314	9 December BJ 098766: Ankara to Tokyo reporting 'Turkey will support the Axis in the spring.'
317	11 December – eleven BJs including four ambassadorial reports by Turks to Ankara, including BJ 098813: Turkish ambassador in Rome reporting the new agreement between Britain, Turkey and the USA.

1942

374 (8611)	27 January BJ 100577/69 and 100519/24: Italian, Ankara to Rome. Churchill read he was to resign and the British cabinet would be reconstructed – sent the intercept to Eden.

Silent from 382 of 23 January 1942 till 385 of 23 February 1942.

452	27 March BJ 102680/82: Sofia to Tokyo, Turkey in a state of extreme anxiety. Two hundred more BJs, including BJ 102687/23 re German casualties and 102689/96: Tehran to Ankara, Russians discriminating against Turks.
454	28 March BJ 102695: Ankara to Chungking re assassination attempt on von Papen; also BJ 102709 (also Ankara to Chungking): 'Turkey is being hemmed in by the Soviets and may have to escape by the Dardanelles if Germany occupies the Crimea.
456	9 April BJ 102755/101 of March 29: Kuibyshev to Ankara; King Boris of Bulgaria will not send troops to Russia but may ask Russia that Turkey would not be allowed to attack Bulgaria if Bulgaria did agree to send troops there.
456	29 March BJ 102755: Kuibyshev to Ankara.
473	4 April: PM to 'C ' – 'your hens seem to be eggbound'.
484 (9155)	9 April: Berlin to Tokyo re German intentions against Turkey, and Kesselring's tactical exercise without troops.
497	15 April: London to Ankara re PM's invitation to Turkey's ambassador to Britain to accompany him to Washington to beg *matériel* from the Americans.
513	21 April BJ 103496/26: Berlin to Tokyo re Turkey's offer to mediate between Germany and Britain.
560	10 May: Ankara to Rome: 'if Turkey had to fight Russia she would fight Britain too'.
563	11 May BJ 104279: Ankara to Lisbon; BJ 104284: Ankara to all stations abroad.
577 and 578	17 May: Madrid to Ankara; Suner reported Allied decision to occupy Turkey. See also 595, 596, 598 and 599.
589 (9555)	22 May: Turkish, Madrid to Ankara.
631	8 June BJ 105334: Madrid to Ankara re British threats to Turkey.
683	1 July BJ 106218: Berlin to Ankara re consequences to the Allies should Turkey join the Axis.
689	2 July BJ 106219: Ankara to Chungking.
700	5 July BJ 106356: Ankara to Lisbon: 'Turkey must declare herself soon'.

706	7 July BJ 106248: Ankara to Tokyo (Kurihara), 'I think we should lean on Turkey'.
718	11 July BJ 106618/158: Sofia to Tokyo reporting Bulgarian view.
721	12 July BJ 106684: Madrid to Tokyo.
729	14 July BJ 106754: Vichy to Ankara (and London and Berlin).
746	17 July BJ 106837: Sofia to Tokyo and Washington to Ankara.
765	21 July BJ 106967: Stockholm to Lisbon.
767	BJs 10692, 996, 998, 107004, 007, 009 report preparations for El Alamein.
774	22 July BJs 106987, 107923 and 37.
788	25 July BJ 107159.
793	26 July BJ 107213: Stockholm to Lisbon; BJ 107221: Cairo to Ankara.
804	30 July BJ 107357: Kuibyshev to Ankara; BJ 107547/80: Vichy to Sofia, second front in France.
814	5 August BJ 107585: Kuibyshev to Ankara.
833 (499 *sic*)	24 August nineteen BJs inc 108167: Berlin to Ankara (lunch with Hitler).
837	26 August BJ 108352: Baku to Tehran re conditions there.
863	3 September BJ 108603: Ankara to Chungking re conditions in Germany as reported by returning Turkish journalists.
869	5 September BJ 108656: London to Ankara, talk with PM.
873	6 September BJ 108714: Ankara to Kuibyshev.
892	12 September BJ 108983: Orbay (London) to Ankara.
895(707)	14 September: 'C' to DMI on suspected leakage of Ultra to ME.
896	12 September: Greek, Ankara to Cairo; Japan, Kabul to Tokyo.
899	15 September BJ 109117: London to Ankara.
902	16 September BJ 109152/849.
929	27 September BJ 109507: London to Ankara.
953	5 October BJ 109747: Madrid to Tokyo.
1026	31 October BJ 110503: Ankara to Lisbon.
1044	4 November BJ 110666/233: Madrid to Ankara.
1107	11 November BJ 110939/29: Japan, Berlin to Ankara; 111188/690: Rome to Tokyo.
1110	16 November BJ: Berlin to Tokyo, 'advocates of peace in England entirely without influence'.
1125 (1449)	20 November BJ 111327: London to Ankara; 111300: Moscow to Ankara; Rome, Madrid to Ankara; 111451/366: Ankara to Tokyo (Kinoshita), British designs on Turkey.
1130	21 November.
1134	22 November: Russian cypher insecurity.
1142	BJ 111451/366 re İnönü.
1145	24 November BJ 11171/383: Ankara to Tokyo.
1148	25 November.
1156	26 November.
1164	27 November BJ 111598: Sofia to Tokyo.
1171/383	27 November: Ankara to Tokyo.
1178	30 November BJ 11713/379: Ankara to Tokyo.
1182	2 December BJ 111767, 70 and 71: Ankara to Tokyo; BJ 111178:

	Berlin to Tokyo.
1207	10 December BJ 112060/245: Sofia to Tokyo.
1210	11 December BJ 112903/249.
1215	12 December BJ 112066/119: Budapest to Tokyo.
1225	15 December BJ 112221: Berlin to Tokyo; BJ 112230/41: Kuibyshev to Belgrade.
1228	16 December BJ 112258/103: London to Ankara.
1234	18 December BJ 112284/4664: London to Lisbon.
1236	19 December BJ 112341: Berlin to Tokyo.
1240	20 December BJ 112341/369 and 40: Berlin to Tokyo.

1943

1286	5 January BJ 112758: Portuguese, Bucharest to Lisbon; Kuibyshev to Ankara, Madrid to Ankara, London to Ankara.
1309 (1311, 1316)	12 January BJ 113021: Berlin to Tokyo on Bulgarian fears of Turkey.
1325	21 January BJ 113328 and 9: Sofia to Tokyo.
1330	25 January BJ 133126 and 113489: Washington to Ankara.
1331 (2129)	26 January: Berlin to Tokyo, Kuibyshev and Bucharest to Ankara.
1332 (2134)	27 January: Ankara to Washington; summary of diplomatic to PM plus seventeen raw BJs.
1337	31 January.
1341	1 February BJ 113603: Bucharest to Ankara, Hitler quote on Turkey.
1342	2 February: summaries (Adana).
1346 (2189)	4 February. Many BJs held during Adana Conference (distribution details supplied. Esp BJ 113744).
1348	6 February BJ 113908, 113855.
1384	13 February BJ 114359: Moscow to Ankara, German living space and dying space.
1387	20 February BJ 114391: Stockholm to Lisbon; Stockholm to Tokyo. FM Tokyo to Kuibyshev.
1429	5 March BJ 14920/21: Japan, Vienna to Tokyo.
1445 (2529)	9 March BJ 128109.
1452	12 March BJ 115903: Japan, Kuibyshev to Tokyo.
1454	13 March BJ 115209/160 of 9/3/43: Japan, Kuibyshev to Tokyo.
1462	15 March BJ 115283/91 of 10/3/43: Japan, Ankara to Tokyo; second front, operations in Balkans? Or just Dodecanese.
1471	16 March BJ 115315: Ankara to Tokyo: PM sidelines.
1476	17 March BJ 115347/96: Ankara to Tokyo.
1479	16 March BJ 115398: Ankara to Tehran.
1482	19 March SHARK broken: PM: 'Congratulate your splendid hens'.
1483	19 March BJ 115440 re Ribbentrop, to Tome.
1488	21 March BJ 115438 to PM via Sargent (FO) 'who wishes you to see it before your interview with Turkish ambassador'.
1491 2	21 March BJ 115492: Vatican to Tokyo, 34 of 17/3 re peace rumours and 115491 (also Vatican to Tokyo) re Ciano.
1496	22 March BJ: Berlin to Tokyo.

1514	25 March (B% = comment from Hut 3). BJ 115629: Buenos Aires to Tokyo.
1522	27 March BJ 115672: Japan, Rome to Tokyo.
1529	28 March SCU (as opp to SLU).
1548	4 April BJ 115903: Bucharest to Tokyo, 37 of 1/4/43; 115910 and 115912: Lisbon to London.
1557 (2831)	3 April.
1558 (2832)	4 April.
1604	24 April BJ 116456, 116391, 116467, 116457.
1613	18 April BJ 116580: Ankara to Tokyo.
1616	19 April BJ 116535/148: Ankara to Tokyo.
1621 (3036)	20 April BJ 116615: Ankara to Tokyo.
1626 (3061)	22 April BJ 116723/155.
1632 (3083)	24 April BJ 116813/53: Ankara to Tokyo.
1638	28 March BJ 115772: Ankara to Tokyo.
1637	26 April BJ 116866: Budapest to Rome.
1650	30 April BJ 116992: Berlin to Tokyo.
1655	1 May: W/T SS message indicating another kidnap attempt.
1659 (3171)	2 May BJ 117985: Berlin to Tokyo.
1661	3 May BJ 117094 and 117095: Rio and Stockholm to Lisbon.
1670	6 May: supplies of BJs in raw form to PM.
1695	10 May BJ 117717: Vichy to Ankara.
1702 (3556)	24 May BJ 117919: Rome to Ankara, Berlin to Tokyo ('C' to PM in Washington of same date).
1703	25 May BJ 117915: London to Rio.
1709	30 May BJ 1118287/296: Rome to Tokyo.
1715 (3449)	6 June BJ 118510: Rome to Ankara; 118069: Ankara to Moscow; 117650: Ankara to London (Greece).
1721 (3465)	7 June BJ 118569, 118058.
1723 (3476)	8 June BJ 118607: Rome to Tokyo.
1726	10 June BJ 118692: Tokyo to all stations re the Anglo-Saxons' efforts to get Turkey into the war.
1729/55 (3510)	11 June BJ 118730: Moscow to Ankara.
1733 (3529)	13 June BJ 118726.
1734 (3528 *sic*)	13 June BJ 118779: Bucharest to Tokyo.
1737	14 June BJ 118826: Berlin to Tokyo.
1734	13 June BJ 118779: Bucharest to Ankara.
1741	16 June BJ 118902/250: Ankara to Tokyo.
1744 (5567)	17 June BJ 118953: Berlin to Tokyo.
1774 (3667)	27 June SHARK of 21/6/43: Japan, Sofia, Vichy to Tokyo.
1779 (3683)	28 June BJ 119325: Sofia and Rome to Tokyo.
1800 (3765)	6 July BJ 119696: Istanbul to Tokyo.
1807	8 July BJ 119772: Sofia to Tokyo.
1824	12 July BJ 119921: Washington to London (Greece).
1881 (3993)	26 July BJ 120354: Istanbul to Tokyo.
1885 (4003)	27 July BJ 120446: Kuibyshev to Ankara.
1895	29 July BJ 120570: Ankara to Lisbon.
1901	31 July BJ 120666: Ankara to Tokyo.
1905	1 August BJ 120791: Ankara to Chungking.

1914 (4077)	4 August BJ 120892: Ankara to Rio.
1920	25 July BJ 122660: Ankara to Tokyo.
1962	25 August BJ 121726/2518: Berlin to Tokyo; BJ 121762: Ankara to Tokyo.
1991	3 September BJ 122407: Berlin to Tokyo.
2017	17 September BJ 122343/5782: Ankara to all stations.
2019	19 September BJ 122788/3509: Ankara to Tokyo.
2024	21 September BJ 122882: Berlin to Tokyo.
2043 (4450)	25 July: naval headlines 810.
2051 (4476)	27 July.
2058 (4501)	29 July.
2064 (4521)	1 October.
2067 (4531)	2 October: Boniface.
2076 (4550)	4 October.
2080 (4563)	5 October: Boniface including three pages on which nation occupied which island of Dodecanese.
2082 (4567)	6 October.
2085 (4574)	6 October: Boniface.
2092 (404)	8 October. BJ 123510/1184: Berlin to Tokyo.
2145	22 October. BJ 124071/1048: Berlin to Tokyo.
2150 (4778)	22 October.
2168 (4804)	26 October. BJ 124258/165: Moscow to Ankara.
2225 (4949)	11 November BJ 124726/406 of 8 November: Ankara to Tokyo.
2249	16 November. Ankara to Tokyo.
2253 (5040)	19 November: naval headlines 868.
2276	12 November, BJ 125337/1347.
2287 (5173)	14 December summaries.
2289	15 December BJ 126571: Ankara to all stations (Cairo proposals). BJ 126601 Ankara (von Papen) to Tokyo.
2290	16 December BJ 126184: Berlin to Tokyo. Ankara to Berlin.
2292	22 December BJ 126184 and BJ 126329/1415: Berlin to Tokyo.

1944

2313(5277)	3 January BJ 126836/1505: Berlin to Tokyo.
2319	7 January BJ 126918: Ankara to Tokyo.
2233	10 January: Ankara to Tokyo.
2342	16 January: Berlin to Tokyo.
2372(5498)	28 January.
2375 (5501)	29 January.
2382	30 January BJ 127666: Ankara to Tokyo.
2382	30 January: Ankara to Tokyo.
2414	5 February BJ 127892: Ankara to Tokyo. BJ 127897: Berlin to Tokyo.
2447 (5694)	9 February BJ 127854/153: Berlin to Tokyo of 4/2.
2559 (5486)	28 February BJ 128743/135 and 128791/165.
2565	1 March BJ 128850/31 and 128877/15.
2592	1 March.
2573	18 March BJ 128944/152592.
2619	14 March BJ 129309: Ankara to Tokyo.

2641 (6044)	15 March BJ 129380: Baghdad to Ankara.
2642	19 March BJ 129533/156.
2646 (6053)	20 March BJ 129551: Berlin to Tokyo.
2654	22 March BJ 129623/99–101 (same date).
2663	25 March.
2673	29 March BJ 129836: Berlin to Ankara
2680	31 March BJ 129933: Ankara to Tokyo. BJ 129907: Berlin to Tokyo.

Gap in numbers and dates between 27 March and 15 April.

2754 (4251)	1 May BJ 131811/425.
2763	BJ 131163: Ankara to Tokyo.
2771	BJ 131233/189/44863: Berlin to Bucharest.
2783 (6477)	13 May.

2895 (6705)	6 June D-Day BJ 131562/467.

'Y' Programmes

This is a list of the Diplomatic and Commercial (home stations) supplied to the Canadian National Security E at Ottawa by GCCS in London on 3 June 1942.

It consists of a list of countries whose diplomatic messages were intercepted for the cryptographers in Berkeley Street, together with the relevant call signs and frequencies in kilocycles; which intercept (or 'Y') station received the messages or – in the case of Turkey and French Colonial which cable censor – which receiving country received the messages, plus comments when necessary:

COUNTRY	CALL SIGN	FREQUENCY	SERVICE TO	'Y' STN	REMARKS
Afghanistan	YAK	18640 13580 9975	Germany	Baldock	Line to BP
			France Germany Italy Paraguay Peru Switzerland USA	Denmark Hill Cupar	
	2nd channel		Brazil	Cupar	According to service running to Axis states
			Chile France Germany Italy Peru Sweden Switzerland		
	LS02	21360	Spain USA	Cupar LQN, LQM, LSO, LST	DADRO
Brazil	PPU	19260	Argentine Chile	Cupar PPH, PPM, PPQ, PPV, PPW, PPK, PUH, PUS	DADRO
			France Portugal Sweden		

COUNTRY	CALL SIGN	FREQUENCY	SERVICE TO	'Y' STN	REMARKS
			Switzerland		
Bulgaria	LZB	7460	China	Sandridge	
			Germany		
			Hungary		
			Italy		
			Sweden		
			USSR		
	LZD	5740	Germany	Sandridge	
			Hungary		
			Italy		
	LZS	105.26	Germany	Cupar	
			Hungary		
			Romania		
Chile	CEA2	17410	Argentine	Cupar	DADRO, CEF, CEG
			Brazil		
			Germany		
			Japan		
			Peru		
Eire	EJK	11470	Vatican City	Whitchurch	Schedules covered
France	FYB	19150	Japan	Whitchurch	
	FYC	15935	Saigon, Hanoi		
	FYC2	9840	Saigon, Hanoi		
	FYM2	82.2	Colonies	C&W	Full cover
	FYN	19.8	Hungary	Denmark Hill	
			Romania		
			Turkey		
	FYQ	14730	Saigon, Hanoi	Whitchurch	
	FYQ2	8865	Saigon, Hanoi	Whitchurch	
			Sweden		
			USA	Whitchurch	
	FYR2	7894	Saigon	Whitchurch	
	FYT2	9930	USA	Whitchurch	
	FYU	1890	Japan	Whitchurch	
			Romania	Whitchurch	
			Saigon, colonies	Whitchurch	
	FYU2	12105	Argentine	Whitchurch	
			Brazil		
			Hungary		
			Japan		
			Portugal		
			Romania		
			Saigon		
			Sweden		
	FYX	16130	Fr Indo-China		
			Portugal	Whitchurch	
			Syria		
Fr Indo-China	FZO	15544	France	Whitchurch	
	FZQ2	7408	France	Whitchurch	

COUNTRY	CALL SIGN	FREQUENCY	SERVICE TO	'Y' STN	REMARKS
	FZS	18388	France	Sandridge	
			Japan		DADRO FZS3
	FZS3	9485	France	Sandridge	
			Japan		FZS
	FZT	17890	France		
			French colonies	Whitchurch	
	FZT2	10515	France	Whitchurch	
Germany	DEY	7632.5	Bulgaria	Denmark Hill	
			Italy		
			Romania		
	DEL	7389	Bulgaria	Denmark Hill	
	DER	10033	Bulgaria	Denmark Hill	
			Romania		
			Turkey		
	DEW	98.36	Italy	Denmark Hill	
			Norway		
			Turkey		
			Yugoslavia		
	DFC	12985	Afghanistan	Brora	
			Thailand		
	DFJ	19700	As DGO/DGY	Brora	
	DFJ	19700	Argentine	Cupar	
			Brazil		
			Chile		
			Peru		
			Thailand		
			Venezuela		
	DFK	7325	As DGO/DGY	Brora	
	DFN	9910	As DGO/DGY	Brora	
	DFO	9730	As DGO/DGY	Brora	
	DFP	7917	As DGO/DGY	Brora	
	DFQ	18700	Afghanistan	Brora	
			Thailand		
	DFS	10920	As DFJ	Cupar	
	DFT	7812.5	As DGO/DGY	Brora	
	DFY	16.55	As DGO/DGY	Brora	
	DFH	10440	As DFJ	Cupar	
	DGO	13225	Japan	Brora	
			Japanese occ		
	DGR	17341	As DFC	Brora	
	DGY	17880	Japan	Brora	
			Japanese occ		
	DGZ	14605	As DFC	Cupar	
	DKD	69.70	Italy	Cupar	
Hungary	HAR	65.64	Bulgaria	Cupar	
			Denmark		
			Italy		
	HAR2	6840	Bulgaria	Sandridge	
	HAT2	9125	Bulgaria	Sandridge	
			Denmark		

COUNTRY	CALL SIGN	FREQUENCY	SERVICE TO	'Y' STN	REMARKS
			France		
			Italy		
			Mexico		
	HAW	57.46	As HAR	Cupar	
Iran	EPA	10810	Syria	Sandridge	
			Turkey		
			USA		
			USSR		
	EPJ	18560	As EPA	Sandridge	
	EPX	16376	Afghanistan	Sandridge	
			?Rome		
Italy and cols	IAC	12445	Colonies	Sandridge	
	IAS	10380	Bulgaria	Sandridge	
			Colonies		
			Hungary		
	IEO	6706	Colonies	Sandridge	
	IGA	8750	Italy	Sandridge	
			Canaries		
	IGB	10718	Italy	Sandridge	
			Spain		
	IGD	10764	Argentine	Sandridge	
			Bulgaria		
			China		
			Colonies		
			Hungary		
			Japan		
			Romania		
			Sweden		
			Thailand		
			Turkey		
			USA		
	IGO	10730	Italy	Sandridge	
	IGZ	18630	Thailand	Sandridge	
	IQA	14736	Argentine	Sandridge	
			China		
			Japan		
			Thailand		
	IQT	55.05	Denmark	Sandridge	
			Germany		
			Hungary		
			Romania		
	IQU	67.07	Germany	Denmark Hill	
			Hungary		
			Portugal		
	IRE	47.62	Germany	Denmark Hill	
	IRF	8930	Germany	Sandridge	
	IRL	19656	Afghanistan	Sandridge	
			Argentine		
			Romania		
	IRS	9966	Argentine	Sandridge	
			Bulgaria		

COUNTRY	CALL SIGN	FREQUENCY	SERVICE TO	'Y' STN	REMARKS
			Colonies		
			Germany		
			Hungary		
			Romania		
			Sweden		
			USA		
	IRV	78518	Bulgaria	Sandridge	
			Colonies		
			Germany		
			Hungary		
			Romania		
			Sweden		
	IRW	19520	Afghanistan	Sandridge	
			Argentine		
			China		
			Japan		
			Thailand		
	IRX	12017	Bulgaria	Sandridge	
			Germany		
			Hungary		
			Japan		
			Romania		
Japan	JMO2(*sic*)	7550	Germany	Brora	
			Italy		
	JM04	15905	As JM02	Brora	
	JNB	13880	Afghanistan	Whitchurch	
			France		
			Sweden		
	JNC	17960	As JMB	Whitchurch	
	JNE	10160	Germany	Brora	
	JNF	15720	Germany	Brora	
	JNL	6810	Germany	Brora	
	JNO	8110	Germany	Brora	
			Italy		
			Switzerland		
	JNP	13740	Italy	Brora	
			Switzerland		
	JNQ2	18945	Italy	Brora	
			Switzerland		
	JUH	11520	Portugal	Brora	
	JUI	7570	Germany	Brora	
			Italy		
			Switzerland		
	JUJ	9265	As JUI	Brora	
	JUL	6730	As JUI	Brora	
	JUM	13705	As JUI	Brora	
	JUW	10980	As JUI	Brora	
	JUW	10980	USSR	Denmark Hill	
	JUX	17950	USSR	Denmark Hill	
	TDH	13520	Germany	Brora	
			Italy		

COUNTRY	CALL SIGN	FREQUENCY	SERVICE TO	'Y' STN	REMARKS
Japan (Shanghai)	XOC	10540	Germany	Sandridge	
	XOH	18155	Germany Italy Switzerland	Sandridge	
Portugal	CUD2	13345	France Germany Italy Japan Portuguese cols Switzerland USA	Sandridge	
	CUK	10905	France Germany Italy Portuguese cols	Sandridge	
	CUT	8095	France Germany Italy Switzerland USA	Sandridge	
	CUW	19180	Brazil Portuguese cols	Sandridge	
	CUX	9195	France Germany Italy Portugal	Sandridge	
	CUY	9195	France Germany Italy Switzerland	Sandridge	
Romania	YOA	9027	France Germany Italy	Whitchurch	
	YOB	25.37	Germany Italy	Brora	
	YOC	94.3	Germany	Whitchurch	
	YOM	10845	Italy	Whitchurch	
	YOP	7333	France Germany Italy	Whitchurch	
Spain	EAA	81.74	Germany	St Albans	Line to BP
	EAN2	9772	France Germany	St Albans	
	EAQ	9860	Argentine Germany USA	Denmark	
Sweden	SAQ	17.2	Italy Switzerland	Cupar	
	SAU	9434	France Italy	Sandridge	

COUNTRY	CALL SIGN	FREQUENCY	SERVICE TO	'Y' STN	REMARKS
	SAV	50	Italy Switzerland USSR	Cupar	
	SDA	7436	Switzerland	Sandridge	
	SDB	10780	France Italy Japan Switzerland USA	Sandridge	
	SDE	13815	France USA	Sandridge	
	SDO	13825	Italy	Sandridge	
	SDQ	15645	Japan	Sandridge	
	SDX	9442	Japan	Sandridge	
	SDY	8967	France Italy Switzerland USSR	Sandridge	
Switzerland	HBA	82.6	Denmark Portugal Spain Sweden Turkey USSR	Brora	
	HBC	9000	Denmark Spain Sweden Turkey USSR	St Albans	
	HBF	18450	Argentine Brazil China Syria	Brora	
	HBG	71	As HBA	St Albans	
	HBH	18480	China Japan Syria	Brora	
	HBM	8665	As HBC	St Albans	
	HBO	11402 12030	As HBH	Brora	
Thailand	HSP	17741	Germany Italy Japan Switzerland	Sandridge	
Turkey	TAE	28.3	Bulgaria Germany Italy Iran Romania Switzerland USSR	C&W	Full cover

COUNTRY	CALL SIGN	FREQUENCY	SERVICE TO	'Y' STN	REMARKS
	TAF	8045	As TAE	C&W	Full cover
	TAG	13090	As TAE	C&W	Full cover
	TAJ	109.09	As TAE	C&W	
USSR	RGE	Various	China	Denmark Hill	
	RNN	6880	Turkey	Sandridge	
	RWZ	13960	Bulgaria	Sandridge	
			Iran		
			Sweden		
			Switzerland		
			Turkey		
	RYS	13960	Bulgaria	Sandridge	
			Iran		
			Spain		
			Syria		
	HVJ	15090	Belgian Congo	Whitchurch	
			Eire		
			USA		

Wartime BJs

Numbers supplied to regular receivers by year (from HW3/162). The DG (Menzies) had copies of all BJs.

RECIPIENTS	1939	1940	1941	1942	1943	1944	1945
Foreign Office	2288	3485	13041	13095	14050	13153	8512
Admiralty	962	4526	7272	6901	5481	5048	3092
War Office	983	3767	5517	6927	5697	5421	3710
India Office	203	1160	3182	2848	1887	2093	2068
Colonial Office	169	1448	3821	3447	1284	1265	1012
Air Ministry	1198	4274	5002	6158	4162	4554	2879
MI5	289	1166	3898	9315	9850	8032	5302
DOT	143	1683	1460	320	60	192	205
Treasury	148	623	1214	617	97	68	195
EB (FO and MEW)	1000	3639	5464	3417	1702	1994	1233
Morton		793	2590	2505	1919	2012	1167
Bridges	563	6048	3614	1534	2036	974	
Dominions Office		378	1185	2515	1086	602	296
RIS now RSS						704	340

Venona

Venona was the name given by the Americans to a long lasting series of decryptions of Russian diplomatic messages between the KGB in the form of the Soviet Consul General in New York and Moscow centre. While it was known that references to a Soviet agent nicknamed 'Gomer' – or 'Homer' – actually referred to Donald Maclean, little else was known about Venona until the NSA released it on the Internet in 1995. Since the second of three tranches released covered the 1943 period and referred (by pseudonyms) to Churchill, Roosevelt, Stalin and the conclusions of several major conferences, it is appropriate to include messages relative to Turkish neutrality in this appendix, and to give a brief account of their emergence.

The Venona material was decrypted by Meredith Gardiner, a US cryptographer. He achieved this by reconstructing the Soviet codebooks. This in turn was achieved because he identified double use of OTP at the Moscow centre end. There are four years' of material, released in three tranches: the first was the period 1944–52 (released in 1994), the second 1943 and the third 1947–52. The Venona traffic has features in common with BJs: the office's date and number; the intercepted station, destination and number; a summary of content by way of heading. There are two notable differences. One is the amount of 'unrecovered' or 'unrecoverable' groups in the early stages, so that the meaning or gist of many intercepts is lost. The second is the practice of reissuing decrypts as and when new information justifies it. Some of the 1943 traffic was reissued in 1974, but with key words and names blacked out by the National Security.

HW3

Papers on GCCS in 1939 – comments by Prof Hinsley on memoranda supplied by J.E. Cooper and Nigel de Grey to Frank Birch in HW3/83 at the PRO.

By 1945, with the result of the war no longer in doubt, GCCS at BP turned its attention to writing its own history, or rather the history of the war through the interpretation of its work. The historians assigned this task included W.F. Clarke, in charge of the German section in 1939, and Frank Birch, his successor. The recently released files of HW3 in the PRO contain memoranda written at his request. Many of these concentrate on the immediate prewar period. These seem to be in response to a conviction that prewar GCCS failed to adapt itself to the ends of a world war and of machine encipherment and that the resulting pessimism about the possibility of everyone reading Enigma messages delayed the success of Turing and Welchman in 1940. Two classical cryptographers, J.E.C. Cooper and Nigel de Grey, were asked for their comments on this piece of received wisdom and to assess the accuracy of Alastair Denniston's memory when he wrote the interwar history of GCCS, to be found in HW3/32. Cooper's comments were reviewed by Prof Sir Harry Hinsley, who wrote the following comment on 1 May 1996:

I believe Josh Cooper is right when he says in his para 8 that AGD understood the wider problem of Sigint better than he was given credit for. It is certainly true that he had to be careful about crossing the boundary between cryptography and intelligence because the Service departments were extremely jealous in insisting that intelligence was their business. It is also true that most of the prewar cryptographers Josh refers to had no interest in intelligence. Neither of these situations was to change until after the outbreak of war – in new circumstances and with no people. Even so, it is to be noted that despite Josh's criticisms of the prewar staff in his para 6 (FO/371/2182), and of the office's amateur structure, the place did remarkably well on the cryptographic side before the war. In addition to its good results on the diplomatic, it made good progress against Italian and Japanese service cyphers. Only against Germany and the Soviets, both diplomatic and service cyphers, did it have no success. But this was due to circumstances that would not change till after the outbreak of war – very little traffic intercepted because of the use of landlines; very difficult cyphers. German diplomatic was not broken until 1943 and German Enigma only broken by the Poles with the aid of stolen documents before mid-1940 (for air force) mid-1941 (for navy) and autumn 1941 (for army).

Josh in para 9 (FO371/2182) is also right to stress that it was AGD who recruited the wartime staff from the universities with visits there in 1937 and 1938 (also 1939, when he recruited me and 20 other undergraduates within two months of the outbreak of war). I believe this was a major contribution to the wartime successes – going to the right places and choosing the right people showed great foresight.

Josh's comment in para 10 (FO/371/21842) that AGD was 'diffident and nervous, a small fish in a big pool that contained many predators' may seem unduly harsh, therefore, but I think it is harsher than Josh intended. There were many predators (the Services seriously thought of winding GCCS down when war came) and Josh would agree, I'm sure, that it was necessary to be diffident and understandable to be nervous. He quite rightly adds at the end of para 20 (FO371/21482) that AGD remembered WW1 very well but 'was tied by the narrow terms of reference imposed on him from above'. This is an accurate conclusion.

The only other paper that calls for comment is the three-page memo, by de Grey. He says that more was achieved cryptographically before the war than is generally recognised, but that the overall effort was limited by lack of funds, lack of imagination and forgetfulness of the lessons about Signals intelligence learnt in war. But he adds that the fault was not all or mainly the fault of GCCS. 'National policy was directed by axemen – very difficult to fight at the time.' I think he exaggerates the lack of imagination and the forgetfulness of the lessons of the previous war. AGD was severely restricted by the axemen – and by the difficulty of doing signals intelligence, as distinct from cryptography, in the interwar years.

Hinsley added his own comment on the spirit of pessimism which allegedly hung over BP in 1940. 'The GAF [Luftwaffe] Enigma was broken early because of Norway but was of limited use operationally, so the breakthrough did not signal great new importance to Bletchley in Whitehall.' Alan Turing told Harry Hinsley he could not break Enigma without the weatherships. These, BP knew, carried German naval Enigma machines and codebooks, for the current months by the coding clerk, for the subsequent month, locked in a safe. Twice Hinsley pinpointed German weatherships for the Royal Navy to board in order to seize not the current month's book – which would have been destroyed by the coding clerk, but the safe which contained the next month's books. Both raids were successful and the books they produced enabled Turing to complete his work on the machine successfully. See Appendix 12 (pp. 565–569) in Hinsley et al., *British Intelligence in the Second World War: Its Influence on Strategy and Operations* (London, HMSO, 1979) vol. 1.

A Note on *Breach of Security*

Breach of Security was edited by David Irving and subtitled 'The German Secret Intelligence File on Events leading to the Second World War' (London, William Kimber, 1968). Pages 121–166 cover intercepted foreign diplomatic cables shown to the Führer; pp. 175–184 decoded material shown to Dr Joseph Goebbels.

The use by Hitler, Ribbentrop, Goebbels and Kaltenbrunner of intercepted diplomatic communications from the neutrals is disclosed in *Breach of Security*. It summarises some of the diplomatic intercepts supplied by the *Forschungsamt*, and the German Foreign Office's Deciphering Bureau – *Chiffierstelle*. The dates on which these were supplied to Hitler are given. They begin on 14 February 1940 and end on 13 November 1943. They emanate from the same capitals as DIR/C – namely Ankara, Washington, Vichy, Cairo, Berne, Rome, Buenos Aires, Santiago da Chile, London, Sofia, Bucharest, Belgrade, Lisbon, Madrid and Tokyo. Their content, as summarised, show they cover the same topics as the BJs, and it must be theoretically possible to marry up the two archives. Some 472 intercepted foreign diplomatic cables were shown to Hitler, according to this compilation, and of these 180 emanated from Turkey.

Who Was Who

British

(1) = served in the First World War
(1a) = served between 1919 and 1939
(2) = served in the Second World War

Adcock, F.E. (1) and (2).

Anstey, W.H. (1).

Birch, Frank (1) and (2). Attached to a department of the FO from 1939. CMG 1945.

Boase, Tom (2). Later Prof, in GCCS's Italian section.

Clark, E. Russell (1) (1a).

Cooper, Josh (2). Head of the Air Force Section in GCCS.

Denniston, A.G. (1) (1a) (2). Head of a department in the FO. CMG 1943.

Ewing, J.A. (1). Director of Naval Education in 1914 and first head of Room 40.

Fetterlein, Ernst (1a) (2). Died 1944.

Forbes, Courtenay (1a)(2).

Foss, Hugh (1a) (2).

Godfrey, Margaret (1a) (2). Wife of Adm Godfrey, DNI.

de Grey, Nigel (1) (2). CMG 1945.

Hall, Adm Reginald. DNI in the First World War.

Hobart-Hampden, Ernest (2).

Hooper, Joe (1a) (2). Later Director of GCHQ.

Hope, G.L.N. (1) (1a) (2).

Hope, H.W.W. Herbert (later Adm) (1). Operational head of Room 40.

Hippisley, Baytum(1).

Hinsley, Harry (2). Later Prof Sir, Vice Chancellor of Cambridge University.

Jones, Gp Capt Eric (2). Later head of GCHQ.

Kendrick, A.D. (1a) (2).

Kenworthy, H.C. (1a) (2).

Knox, A.D. (2). Head of ISK at Bletchley Park.

Lambert, Leslie (1) (1a) (2). Also broadcaster and conjuror.

Last, Hugh (2). Professor of Roman History.

Maine, Henry (1a) (2).

Montgomery, Revd William (1).

Parlett, Sir Harold (1a). Previously Japanese counsellor at the Tokyo embassy.

Rotter, E. (1). Paymaster Captain.

Sinclair, Evelyn. Sister of Adm Sinclair, head of SIS 1922–39.

Sinclair, Adm Hugh, head of SIS.

Strachey, Oliver (1a) (2). Formerly of MI1B, later head of ISOS at Bletchley.

Tiltman, John (1a) (2). Head of the military section in GCCS.

Travis, Edward (1a) (2). Head of Bletchley Park 1942–52.

Welchman, Gordon (2). Also author of *The Hut Six Story*.

Welsford, Rhoda (1a) (2). Worked with Anthony Blunt at the Courtauld Institute.

Turks

Saraçoğlu, Sukru
Menemencioğlu, Numan
İnönü, Ismet
Acekalin
Rauf, Orbay

Ambassadors

Oshima, Hiroshi
Kurihara, Sho
de Peppo
Quaroni

FO Officials

Butler, R.A.
Cadogan, Sir Alexander
Clutton, George (GL)
Dixon, Pierson
Helm, Knox
Jebb, Gladwyn
Falla, Paul
Knatchbull-Hugessen, Sir Hughe
Lawford, J.
Reilly, Patrick
Rendel, George
Sargent, Sir Orme 'Moley'

Notes

Introduction

1 DIR/C is the name given to Churchill's files of secret intelligence.

2 The following official histories cover Turkish neutrality from a British point of view: G.E. Kirk's *The War and the Neutrals;* Oxford, Oxford University Press, 1954; W.N. Medlicott, *The Economic Blockade*; London, HMSO, 1952; vol. 1, chapters 8 and 18; Sir Llewelyn Woodward's 5-volume *British Foreign Policy in the Second World War*; London, HMSO, 1963; vol. 3.

3 While this has been massively documented, Robin Maugham's memory of Churchill's electoral defeat in 1945 is worth recording. Churchill told him at a party: 'What I shall miss most of all are the . . . cables being brought in at the start of every day' (quoted in Michael Woodbine Parish, *Aegean Adventures 1940–3*; Lewes, the Book Guild, 1993).

4 Handwritten undated notes on the origin and wartime work of Room 40, by A.G. Denniston, lodged in the Churchill Archives in Churchill College, Cambridge. See also Patrick Beesly, *Room 40: British Naval Intelligence 1914–18*; London, Hamish Hamilton, 1982, pp. 16 and 20. See also Appendix 4.

5 A quote from Richard Ullman, *Anglo-Soviet Relations: vol. 3 The Anglo-Soviet Accord*; Princeton, Princeton University Press, 1972; chapter 7.

6 See especially Ronald Lewin, *Ultra Goes to War: The Secret War;* London, Hutchinson, 1979.

7 See Keith Jeffrey (ed) 'The Government Code and Cipher School: A Memorandum by Lord Curzon', in *Intelligence and National Security*, vol. 1, no. 3, 1986.

8 See HW1/12, 'Government Code and Cipher School', which only covers the diplomatic section for the period 1919–26.

9 D.C. Watt, *How War Came: The Immediate Origins of the Second World War*; London, Heinemann, 1989.

10 See Peter Smith and E. Walker, *War In the Aegean*; London, Kimber, 1974; and Jeffrey Holland, *The Aegean Mission: Allied Operations in the Dodecanese, 1943*; Westport, Connecticut, Greenwood Press, 1988.

11 F.H. Hinsley et al, *British Intelligence in the Second World War: Its Influence on Strategy and Operations* (abridgement); London, HMSO, 1993. See also Hinsley (co-ed) *Code-breakers: The Inside Story of Bletchley Park*; Oxford, Oxford University Press, 1993.

12 See Louis and Blake (eds) *Churchill*; Oxford, Oxford University Press, 1994, p. 4.

Chapter 1

1 See Trumbull Higgins, *Winston Churchill and the Dardanelles: A Dialogue in Ends and Means*; New York, Macmillan, 1963, p. 105; and Martin Gilbert, *Winston S. Churchill*; London, Heinemann, 1971, vol. 3, with accompanying companion volumes for the period November 1914–April 1916.

2 See Chapter 3.

3 Reported in PRO ADM223/147 in an appreciation of the strengths and weaknesses of the Turkish soldiery.

4 D.C. Watt, *How War Came: The Immediate Origins of the Second World War, 1938–9*; London, Heinemann, 1988, p. 284.

5 Much to the annoyance of the British service attachés in Ankara, 'The Turks like him [Kelly] enormously': Lady Kanfurly, *To War with Whitaker: The Wartime Diaries of the Countess of Kanfurly 1939–45*; London, Heinemann, 1994, p. 180.

6 Harold Macmillan, *War Diaries: Politics and War in the Mediterranean, January 1943–May 1945*; London, Macmillan, 1973.

7 See Larry Weisband, *Anticipating the Cold War: Turkish Foreign Policy 1943–5*; Princeton, Princeton University Press, 1973, p. 52.

8 See Ronald Lewin, *Ultra Goes to War*; London, Hutchinson, 1978, p. 188.

9 Patrick Beesly, *Room 40: Naval Intelligence 1914–18*; London, Hamish Hamilton, 1978, pp. 16–18. Beesly quotes extensively from an undated handwritten memorandum by A.G. Denniston lodged in the Churchill College archives and reproduced here at Appendix 6. See Christopher Andrew, *Secret Service: The Masking of the British Intelligence Community*; London, Heinemann, 1985, p. 307; and Martin Gilbert, op. cit., p. 359. For Churchill's Room 40 charter see HW3/4 at the PRO.

10 Ewing and Hall: see Beesly, op. cit., pp. 125–27.

11 See Barbara W. Tuchman, *The Zimmermann Telegram*; London, Constable, 1959, p. 3; for the names of those who broke it: William Montgomery and Nigel de Grey. See also Sir William James, *The Sky Was Always Blue*; London, Methuen, 1951.

12 The main source is A.G. Denniston, 'The Government Code and Cipher School between the Wars' (ed Dr Christopher Andrew) in *Intelligence and National Security*, vol. 1, no. 1, 1936, pp. 48ff.

13 Denniston, op. cit., p. 55.

14 For more on OTP, see Chapter 2.

15 On Ambassador Oshima see Carl Boyd, *Hitler's Japanese Confidant: Oshima Hiroshi*; Kansas City, University of Kansas Press, 1989.

16 This information comes from Dr John Ferris, and from the National Archives of Canada. (See Appendix 2.)

17 See Appendix 8, and Prof Bradley Smith, *The Ultra Magic Deals: The Most Secret Special Relationship 1940–6*; Los Angeles, Presidio, 1993.

18 BJs or 'blue jackets', so called from the blue folders in which they were circulated. DIR or DIR/C Archive in Hinsley stands for Director and refers to the Chief of the British Secret Service, Gen Sir Stewart Menzies, and identifies the files Menzies ('C') brought constantly to Churchill.

19 Diplomatic deciphering from 1939 to 1942 took place in the main building at Bletchley Park, while 'High-grade' sigint (Enigma, later also 'Fish') was carried out in Huts 3, 4, 6 and 8, in the grounds of the Park (information from Prof Hinsley). Turkish material was accesible partly because of Cable & Wireless and partly because the traffic was in French both ways, and did not require translation. For this reason GCCS did not need a Turkish specialist.

20 See John Charnley, *Churchill: The End of Glory*; London, Hodder and Stoughton, 1991.

21 The C-in-C Middle East, Gen Sir Henry Maitland Wilson, was related to Field Marshal Maitland Wilson who was in charge of military affairs in the Mediterranean at the time of the Dardanelles assault.

22 See J. Ferris, 'Indulged in all too little: Vansittart, Intelligence and Appeasement' in *Diplomacy and Statecraft*, vol. 6, no. 1, 1995, pp. 122–51.

23 J.M. Gwyer and J.R.M. Butler, *Grand Strategy*; vol. 3, London, HMSO, 1976, pp. 343–4; also quoted in Michael Howard, *The Mediterranean Strategy in the Second World War*; London, Weidenfeld and Nicolson, 1968.

24 Howard, op. cit., p. 34.

25 Howard, op. cit., p. 37.

26 See David Kahn, *Seizing the Enigma: the Race to Break the German U-boat Codes, 1943–5*; Boston, Houghton Mifflin, 1991.

27 David Dilks (ed), *The Diaries of Sir Alexander Cadogan OM 1938–45*; London, Cassell, 1971, p. 433.

28 Quoted from a BJ in DIR/C (HW1/892).

Chapter 2

1 See especially John Ferris, 'Whitehall's Black Chamber: British Cryptology and the Government Code and Cipher School 1919–29' in *Intelligence and National Security*, vol. 2, no. 1, 1987, pp. 54–91.

2 See DENN 1/3 (handwritten on Admiralty letter heading) and DENN 1/4 in Churchill College, Cambridge.

3 See DENN 3/1 (handwritten on Admiralty letter heading) and DENN 4/1 in Churchill College, Cambridge.

4 See Appendix 8 for list of names of British cryptographers.

5 See John Ferris in his review of F.H. Hinsley and Alan Stripp (eds) *Code-Breakers*; (Oxford, Oxford University Press, 1993) in *Intelligence and National Security*, vol. 9, no. 3, 1994, pp. 560–1.

6 Ibid.

7 See Appendix 8.

8 See Patrick Beesly, *Room 40: British Naval Intelligence 1914–18*; London, Hamish Hamilton, 1982.

9 Rotter or Hope. See Appendix 8 and see Beesly, op. cit., p. 15.

10 A.G. Denniston, in his draft manuscript history of Room 40, 2 December 1944, DENN 1/4, asserts that both were vital to the early success of the enterprise. Hope later became Room 40's operational head.

11 Beesly, op. cit., p. 18. See Appendix 4 for the document *in extenso*. This is also used by Martin Gilbert, *Winston S. Churchill*; London, Heinemann, 1971, vol. 3, and Christopher Andrew, *Secret Service: The Making of the British Espionage Establishment*; London, Heinemann, 1985, p. 307.

12 Beesly, op. cit., p. 80 and Appendix 4.

13 Admiral Usedüm, the German Inspector-General of Coast Defences and Mines at the Dardanelles.

14 Minute of 22 March 1915 in Martin Gilbert (ed), *Winston S. Churchill*; vol. 3, p. 359.

15 Beesly comments, op. cit., p. 82: 'This may seem a somewhat unbelievable story, but then so are most of the stories about Hall, and most of them are true!' Hall's papers are in Churchill College, Cambridge. See also Gilbert and Andrew, op. cit.

16 See India Office Records L/MIL/7/2541.

17 See Christopher Andrew, 'The British Secret Service and Anglo-Soviet Relations in the 1920s' and 'British Intelligence and the Breach with Russia in 1927', both *Historical Journal*, vol. 20, no. 3 (1977), pp. 653–70 and vol. 25, no. 4 (1982), pp. 957–64 respectively.

18 He in turn nurtured his specialists, reducing the stress of their work by instituting short working hours and a six-week holiday, and by writing to the FO of 'their talents . . . amounting almost to genius'. (PRO HW3/62 X356, 1937). He is said to have been unable to obtain funds for the purchase from the Treasury, so bought Bletchley Park with his own money.

19 See D. French, 'The Dardanelles, Mecca and Kut: Prestige as a Factor in British Eastern Strategy, 1914–16' in *War and Society*, vol. 5, no. 1 (1987) and 'The Origins of the Dardanelles Campaign Reconsidered' in *History* (1983) and 'Perfidious Albion Faces the Powers' in *Canadian Journal of History*, vol. 28, no. 3.

20 See Richard Ullman, *Anglo-Soviet Relations*, vol. 3 *The Anglo-Soviet Accord*; Princeton, Princeton University Press, 1972, Chapter 7. Hankey minuted: 'Marta is a very ingenious cipher which was discovered by great cleverness and hard work. The key of the cipher is changed daily and sometimes as often as 3 times in one message. Hence if it becomes known that we decoded the messages, all governments of the world will probably soon discover that no messages are safe.' In fact the discovery was made by Fetterlein with two Russian-speaking assistants; a secret memorandum from Trotsky to Lenin reveals the Russians knew Fetterlein was employed by the government in a cryptographic capacity, and that alone would have alerted them to the danger to their cipher security. (Trotsky Archive T/628 of 19/12/20.)

21 The best account of this ferocious diplomatic confrontation is in Christopher Andrew, op.

cit., pp. 266–70.

22 Howard to Department, 10 July 1937, Registry no. X5264/113/504 of 13 July 1937, Chief Clerk's Department, Domestic Files 87–225, opened in 1988, PRO FO366/1000.

23 PRO WO32/4897. Inter-service committee on organisation of cryptography.

24 PRO WO32/4895. Inter-service committee on organisation of cryptography, which met from 1923 to 20 October 1939. Hugh Sinclair memorandum of 9 May 1924. The file contains memoranda on GCCS by the Foreign Office.

25 See esp William Friedman, *Sources in Cryptologic History no. 3: The Friedman Legacy*; National Security Agency, 1992.

26 See PRO HW3/32.

27 Sir Hughe Knatchbull-Hugessen chaired a committee which reported in the late 1930s on the possibilities of widening the entrance requirements for the diplomatic service and advised against.

28 See PRO HW3/32 and DENN 1/4, A.G. Denniston, 'The Government Code and Cipher School between the Wars', 2 December 1944, and the published version in *Intelligence and National Security*, vol. 1, no. 1, 1986, p. 50.

29 Peter Hennessy, *Whitehall*; London, Jonathan Cape, 1990, p. 103.

30 Christopher Andrew, op. cit., p. 454. See also notes by J.E. Cooper and Nigel de Grey and comments of F.H. Hinsley in Appendix 5.

31 See Nigel West, *GCHQ: The Secret Wireless War 1900–1986*; London, Weidenfeld and Nicolson, pp. 38, 123, 174/5, 181, 185, 187, 206–17.

32 Traffic Analysis. See West, op. cit.; Denniston's narrative in PRO HW3/32 and G. Welchman, *The Hut Six Story: Breaking the Enigma Codes*; New York, McGraw Hill, 1982; and D. Kahn, *Seizing the Enigma*; London, Souvenir Press, 1991, p. 184.

33 Evaluation – or assessment or 'discrimination' (Canadian jargon) – is a complex subject which by 1945 the leading classical cryptographers at Bletchley Park continued to debate. Was their function to provide intercepts – or intelligence? At what point did one shade into the other? Nigel de Grey's paper on the subject would repay detailed study (PRO HW3/33).

34 Most secret diplomatic cables to and from the FO were in OTP.

35 OUP as OTP supplier. The go-between was Edward Travis, c/o Mansfield College. The volume of business he generated was such that HMSO (the paymaster) became the Press's chief outside account, and many skilled workers were kept busy tapping out random numbers throughout the hostilities. A satellite printing works was set up in nearby Juxon Street to handle OTP business that exceeded the capacity of the main printing works. Retired pressworkers are still reluctant to talk about their secret wartime work, and since no accounts were to be submitted in writing, tracing the production of OTPs has been difficult. PRO FO366/1059 shows that Mansfield College, Oxford, became the 'construction' [codemaking] department of GCCS where some seventy Oxford girl graduates were employed by Edward Travis, head of 'construction' (i.e. encipherment) at GCCS and deputy head, in supplying the figures to the press. I asked one retired printer, Harold Dotterill, if the comps were allowed to produce their own random figures: the answer was no. (I am grateful to Peter Foden for assisting me through the day books and order books of the war years, and to Mr Dotterill for showing me the 'code' and 'decode' process whereby print security was guaranteed.)

36 Nigel West, op. cit., p. 133.

37 Private information.

38 In fact HW3 shows that he did not receive all BJs.

39 Sir Patrick Reilly: private information.

40 John Ferris, 'Indulged in all too little: Vansittart, Intelligence and Appeasement' in *Diplomacy and Statecraft*, vol. 6, no. 3 (March 1995) pp. 122–75.

41 See Appendix 8.

42 House of Lords Library: Lloyd George Papers, file F/209.

43 See R. Ullman, op. cit., pp. 308–9. This quotes from Trotsky's Archives T-628: 'England has organised a network of intercept stations designed particularly for listening to our radio. This accounts for the deciphering of more than 100 of our codes. The keys are sent from

London where a Russian subject Feterlain [*sic*] has been put at the head of cipher affairs having done such work before in Russia.' For Feterlain read Fetterlein who joined GCCS in 1922 as head of the Russian department.

44 See 'The Professional Career of A.G. Denniston' by the present author in K.G. Robertson, (ed.), *British and American Approaches to Intelligence*; London, Macmillan, 1986.

45 Lord Gladwyn [Gladwyn Jebb] remembers taking a BJ to Chamberlain's office in the House of Commons in 1938. The FO regarded it as further evidence of the futility of appeasement and hoped it would influence Chamberlain. But the Prime Minister simply glanced at it, threw it down and addressed the young Jebb bitterly on the subject of the FO's disloyal practice of trying to influence the government's foreign policy by the selective use of diplomatic intercepts. (Private information from Lord Gladwyn.)

46 PRO HW3/32.

47 See P. Paillole, *Notre Espion chez Hitler*; Paris, Laffont, 1985, p. 270. Bertrand here confirms that Capt Braquenie was the head [French] cryptographic specialist. Both he and Col Langer of the Polish secret service signed the Dennistons' visitors' book on 9 December 1939, proving that he and Bertrand stayed with Cdr Denniston and worked with him at Bletchley. See also PRO HW3/32: 'Naturally the Military Section worked in close cooperation with the military intercepting station at Chatham, and it was thanks to this that the section, and GCCS as a whole, had, in 1937, their first glimpse of Wehrmacht and Luftwaffe material and of German police transmissions. Knox failed in his efforts on naval Enigma, led (*sic*) the team which started to investigate this new problem. Tiltman, deep in other problems, broke in to contribute one vital link. An ever closer liaison with the French, and through them with the Poles, stimulated the attack. Fresh ideas flowed, even from those selected from a university as recruits in the event of war. I think it may be rightly held that this effort of 1938 and 1939 enabled the party at B/P to read the current traffic of the GAF (*sic*) within five months of the outbreak of war.' (Draft narrative 2 December 1944, copies in PRO HW3/32, DENN 1/4, and Denniston, op. cit., p. 62).

48 A.J.P. Taylor, *English History 1914–1945*; Oxford, Oxford University Press, 1965, p. 4.

Chapter 3

1 See D.C. Watt, *How War Came: The Immediate origins of the Second World War, 1938–9*; London, Macmillan, 1989, pp. 271ff.

2 See Chapter 2.

3 Eden did not assume the full title Secretary of State for War until May 1940.

4 See John Ferris, 'Vansittart, Intelligence and Appeasement' in *Diplomacy and Statecraft*, vol. 6 no. 1 (1995), pp. 133ff.

5 See Selim Deringil, *Turkish Foreign Policy in the Second World War*; Cambridge, Cambridge University Press, 1989, pp. 92ff, 205–6.

6 David Dilks (ed), *The Cadogan Diaries*; London, Cassell, 1971 p. 255.

7 See Gerard Mangune (ed), *The International Straits of the World*; Dordricht, 1987.

8 AIR23/6935; see also Hinsley, op. cit., vol. 1.

9 Martin Gilbert, op. cit., vol. 6, pp. 677–8.

10 Gilbert, ibid p. 880.

11 PRO FO195/1239; Deringil, op. cit., p. 93.

12 PRO FO195/1239, PRO WO190/893/22832 (see folder at back).

13 PRO FO195/2462, Hugessen to Nichols, 7 July 1940.

14 Though France was out of the fighting Anglo-French sigint co-operation was to continue effectively for another two years. From 20 May 1940 until 14 June the French cryptographic team at Bruno intercepted and decrypted 3,074 German Luftwaffe messages, and on 21 May the first intercepts were sent from Bletchley Park to the British Military Mission in France. Hugh Skillen, *Spies of the Air Waves*; London, Skillen, 1988, p. 103.

15 Deringil, op. cit., p. 102.

16 WO 190/893/22832.

17 PRO FO195/2462, Rendel to Department, 15 January 1940.

18 FO371 30076.

19 PRO FO371/30153, Sargent's handwritten minute, 20 August 1940.

20 Franz Halder, *The Halder War Diary 1939–42* (ed. by Charles Burdick and Hans-Adolf Jacobsen); New York, Greenhill Books, 1988, p. 65.

21 Halder, ibid.

22 Quoted in Deringil, op. cit., p. 105.

23 Quoted in Deringil, from the 3-volume *Kriegstagebuch*; Kohlhammer, 1964, vol. 2, p. 151.

24 PRO FO371/330076, Sargent's handwritten minute.

25 See James Marshall-Cornwall, *Wars and Rumours of Wars*; London, Leo Cooper/Secker and Warburg, 1982.

26 Eden memorandum on Turkey: Hugessen told the FO, 'This will have been seen by No. 10' – i.e. Churchill read a BJ report on Eden in Turkey. See PRO FO371/30076, 4 January 1941. This is one of the few references to Turkish intercepts in the FO files.

27 Winston S. Churchill, *The Second World War: vol. 3 The Grand Alliance*; London, Cassell, 1950, p. 9.

28 Halder, op. cit., p. 118.

29 Irving, op. cit., p. 128.

30 DO(41) 6th meeting of 20 January quoted in Hinsley, op. cit., vol. 1 p. 443.

31 Hinsley, op. cit., vol. 1 p. 443.

32 Churchill, op. cit., p. 18.

33 Irving, op. cit., pp. 126–27.

34 Hinsley, op. cit., p. 352.

35 Churchill, op. cit., pp. 30–1. An Enigma decrypt of 18 January shows German hutments being shipped to Bulgaria and a Luftwaffe mission in Romania discussing long-term fuelling arrangements. See Hinsley, op. cit., p. 355.

36 Hinsley, ibid p. 355; Gilbert, op. cit., p. 1003, n. 3.

37 PRO WO190/893/22832, nos 3A and 5A, 15 January 1941; Hinsley, op. cit., p. 446.

38 Hinsley, op. cit., p. 358.

39 WO190/893.

40 Hinsley, op. cit., p. 404.

41 Dalton's diary, lodged in the London School of Economics.

42 PRO WO190/983/22832, 79A, 6 February 1941.

43 Gilbert, op. cit., p. 1003.

44 Gilbert, ibid p. 649.

45 Pierson Dixon, *Double Diploma: The Life of Sir Pierson Dixon, Don and Diplomat*; London, Hutchinson, 1968, pp. 57 and 66.

46 Irving, op. cit., p. 172.

47 Churchill, op. cit., p. 65.

48 PRO PREM3/206/3 and 173, Confidential Print of 29 September 1941.

49 Deringil, op. cit., pp. 119–20.

50 Churchill, op. cit., p. 86.

51 Churchill, op. cit., p. 109.

52 Churchill, op. cit., p. 109.

53 Halder, op. cit., p. 358.

54 See *Documents of German Foreign Policy*, Series D, vol. 12, p. 286.

55 Hinsley, op. cit., p. 413 and PRO CAB105/4. This was the first time that Luftwaffe Enigma decrypts were sent to Allied field commanders (Hinsley ibid p. 407; also PRO AIR40/2323, pp. 828–904).

56 Churchill, op. cit., p. 119.

57 Halder, op. cit., p. 373.

58 See HW3/62.

59 Churchill, op. cit., p. 149.

60 Churchill, op. cit., pp. 149–50. Italics added.

61 Gilbert, op. cit., p. 1073.

62 Gilbert, op. cit., p. 1052, and Frantiscez Moravec, *Master of Spies*; London, Bodley Head, 1975, p. 204.

63 WO190/893, 22832.

64 Hinsley, op. cit., pp. 410, 412 (BJ).

65 PRO WO190/893/22832. See folder.

66 PRO WO190/893/22832. See folder.

67 Deringil, op. cit., p. 120.

68 Churchill, op. cit., p. 227: see also Warren F. Kimball, *Churchill and Roosevelt: the Complete Correspondence*; vol. 1: October 1933–November 1942, Princeton, Princeton University Press, 1984.

69 Churchill, op. cit., p. 127.

70 Gilbert, op. cit., p. 1086.

71 Hinsley, op. cit., p. 71.

72 Hinsley ibid p. 422. See also PRO CAB105/4.

73 PRO FO371/30153.

74 Hinsley, op. cit., pp. 407–8; see also PRO CAB105/4.

75 Hinsley, ibid p. 319.

76 See Ronald Lewin, *Ultra Goes to War*; London, Hutchinson, 1978, pp. 104ff.

77 Halder, op. cit., p. 404.

78 See Deringil, op. cit., p. 121.

79 Hinsley, op. cit., p. 278.

80 Hinsley, op. cit., pp. 379–427.

81 PRO HW1/6, decrypted 24 June 1941.

82 Hinsley, op. cit., p. 154.

83 Halder, op. cit., p. 155; Harvey, op. cit., p. 156.

84 PRO FO371/30068. R139D/650/G44, Clutton, minute on supplies to Turkey, July 1941.

85 Irving (ed), op. cit., p. 132.

86 Gilbert, op. cit., pp. 138; HW1/13.

87 Irving (ed), op. cit., p. 132.

88 Hinsley, op. cit., vol. 2 pp. 82–3.

89 Hinsley, op. cit., vol. 2, p. 840.

90 Hinsley, op. cit., vol. 2. *passim*, especially p. 836 for Churchill and BJs.

91 See Frank Weber, *The Evasive Neutral: Germany, Britain and the Quest for a Turkish Alliance in the Second World War*; Missouri, Missouri University Press, 1979, p. 109.

92 Harvey, op. cit., p. 168.

93 Halder, op. cit., p. 517.

Chapter 4

1 James Marshall-Cornwall, *Wars and Rumours of Wars*; London, Leo Cooper, 1984.

2 PRO FO371 44064 Dill to Churchill dated 5 January 1944. Also PRO PREM3/447/6, p. 330, no. 387: Grand no. 125. Churchill's doodle suggests he was giving the suggestion some thought.

3 Hinsley, op. cit., p. 173.

4 For the letter and Milner-Barry's comment, see *Intelligence and National Security* vol. 6 (1986).

5 Letter to the present writer from the Archivist at Government Communications Headquarters of 2 February 1995.

6 See Appendix 2 for alphabetical list of countries targeted, call signs, frequencies in kilohertz, which 'Y' station provided interception and which countries received the messages.

7 See Chapter 1 in connection with the crisis in Smyrna in October 1922.

8 See Appendix 2.

9 A captured German codebreaker called Schmidt, under interrogation, told British authorities that 'the intercepted messages of the Turkish embassy in Moscow and the American Embassy in Berne were deemed of especial value'. He also asserted that Turkey was among the thirty-four countries whose secret communications the Germans were reading at this time. (Deringil, op. cit., p. 61).

10 See Trumbull Higgins, *Winston Churchill and the Second Front: 1940–43*; Oxford, Oxford University Press, 1957, pp. 77–78.

11 See Richard Lamb, *Churchill as War Leader*; New York, Carroll and Graf, 1991.

12 PRO FO371/30124. Also Marshall-Cornwall, op. cit., pp. 178–79.

13 PRO FO371/30068.

14 See Pierson Dixon (ed), *Double Diploma: The Life of Sir Pierson Dixon, Don and Diplomat*; London, Hutchinson, 1968, pp. 42–44 and addendum pasted into the prelims giving an account of the imagined talk between Mustapha Kemal and Loraine which was written by Sir Charles Mott-Radclyffe, as a fantasy on the voluminous telegrams sent back to London by Loraine in the 1930s.

15 PRO PREM3/445/2 Ismay to Churchill, 8 August 1941.

16 Most people called the country Iran, as now, but Churchill was keen to use the traditional name Persia, so out of deference to the war leader, this author will do the same!

17 PRO HW1/38, BJ 095069, Moscow to Ankara, decrypted 1 September 1941.

18 David Irving (ed), *Breach of Security*;, op. cit., *passim*; also Deringil, op. cit., p. 61.

19 *Documents on German Foreign Policy* (*DGFP*), Series D, vol. 12, doc. no. 113, pp. 201–2.

20 H.R. Trevor-Roper (ed), *Hitler's Table Talk 1941–4*; London, Weidenfeld and Nicolson, 1953.

21 PRO DIR HW1/38, BJ 095114, Ankara to Rome, decrypted 5 September 1941.

22 PRO FO954/324 folio 388.

23 *DGFP*, Series D, vol. 12, p. 179.

24 Trevor-Roper, op. cit., p. 339.

25 *Principal War Telegrams and Memoranda*; London, Kraus, 1976. See also PRO PREM3/446/10, no. 573, 29 January 1943, Jacob to PM: 'The Foreign Office have always maintained the relations with Turkey are so delicate that they should not be handled in any way by the Minister of State [Macmillan].'

26 PRO HW1/49, BJ 095195: Kabul to Rome, decrypted 5 September 1941.

27 PRO HW1/49: Churchill to Eden, 6 September 1941.

28 PRO HW1/64, BJ 095419: Kabul to Rome, decrypted 13 September 1941.

29 PRO HW1/64: Ankara to Tokyo, decrypted 13 September 1941, BJ 095419.

30 PRO HW1/64, BJ 095419: Sofia to Rome, decrypted 13 September 1941.

31 PRO HW1/67, BJ 095417: Churchill to Pound on BJ decrypted 15 September 1941.

32 Churchill, op. cit., p. 412.

33 Gilbert, op. cit., p. 1196.

34 Churchill, op. cit., p. 767.

35 PRO HW1/93, BJ: Washington to Ankara, decrypted 26 September 1941. Diplomatic distribution (i.e. MEW, not service ministries, PID, DoT, Sir R. Hopkins).

36 PRO HW1/93, BJ: London to Tokyo, decrypted 27 September 1941.

37 PRO HW1/79, BJ 095665: Vichy to Ankara, decrypted 20 September 1941.

38 *sic.* PRO HW1/79, BJ 2019141: decrypted 20 September 1941.

39 PRO HW1/79, BJ 095666: Ankara to Tokyo, decrypted 20 September 1941.

40 PRO HW1/82, BJ 095748: Berlin to Tokyo, decrypted 24 September 1941.

41 PRO HW1/79, BJ 095666/1609 and 1610: French ambassador to Ankara to Algiers, decrypted 20 September 1941.

42 BM typed letter of 24 September 1941.

43 PRO HW1/108, BJ 096091/3540: Greek chargé Cairo to London, decrypted 2 October 1941.

44 PRO HW1/109, BJ 096081: Ankara to Rome, decrypted 2 October 1941.

45 PRO HW1/110, BJ 096132: Stockholm to Berlin, decrypted 3 October 1941.
46 PRO HW1/112, BJ 096137: Ankara to Tokyo, decrypted 3 October 1941.
47 PRO FO371/30085: R8965/79/44, Clutton handwritten note of 9 October 1941.
48 PRO HW1: Ankara to Tokyo, decrypted 3 October 1941. The Germans would not, of course, have had access to the cable facilities of Cable & Wireless in Istanbul, like the British.
49 Hinsley, op. cit., vol. 2 p. 84fn and PRO HW1/136 BJ, decrypted 19 October 1941.
50 Churchill, op. cit., vol. 4, p. 484.
51 PRO HW1/110(7709) BJ: Stockholm to Berlin, decrypted 3 October 1941.
52 PRO HW1/159 (7858), BJ 096774: Berlin to Tokyo, decrypted 21 October 1941.
53 Trevor-Roper, op. cit., p. 546.
54 PRO PREM3/446: Cadogan handwritten minute.
55 PRO HW1/206, BJ 097561: Ankara to Tokyo, decrypted 11 November 1941 and HW1/207, BJ 097604: Berlin to Tokyo, decrypted 12 November 1941. Distribution: DIR 3, FO 3, PID, ADM, WO 3, IO 2, AIR, DoT, Sir R. Hopkins, MEW 2, Dominions Office, Colonial Office: 21 copies total.
56 PRO HW1/— BJ 095604: Ankara to Tokyo, decrypted 12 November 1941.
57 PRO HW1/281, on BJ 098360, decrypted 11 November on BJ 098360 circulated 30 November 1941.
58 Churchill, op. cit., p. 475.
59 PRO HW1/314, BJ 098766: Ankara to Tokyo, decrypted 9 December 1941.
60 PRO FO371/33133, Rendel to Department, 3 January 1942.
61 Ibid.
62 PRO FO371/33133. Sargent was another of Hugessen's confidants, the latter writing regularly and at length to him, as much to clear his own mind on the appropriate British diplomatic response to Turkey as to inform the FO.
63 PRO HW1/374 (8611), BJ 100577/69: Ankara to Rome, decrypted 27 January 1942; see also Deringil, op. cit., p. 61.
64 PRO PREM3/445/4, 21 January 1942, Hugessen to department.
65 PRO PREM3/445/4, PM to COS, January 1942.
66 PRO FO371/R953/486/44: Telegram no. 290.
67 Whether this was official witholding or a symptom of the developmental stage of the handling of DIR it is difficult to say, but both Hinsley and GCHQ think it is the latter.
68 Private information from A.G. Denniston's pocket diary for 1942. Both aspects of the truncated GCCS – diplomatic and commercial – were to flourish from then on, due to the needs of the FO in respect of diplomatic intercepts, and to those of the MEW for updatable economic information, particularly of Spanish exports of tungsten, wolfram and antimony to Germany.
69 David Dilks (ed), op. cit., p. 433.
70 Typed letter dated 26 March 1942 in BM Emrys Evans archive.
71 PRO HW1/452, BJ 102680/82: Sofia to Tokyo, decrypted 27 March 1942. Distribution twenty including PID and Morton.
72 PRO HW1/456/1311, BJ 102371/1191: Ankara to Chungking; and 102755/10: Kuibyshev to Ankara, both decrypted 29 March 1942.
73 Deringil, op. cit., p. 119, quoting *DGFP* D/x11.
74 PRO HW1/456, BJ 102755: Kuibyshev to Ankara, decrypted 24 March 1942.
75 Trevor-Roper, op. cit., p. 378.
76 PRO HW1/484/9155: Kuibyshev to Ankara, decrypted 9 April 1942.
77 Churchill, op. cit., vol. 4, p. 284.

Chapter 5

1 Trumbull Higgins, *Winston Churchill and the Second Front 1940–2*; New York, Oxford University Press, 1957. Higgins described Turkey in 1941 as a neutral state whose large and

poorly equipped army would continue to attract Churchill's encouraging smiles and ultimately futile favours for three full years to come.

2 Higgins, op. cit., and John Ehrman, *Grand Strategy* vol. 5; London, HMSO, 1956.

3 Italics added.

4 PRO HW1/497 of 15 April 1942: 'I shall shortly be going to America. Will you be willing to accompany me?' The Ministry of Foreign Affairs in Ankara immediately concurred. Distribution to Director (Menzies) and Churchill only.

5 PRO HW1/513, BJ 103496–26 of 21 April. Japanese ambassador in Berne of 17 April 1942.

6 Italics added. PREM3/446/1D, p. 513.

7 PRO FO371/33403. Peter Lawford minuted on 26 August: 'The Prime Minister is the symbol of the national war effort in Turkish eyes, and a personal glimpse of their hero would undoubtedly "make" their visit to this country.' Dixon minuted: 'excellent'. The PM interview did not last more than fifteen minutes. He and M. Yalin spoke to each other in French, on WW1, Enver and Atatürk. Yalin asked that Turkey should be at the peace conference. 'The PM's reply satisfied the Turks less than Eden's interview.'

8 Deringil, op. cit., p. 117.

9 PRO HW1/560, BJ 10472: Ankara to Rome, decrypted 10 May: De Peppo quoting Saraçoğlu verbatim.

10 PRO HW1/563, BJ 104279: Ankara to Lisbon, decrypted 11 May 1942.

11 PRO HW1/563, BJ 104284: Ankara to all stations, decrypted 11 May 1942. İnönü proved the best survivor of the lot and was still active in Turkish politics until the late 1960s.

12 Churchill, op. cit., vol. 4 p. 769; see also PRO PREM3/446/8, PM to Eden, 12 May 1942. 'Your last sentence leads swiftly to our usual conclusion, viz to do nothing.' Eden thought Churchill was attacking him because he thought saying anything to the Turks was risky. Churchill tried to pacify him by pointing out he said 'our' not 'your' – i.e. the FO. It was not difficult to see through this as brazen flannel – the puzzle is why Eden appears not to have done this.

13 PRO HW1/577, BJ: Madrid to Ankara, decrypted 17 May 1942; and 589/9555: Madrid to Ankara, decrypted 22 May 1942.

14 PRO HW1/631, BJ 105334: Madrid to Ankara, decrypted 17 May 1942.

15 PRO HW1/689, BJ 106218: Ankara to Chungking, decrypted 2 July 1942.

16 PRO HW1/700, BJ 106356: Ankara to Lisbon, decrypted 5 July 1942.

17 Kurihara was ordered to stay in Istanbul and not move to Ankara, reflecting Japanese preference for the international information available in the former capital.

18 PRO HW1/706, BJ 106428: Ankara to Tokyo, decrypted 7 July 1942.

19 PRO HW1/718, BJ 106618: Sofia to Tokyo, decrypted 11 July 1942; PRO HW1/746, BJ 106837: Sofia to Tokyo, decrypted 17 July 1942; PRO HW1/721, BJ 106684: Madrid to Tokyo, decrypted 12 July 1942; and PRO HW1/729 of 14 July 1942; PRO HW1/729, BJ 106754: Vichy to Ankara, decrypted 14 July 1942.

20 PRO HW1/793, BJ117213: Stockholm to Lisbon, decrypted 26 July 1942: 'I was told from an official source that the Reich would accept [group missing 'peace'?] based on the status quo conditional, however, on Germany's retention of the territories captured from Russia.'

21 PRO HW1/793, BJ 107221: Cairo to Ankara, 26 July 1942; reporting Saraçoğlu's far running thoughts: 'please keep the whole conversation absolutely secret.'

22 PRO HW1/804, BJ 107357: Ankara to Tokyo, decrypted 30 July 1942.

23 PRO HW1/814, BJ 107585: Kuibyshev to Ankara, decrypted 5 August 1942.

24 PRO HW1/793, BJ 107221: Cairo to Ankara, decrypted 26 July 1942.

25 PRO FO371/33376: Cadogan handwritten memorandum.

26 PRO HW1/833(499), BJ 108167: Berlin to Ankara, decrypted 24 August 1942. There are no less than 23 BJs in this one DIR file; copies of all of them were sent to Washington.

27 PRO FO371/33376: Hugessen to Department, 29 August 1942.

28 FO371/33376 and PREM3/446/8.

29 PRO FO371/33376: Clutton to Department, 31 August 1942.

30 PRO FO371/R4087/24/24: Clutton handwritten minute, 22 June 1942.

31 Deringil, op. cit., pp. 140–1; FO371/, R5618/2713/44. 44 is the FO code for Turkey.

32 PRO HW1/869, BJ 108656 28 August 1942. The day before British diplomatic cryptanalysis broke the 'Floradora' (German diplomatic) cipher and passed the results to Adcock of Berkeley Street to process for the FO. Prof Frank Adcock, a veteran cryptographer and long-term friend and associate of Denniston's, moved with him (and many others) to Berkeley Street in February 1942. Adcock later became Professor of Ancient History at Cambridge. See P.W. Filby, in *Intelligence and National Security*, vol. 6 no. 3, 1988, pp. 272–84 which is the definitive article on Berkeley Street's war work. See also Martin Gilbert, *Winston S. Churchill: The Road to Victory 1941–5*; London, Heinemann, 1986, p. 869.

33 PRO HW1/892, BJ 109983: London to Ankara, decrypted 11 September 1942.

34 PRO HW1/929, BJ 109491: Berlin to Tokyo, decrypted 27 September 1942.

35 PRO HW1/895(707), BJ 14518: Berlin to Ankara, decrypted 14 September 1942.

36 PRO HW1/896, BJ 109039/4446: Ankara to Cairo, decrypted 12 September 1942. This is an early appearance of a second number on a BJ. This number (typed rather than rubber-stamped as the main number invariably was) was the office number given to reassure recipients that they had a complete set of records of intercepts sent from one particular station, e.g. Ankara, to another, e.g. Tokyo.

37 PRO HW1/899, BJ 109117/276: London to Ankara, decrypted 14 September 1942.

38 PRO HW1/902, BJ 109152/849: Berlin to Ankara, decrypted 15 September 1942.

39 PREM 3/446/8. Hugessen and the FO would have privately noted that this may have been true but was certainly not the whole truth.

40 PRO PREM3/446/8: Churchill to Eden, 12 October 1942.

41 PRO PREM3/446/8: Churchill to Eden, 12 October 1942.

42 His staff in Ankara was of high calibre, especially Knox Helm and John Sterndale-Bennett, the former a career diplomat who had come up the hard way in the Levant Consular Service, eventually to become the last Governor General of the Sudan. But the FO thought his views on pressurising Turkey too radical.

43 These letters were certainly not part of the 'Cicero' corpus, as he dictated them to an English secretary, Miss Brown, who would have got them into the diplomatic bag before they got back to the ambassadorial residence. See Hugessen's notes on Cicero, Moyzisch and 'his period of some difficulty', kindly lent to me by his daughter.

44 There are no files of DIR between numbers 929 and 1107.

45 Elizabeth Barker, *Churchill and Eden at War*; London, Macmillan, 1978, p. 207.

46 Churchill, op. cit., pp. 626–28.

47 PRO FO371/37400. In fact there was little to be done about individual cases but pressure from both Allied and Axis countries combined to induce İnönü to rescind the Tax law in October 1944.

48 Harvey, *War Diaries*; vol. 2 p. 180.

49 Barker, op. cit.

50 PRO HW1/1107, BJ 110939: Rome to Tokyo, decrypted 16 November 1942, standard distribution. And BJ 111188/690: Rome to Tokyo, decrypted 16 November 1942.

51 Churchill, op. cit., vol. 4 pp. 623ff.

52 Ibid p. 625.

53 PRO HW1/1125(1449), BJ 111327: London to Ankara, decrypted 20 November 1942.

54 PRO HW1/1125, BJ: 111300: London to Ankara, decrypted 20 November 1942.

55 PRO HW1/1145, BJ: Ankara to Tokyo, decrypted 24 November 1942 also PRO HW1/1148: Sofia to Tokyo; PRO HW1/1156, BJ: Ankara to Tokyo, decrypted 26 November 1942, and PRO HW1/1164, BJ 111598, decrypted 27 November 1942; also PRO HW1/1171/383 BJ: decrypted 27 November 1942.

56 PRO HW1/1178, BJ 111713 and HW1/1142, BJ 111451: Ankara to Tokyo, decrypted 30 November 1942.

57 PRO FO371/37491; exchange of memos and letters between Sir Alexander Hardinge, the King's Private Secretary, George Clutton and Sir Alexander Cadogan.

58 PRO HW1/1182, BJ 111767, 70, 71/ 383: Ankara to Tokyo, decrypted 2 December 1942.

59 PRO HW1/1210, BJ 112093/249: Sofia to Tokyo, decrypted 2 December 1942.

60 Churchill, op. cit., vol. 4 p. 625.

61 Churchill, op. cit., vol. 4 p. 622.

62 PRO HW1/1240, BJ 112341 and 369/400: Ankara to Tokyo, decrypted 20 December 1942, BJs 112341/369 and BJ 112370: Berlin to Tokyo, decrypted 20 December 1942.

63 PRO FO371/37645: Sterndale-Bennett to Sargent, 18 December 1942. On 13 December GCCS broke the four-rotor key SHARK, so the blackout on U-boat traffic was over. (Hinsley, op. cit., vol. 1 p. 226 and vol. 2 p. 667.)

64 The security of Ultra is a recurring theme of the DIR file. The main question was, what was and what was not, to be sent to the Russians, and through what channel. What no one at BP or the FO knew is that the DIR was available to the least mentioned but possibly most important member of the famous five Cambridge Soviet spies – John Cairncross. We may never know the volume and extent to which Stalin used his knowledge of DIR via this route, but it has been asserted that without it the Battle of Kersh would have been lost. See Christopher Andrew and Oleg Gordievsky, *KGB: The Inside Story of its Foreign Operations from Lenin to Gorbachev*; London, Hodder and Stoughton, 1990, pp. 248, 600. See also Churchill, op. cit., vol. 4, p. 602.

65 PRO HW1/1286, BJ 112758: Bucharest to Lisbon, decrypted 5 January 1943.

66 PRO FO371/37645.

67 PRO HW1/1309, BJ 113201: Berlin to Tokyo, decrypted 5 January 1943.

68 David Dilks (ed), op. cit., p. 394. Hugessen was nicknamed Snatch by the FO.

69 PRO FO371/37505.

70 PRO PREM3/446/1.

71 PRO HW1/1325, BJs 11328 and 11329: Sofia to Tokyo, decrypted 21 January 1943.

72 PRO HW1/1330, BJ 113489: Washington to Ankara, decrypted 25 January 1943.

73 PRO HW1/1331, BJ 113524: Washington to Ankara, decrypted 25 January 1943; HW1/1332, BJs 113499, 519, 521, 540, 541, 545, 548, 557: Budapest to various capitals, decrypted 27 January 1943.

74 PRO FO371/37503: Hugessen to Department, 28 January 1943.

75 Ian Jacob, unpublished typescript journal in Churchill Archives, Churchill College, Cambridge, p. 122.

76 PRO FO371/44148: PM to Eden, Eden to PM, 19 January 1943.

77 PRO FO371/37466: Hugessen to department. 'Modesty forbids me to tell you that my staff had nothing whatever to do with it.'

78 PRO FO371/37503, R1084/265/44, no. 240, Hugessen to FO, 7 February 1943.

Chapter 6

1 Churchill, op. cit., *The Hinge of Fate* and *Closing the Ring*; London, Cassell, 1951 and 1952. Martin Gilbert, *The Road to Victory: Winston S. Churchill 1941–5*; London, Heinemann, 1986, pp. 322ff.

2 Churchill, op. cit., *The Hinge of Fate*, pp. 629–41.

3 See e.g. David Carlton, *Anthony Eden*; London, Allen Lane, 1981, p. 207: 'Eden's difference with Churchill over Adana was to have considerable long term significance.'

4 Churchill, op. cit., p. 627.

5 PRO FO371/37645: War Cabinet to Churchill, 25 January 1943.

6 Hugessen gives a vivid account of his and the president's departure from a small town outside Ankara, to preserve secrecy, which the arrival of a snowstorm and many Turkish labourers to clear the roads and railway totally aborted. See *Diplomat in Peace and War*; London, John Murray, 1949, pp. 129ff. For the environs of Adana see Adrian Seligman, *No Stars to Guide*; London, Hodder and Stoughton, 1947.

7 Typo in the printed text.

8 PRO FO371/37465, R795/55 G44 and R709/TOO21302/3; Ivan Maisky to FO of 31 January 1943; Churchill, op. cit., p. 628.

9 Churchill, op. cit., pp. 630–8.

10 Ibid.

11 Quoted in Arthur Bryant (ed), *The Turn of the Tide: Alanbrooke 1939–45*; London, Collins, 1957, pp. 572–3.

12 This and following quotes are all from Ian Jacob, unpublished typescript journal of the Adana Conference, Churchill College Archives, Cambridge, JACB 1/16.

13 Jacob made a sketch of this, available in the Churchill Archive.

14 Jacob, op. cit., p. 127.

15 Jacob, op. cit., p. 128. See also PRO FO/371/44083 for George Clutton's minute on problems of maintaining living standards for British personnel in Turkey – 'a backward country and financially very dicky'. These are rare occurrences of Britons observing upcountry Turkey.

16 Jacob, op. cit., p. 132.

17 See Sir Hughe Knatchbull-Hugessen, *Diplomat in Peace and War*; London, John Murray, 1949, pp. 112ff.

18 PRO FO371/37645: Clutton handwritten minute.

19 See Sir Hughe Knatchbull-Hugessen, *Diplomat in Peace and War*; London, John Murray, 1947.

20 Jacob, op. cit., p. 133.

21 Jacob, op. cit., p. 135.

22 Jacob, op. cit., p. 136.

23 Interview with Falla. See also Churchill, op. cit., p. 636.

24 Jacob, op. cit., pp. 137–8.

25 Hugessen manuscript diary for 1943 in the Churchill Archives at Churchill College, Cambridge.

26 PREM3/446/10, p. 564.

27 PREM FO371/37645, Churchill to Eden.

28 Jacob, op. cit., pp. 139–40.

29 Jacob, op. cit., p. 141.

30 Jacob, op. cit., p. 143.

31 Summarised in Churchill, op. cit., vol. 4, p. 636; in full in PRO FO954 and PRO PREM3/446 *passim*.

32 Barker, op. cit., p. 208.

33 Jacob, op. cit., pp. 147, 150–51, 152.

34 PRO FO3711/37465 R709: Stratagem c/3 on 31 January 1943.

35 Sir James Butler (ed), *History of the Second World War*; UK Military Series *The Mediterranean and Middle East*: Maj-Gen I.S.O. Playfair with Brig C.J.C. Molony et al, vol. 4 'The Destruction of the Axis Forces in Africa'; London, HMSO, 1966.

36 David Dilks (ed), *The Diaries of Sir Alexander Cadogan O.M. 1938–45*; London, Cassell, 1971, p. 509.

37 Irving, op. cit., p. 178. The document is dated 14 February 1943.

38 Churchill, op. cit., vol. 4 p. 638.

39 Deringil, op. cit., pp. 146 and 214.

40 PRO FO371/30076.

41 PRO FO371/37645 709: unparaphrased version of a Most Secret Cipher Telegram, February 1943, not One Time Table (=2130z/31 (NOCOP) 9 i.e. no copies).

42 Lord Moran, *The Struggle for Survival*; London, Constable, 1966, pp. 83–6. He later noted that Churchill's failure to induce İnönü to declare war on the Axis at their next meeting at Cairo in November 1943 made him physically ill.

43 Arthur Bryant (ed), *The Alanbrooke Diaries*; London, Collins, 1957, p. 571. Jacob, op. cit.

44 Hugessen's MS diary, CCC, op. cit.

45 PRO HW1/1346, BJ 113743, and ISOS (intelligence source Oliver Strachey, the GCCS cryptographer who solved the Abwehr cipher): Ankara to Berlin contain the aborted plan to poison Churchill and see earlier Chapter 1.

46 This text appears in a telegram from CSS ('C') 'for Gibraltar' encoded by B.L. at 13.30 hours on 4 February 1943. 'Two copies based on VD [?SD] most secret material.' Both the SD and Abwehr cipher systems had been broken and were referred to as ISOS. The text quoted above is supported in the HW1 files by intercept X111/31 Tangier to Berlin 1529 of 5 February, for PARSIFAL: 'Schultze [2nd Press Attaché, Tangier] has despatched two Wasani men and one Torres, and he himself took one Wasani man, to the frontier at Alcazar, on 4th January [*sic*] with an assignment against Churchill. If the attack on Churchill does not succeed, they are to use the material given them for acts of sabotage. (signed) Schultze.' 'C' passed this via SCU (special ?cipher unit) zzzzz as follows: 'a) tested source reports at least four saboteurs with necessary material crossed frontier on February 4th to take action against Churchill. b) inform Brigadier and Eisenhower immediately. Distribution C.S.S. and Section s [i.e. at Bletchley Park]. Encoded by Baker at 2015 hours on 5 February.' The text of two Isosicles (jargon for ISOS) was passed to 'C'. '1) X111/31 Please dispatch urgently 20 to 50 machine pistols with ammunition, magnetic mines adhesive mines [*Klebminen*]. Also poisons for [adding to] drinks and effective upon bodily contagion. Some saccharine for a diabetic female relative of TONI MUH 2) 10 magnetic mines went off today to be used against USA tanks. Organisation for the housing of the material and distribution of required amounts, also immediate operation, taken care of at our end. MUHAM.' PRO HW1/1346, BJ 113743.

47 PRO PREM3/446/14, PM to Stalin, 6 February 1943.

48 PRO FO371/37516, Cadogan to Department, 6 February 1943.

49 The document was written, on internal evidence, by Cadogan.

50 Churchill, op. cit., vol. 4 pp. 713–4.

51 It is to be found in HW1/1348.

52 PRO HW1/1346, BJ 113744, 4 February 1943: Ankara to Vichy.

53 PRO HW1/1210, BJ 112093: Sofia to Tokyo, decrypted 10 February 1943; ticked by Churchill.

54 PRO HW1/1348, BJ 113849: Ankara to Tokyo, decrypted 6 February 1943.

55 See also PRO HW1/ 1387, BJ 11439 of 20 February 1943: 'Turkey's role is to sound German views on how to avoid the Bolshevisation of Europe, and a separate peace between Germany and the Western Allies.'

56 Malcolm Muggeridge (ed), *The Ciano Diaries 1939–45*; New York, Doubleday, 1946, p. 71.

57 PRO HW1/1240, BJ 112341 and 112369: Ankara to Tokyo, both decrypted 20 February 1943.

58 PRO HW1/1240, BJ 112370/29: Berlin to all points south and east (Ankara, Vichy, Rome, Madrid, Berne). This BJ, like others in this period, was shown to G20 in Washington.

59 PRO HW1/1348: Ankara to all stations, decrypted 6 February 1943.

60 PRO FO371/37516, FO to MEW7301: 'price not to be the determining factor. Both we and the Germans are going to pay heavily for the chrome but it will be the Turks who will fix the price.'

61 PRO FO371/34461: Clutton handwritten minute re Jackson, sent by the State Department to add muscle to the FO's dithering over chrome shipments.

62 PRO FO371/37460 and PRO PREM3/446.

63 PRO FO371/37509 and PRO FO 371/37399. Sir Orme Sargent minuted 'the great importance attached to chrome not only from the point of view of Anglo-Turkish relations but because it is also the touchstone of Turco-German relations.'

64 PRO FO371/ 37491, R/123/123/44, Clutton, minute of 8 April 1943.

65 PRO FO371/37509, FO371/37465 – including 'we know from other sources'.

66 PRO HW1/1348, BJ 113731: Ankara to Tokyo, decrypted 6 February 1943. In the same files BJ 113849 carried Oshima's report to Tokyo that no change was expected in Berlin in Turkish policy towards Germany (decrypted 6 February 1943); also PRO HW1/1348, BJ 113855: Ankara to Lisbon, decrypted 6 February 1943: 'the Adana meeting was to urge Turkey into the war; and it failed. The plan was to polish off Tunisia, occupy Crete and the Dodecanese, attack the Balkans, occupy Thrace.' Neutrality was a word to be avoided, but the

Turks would plead lack of armaments. Churchill marked this 'important', for Alanbrooke to read.

67 PRO HW1/1377, to 'C': Moscow to Ankara, decrypted 13 February 1943.

68 PRO FO371/37509: Ankara to London, 1 March 1943.

69 PRO HW1/1627, BJ 115283/91: Bucharest to Lisbon; Ankara to Tokyo, decrypted 15 March 1943.

70 PRO HW1/1346/2189, BJ 115249 decrypted 4 February 1943. PRO PREM3/446/2. PRO PREM3/446/4 of 3 March: PRO FO371/37466 of 22 March 1943. Knox Helm in Ankara pressed for a multilateral guarantee from Britain to Turkey, but the FO rejected the suggestion. Also in Ankara Adm Kelly observed that 'an imperialistic Russia is more frightening than a thorough-going Communist Russia' – to which Dixon minuted 'good point'. Kelly was Churchill's personal appointee in Ankara and continually riled the Southern Department – e.g. 'we do not want a number of Admiral Kellys throwing spanners into the works in the course of independent conversations'. Meanwhile the air attaché in Ankara was having his nose put out of joint by the admiral and indulging in *Schadenfreude*.

71 PRO HW1/1638, BJ 115772: Ankara to Tokyo, decrypted 28 March 1943.

72 PRO HW1/1387, BJ 114391: Stockholm to Lisbon, decrypted 20 February 1943.

73 PRO HW1/1557/2831 BJ, decrypted 3 April 1943, HW1/1558/2832 decrypted 4 April 1943; HW1/1604 BJ 116456; BJs 116391, 116467, 116457.

74 PRO FO371/37460, FO to Ministry of Economic Warfare, 30 January 1943.

75 PRO FO371/37640: Sargent to Ankara, 7 February 1943; Deringil, op. cit., p. 147.

76 It is unlikely that Wilson would have access to these diplomatic comments on his Ankara visit, since GHQ Cairo received Boniface/Enigma but not diplomatic messages.

77 PRO HW1/1621, BJ 116615: Ankara to Tokyo, decrypted 20 April 1943.

78 PRO HW1/1621/3036, BJ 116613: Ankara to Tokyo, decrypted 4 April 1943. PRO HW1/1621/3036, BJ 11613: Ankara to Tokyo, decrypted 20 April 1943.

79 PRO FO371/37467, WO 208/892.

80 PRO FO371/36467, Cadogan to Department, 15 April 1943.

81 PRO FO371/R5310/55/44. FO371/34461, Sargent to Department.

82 PRO FO371/36467, Sargent, minute of 27 April 1943.

83 PRO HW1/1626, BJ 116723: Ankara to Tokyo, decrypted 22 April 1943.

84 PRO HW1/1626/3061, BJ 116723: London to Tokyo, decrypted 22 April 1943. PRO HW1/1632/3083, BJ 116798: Ankara to Tokyo, decrypted 24 April 1943.

85 Churchill, op. cit., vol. 4 pp. 782–99. Frank G. Weber, *The Evasive Neutral: Germany, Britain and the Quest for a Turkish Alliance in the Second World War*; Missouri, Missouri University Press, 1979, p. 47, and Gerard Mangune (ed), *The International Straits and the World*; Dordrecht, Kluwer, 1987. PRO HW1/1661/3171 BJ 117985, Berlin to Tokyo, decrypted 2 May 1943.

86 PRO HW1/1702, BJ 11719: Rome to Ankara, decrypted 24 May 1943; PRO HW1/1703/118, BJ 117915: London to Baghdad, decrypted 25 May 1943; PRO HW1/1707, Ultra summaries for Commodore Spencer (Churchill) 'to be handed over personally, then to retrieve document for destruction by yourself'. PRO HW1/1709, 445 (15R), sent 30 May 1943; PRO HW1/1715, BJ 118510: Rome to Ankara, decrypted 27 May 1943; PRO HW1/1716, BJ 118510: Rome to Ankara, decrypted 1 June 1943.

87 PRO HW1/1659/3171, BJ 117985: Berlin to Tokyo, decrypted 2 May 1943.

88 PRO HW1/1721, BJ 118658: Budapest to Tokyo, decrypted 7 June 1943.

89 PRO HW11/1715/3449, BJ 117650: Ankara to Moscow, decrypted 6 June 1943. PRO HW1/1716/3454 BJ of 6 June. HW1/1721/3465, BJ 118569: Vatican to Tokyo, decrypted 7 June 1943. HW1/1723/3476, BJ 118607: Rome to Tokyo, decrypted 8 June 1943. HW1/1721, BJ 118658, decrypted 7 June 1943. HW1/1729/55/3510, BJ 118730: Moscow to Ankara, decrypted 11 June 1943.

90 PRO HW1/1914/44077, BJ 129892: Ankara to Rio de Janeiro, decrypted 4 August 1943. HW1/1921, BJ 122660: Ankara to Tokyo, decrypted 25 August 1943.

Chapter 7

1 Churchill, op. cit., vol. 5 *Closing the Ring*, p. 181. Churchill was determined that the world should know his version of events, organised his directives and memoranda into accessible form before the end of 1943 and published his account in 1952.

2 See Sheila Lawlor, *Churchill and the Politics of War, 1940–1*; Cambridge, Cambridge University Press, 1994, for a definitive analysis of the part Churchill's own war histories plays in the historiography of the Second World War. The author concludes (p. 11), 'it is Churchill's history which is reflected in much subsequent interpretation'.

3 Brig C.J.C. Molony, *The Mediterranean and the Middle East*, vol. 5 and vol. 6 pt 1 *The Campaign in Sicily and the Campaign in Italy: 3 September 1943 till March 1944*; London, HMSO, 1973. Also F.H. Hinsley (with E.E. Thomas, C.F.G. Ransom and R.C. Knight); *British Intelligence in the Second World War: its Influence on Strategy and Operations*, vol. 3 pt 1 pp. 119–35.

4 John Ehrman, *Grand Strategy*, vol. 5; London, HMSO, 1956; Michael Howard, *Grand Strategy*, vol. 4 and his *Strategic Deception in the Second World War*; London, HMSO, 1990; Capt Stephen Roskill, *The War at Sea*, vols 1–3; London, Collins, 1954–61.

5 William Jackson, reviewing Hinsley, op. cit., vol. 3, pt 2 in *The Sunday Times*, 22 February 1992.

6 WO190/ 893 reference 22832.

7 Jeffrey Holland, *The Aegean Mission: Allied Operations in the Dodecanese, 1943*; Westport, Greenwood Press, 1988, pp. 167ff. See also Smith and Walker; *War in the Aegean*; London, Kimber, 1974.

8 PRO HW1/1800(3765), BJ 1196696: Istanbul to Tokyo, decrypted 6 July 1943.

9 By summer 1943 diplomatic intercepted traffic distributed in Whitehall had become known as Dedip.

10 Walker, op. cit., p. 58.

11 Soviet historians have given some of the credit for the Red Army's great tank battle victory in the Kursk salient to (among others) a British cryptographer working at Bletchley, who supplied the Russians with priceless information, derived from Boniface, on the thickness of German tank armour, enabling Soviet war workers to produce armour-piercing weaponry capable of knocking out the German tanks. (He was not, of course, authorised to do so.) His name was John Cairncross. (See C. Borovik, *The Philby Files*; London, Little Brown, 1994, p. 377.)

12 Arthur Bryant (ed), op. cit.; Alanbrooke diary entry for 28 October 1943.

13 Hugessen's manuscript diary entry for that date: typescript in Churchill College, Cambridge. Hugessen wished to appoint a British disabled ex-serviceman to the job but the FO said no (information from his daughter). See also F. von Papen, *Memoirs*; London, Deutsch, 1949, pp. 514ff: see also Chapter 8.

14 PRO W1/1881(3993), BJ 120354: Istanbul to Tokyo, decrypted 26 July 1943.

15 Churchill, op. cit., p. 84.

16 PRO HW1/1885(4003): Kuibyshev to Ankara, decrypted 27 July 1943. Kuibyshev was 500 km east of Moscow. The entire international diplomatic corps was relocated there in September 1941 on Stalin's orders, returning to Moscow in late 1943.

17 See L. Marsland Gander in *The Daily Telegraph* of 9 November 1943.

18 See Beesly, op. cit., p. 80.

19 These telegrams can be found in PRO PREM 31319, pp. 67, 84, 99, 161–3, 164, 165, 166–72, 184, and in *Principal War Telegrams and Memoranda* pt 3; London, Kraus, 1976.

20 See Hinsley, op. cit., vol. 3, pt 1, p. 618.

21 Trumbull Higgins, *Winston Churchill and the Second Front 1940–3*; Oxford, Oxford University Press, 1957, and Smith and Walker, op. cit., pp. 48 and 268ff.

22 Holland, op. cit., p. 168.

23 Churchill, op. cit., p. 182.

24 PRO HW1/2043(4450) naval headlines 810 of 25 July 1943.

25 The following PRO DIR/C HW1 files, all from 1943, contain messages directly relevant to British handling of the Dodecanese campaign: 2006; 2043(4550) of 25 July, naval headlines 810; 2051(4476) of 27 July; 2058 (4501) of 29 July; 2067 (4531) of 2 October; 2076 (4550) of 4 October; 2080 (4563) of 5 October; 2082 (4567) of 6 October; 2085 (4574) of 6 October; 2094 (4041) of 9 October; 2097, 2118 (4690) of 16 October; 2122 (4700) of 18 October; 2132 (4774) of 21 October; 2142 (4757) of 21 October; 2150 (4778) of 22 October; 2162 (4804) of 26 October; 2163 (4804) of 26 October; 2185, 2187 (4855) of 31 October; 2190 of 1 November; 2202 (4888) of 3 November; 2212, 2219 (4935) of 5 November; 2220 (4938) of 10 November; 2221 (4940) of 7 November; 2222 (4943) of 8 November; 2226 (4951) of 9 November; 2234 (4973) of 10 November; 2236 (4978) of 11 November.

26 1st Bn Durham Light Infantry, 29th Sqn RAF Regt with light AA weapons and 7th Sqn SAAF with seven Spitfires.

27 HW1/2051, intelligence report of Aegean situation, 27 September 1943.

28 TOO: Alternative acronym for OTP.

29 JP 5477: CX/MSS/ZTPGM 37717 to BB AM WO ADY (Broadway Buildings, Air Ministry, War Office, Admiralty): BJ 137725.

30 PRO HW1/2067 (4531) of 2 October 1943.

31 PRO HW1/2076 (4550) of 4 October 1943.

32 PRO HW1/2080 (4563) of 15 October 1943.

33 All from PREM 3/3/3 and *Principal Telegrams and Memoranda: Middle East Vol. 2* last section; London, Kraus, 1976.

34 The legend B% here might indicate input from Broadway Buildings (MI6) or more likely Hut 3 at Bletchley Park – elsewhere 'comment'. It is worth noting that the % symbol is also used regularly on those Venona decrypts which have recently been released by the National Security Agency on the Internet, indicating input from the cryptographic, assessment, discrimination or translation sections.

35 PRO HW1/2080 (4563) of 4 October and 2082 (4567) of 6 October 1943.

36 The report has the symbol C% indicating that 'C' had added his comment to the message.

37 Churchill, op. cit., p. 191.

38 Portal seems to have been too weak to deal with Tedder, as indeed he was with 'Bomber' Harris.

39 *Principal Telegrams and Memoranda* pt 3, document dated 1 November 1943.

40 PRO PREM 31319, D170/3: PM to COS: 'In 48 hours we shall know whether it is necessary to throw in the sponge all along the line.'

41 PRO HW1/2097 of 9 October 1943. Naval headlines 827 reported the minelayer *Bulgaria* laying mines off Cos.

42 PRO HW1/2145 decrypted 22 October 1943.

43 PRO HW1/2190 decrypted 1 November 1943.

44 PRO PREM 31319, p. 99, T1616/3.

45 PRO HW1/2822 (4935) decrypted 5 November 1943.

46 PRO HW1/2085 (4574) decrypted 6 October 1943.

47 PRO HW1/2219 (4574) decrypted 6 October 1943. PRO HW1 2080, decrypted 5 October 1943, carries three pages on which nation occupied each island.

48 PRO HW1/2220 (4938) decrypted 10 November 1943.

49 PRO HW1/2221 (4940) decrypted 7 November 1943.

50 'C' marked this 'important'.

51 PRO HW1/2238 (4984) decrypted 12 November 1943.

52 Hinsley, op. cit., vol. 3 pt 1 p. 127.

53 Ibid p. 134.

54 PRO HW1/2225 (4949), BJ 124726/406: Ankara to Tokyo, decrypted 11 November 1943.

55 Referred to by Churchill as 'Boniface'.

56 Stephen Roskill, *Churchill and the Admirals*; Collins, 1977, p. 328. Adm Willis's despatch on the Aegean operation was heavily censored before publication 'in order to eliminate all

references to the fact that British warships had made frequent use of Turkish territorial waters in order to prolong their patrols off the islands without returning to Alexandria to refuel.' See Adm Willis's *Memoirs* (Bibliography) and *Supplement to the London Gazette* of 8 October 1948.

57 A handwritten note at the head of the paper signed by CSS secretary requires 'all copies to be destroyed after passing to addressee – Following from Duty Office Hut 3 [at Bletchley Park].' The full Oshima paragraph is important enough to be worth quoting in its entirety: 'Menemencioğlu stated that the Soviet Ambassador to Turkey also was to have taken part in the conversations but he was unable to do so for reasons connected with his aeroplane, and the talks [at Cairo] took place between the British, the Americans and the Turks. Having decided, at the Tehran Conference, on Turkey's participation in the war, Roosevelt and Churchill pressed strongly for it, but there was considerable difference in the degree of their desire to secure it, for whereas Churchill's stand was one of threatening to suspend the supply of goods to Turkey, Roosevelt took up no such attitude. Eden adopted a most menacing line. It is clear that the Soviet Union also earnestly desires Turkey's entry into the war. When von Papen asked him whether, in the event of Turkey's non-participation, Great Britain and America would, in practice, apply sanctions, Menemencioğlu replied that he was firmly convinced that even England [? was not so strong as to enforce sanctions at the risk of making an enemy of Turkey] and America in any case would have no part in them. He had further stated categorically that Turkey had not given any promise to the British and Americans at the said Conference that she would come into the war under any conditions. (Ribbentrop added the comment that realising that Turkey, while not directly participating in the war, might grant the use of land and air bases in Turkish territory, the German Government had made it clear to the Turks that in such an event they would *consider that Turkey had entered the war.*' (Emphasis added.) PRO HW1/2292, BJ 12184: decrypted 16 December 1943; also PRO HW1/2279, BJ 126571: Berlin to Tokyo, decrypted 15 December.

58 Churchill, op. cit., *Closing the Ring* pp. 198–99 and 345–46.

59 *Foreign Relations of the United States* vol. 3; Washington, DC, Government Printing Office, 1964, pp. 476–82.

60 See Laurence Weisband, *Anticipating the Cold War: Turkish Foreign Policy 1943–5*; Princeton, New Jersey, Princeton University Press, 1973, pp. 173, 176.

61 The Earl of Avon, *The Eden Memoirs: The Reckoning*; London, Cassell, 1965, p. 419. See also Deringil, op. cit., p. 155.

62 Weisband, op. cit., p. 177 n 30.

63 PRO HW1/2145, decrypted 22 October 1943.

64 Churchill, op. cit., p. 173.

65 Irving, op. cit., p. 183.

66 See next chapter and Eleysa Basna, *I Was Cicero*; London, Andre Deutsch, 1962, and Ludwig Moyzisch, *Operation Cicero*; London, Wingate, 1947, pp. 148–65.

67 Deringil, op. cit., p. 157.

68 *FRUS*, vol. 3, op. cit., pp. 164–67, 174–75; and Weisband, op. cit., p. 178–79.

69 Churchill, op. cit., p. 362.

70 Deringil, op. cit., p. 215.

71 Sir Llewelyn Woodward, *British Foreign Policy in the Second World War*; London, HMSO, 1975, especially vol. 6, pp. 639ff.

72 I am grateful to Randal Gray for help over the Dodecanese chronology.

73 Holland, op. cit., p. 95.

74 Stephen Roskill, *Churchill and the Admirals*; London, Collins 1977, p. 222.

75 *Principal War Telegrams and Memoranda* vol. 3; London, Kraus, 1976.

76 PRO HW1/2253 (5040) naval headlines 868.

77 PRO PREM3/446/17.

78 Churchill, op. cit, vol. 5.

79 Lord Ismay; *Memoirs*; London, Heinemann, 1960, p. 331.

80 PRO HW1/2276, BJ 125337/1347 decrypted 12 December. See also Weisband, op. cit., p. 189.

81 Churchill, op. cit., p. 328.
82 Weisband, op. cit., p. 195.
83 *FRUS*, op. cit., pp. 476–82, and especially p. 478.
84 PRO HW1/2447 (5694), BJ 127854/77: Berlin to Tokyo, decrypted 9 February 1944.
85 Deringil, op. cit., p. 216.
86 Eden, op. cit., p. 429.
87 Churchill, op. cit., p. 357.
88 PRO HW 1/2287 (5173) of 14 December 1943: summaries.
89 PRO HW1/2289, BJ 126571: Ankara to all stations, decrypted 15 December 1943.
90 PRO HW11/2289, BJ 126101: Berlin to Tokyo, decrypted 15 December 1943.
91 PRO HW1/2289 BJ 126184/1460: Ankara to Berlin.
92 This instruction was not carried out, as is evidenced by its appearance in HW1.
93 PRO HW1/2289 MSS, BJ 126571: Berlin to Tokyo, decrypted 15 December 1943.
94 PRO HW1/2292, BJ 126184/1415: Berlin to Tokyo, decrypted 15 December 1943.
95 PRO HW1/2289, BJ 126571: Berlin to Tokyo, decrypted 15 December 1943.
96 PRO HW1/2298, BJ 126329: Berlin to Tokyo and all stations, decrypted 21 December 1943.
97 HW11/2309.

Chapter 8

1 Ludwig Moyzisch, *Operation Cicero*; London, Wingate, 1947. Walter Schellenberg, *The Schellenberg Memoirs*; London, Andre Deutsch, 1959, pp. 376ff. Eleysa Basna (with Hans Nogly), *I Was Cicero*; London, Andre Deutsch, 1962, esp pp. 62ff. Fritz von Papen, *Memoirs*; London, Andre Deutsch, 1952. Sir Hughe Knatchbull-Hugessen, *Diplomat in Peace and War*; London, John Murray, 1949. Hugessen also produced comments on Moyzisch's story in August 1956, in a series of papers kindly lent to me by his daughter, Alethea Knatchbull-Hugessen. He denied accompanying Basna on the piano and dismisses much of what Basna may be assumed to have told Moyzisch. Basna's own story was published six years later, and answers many of the questions Hugessen raises about what he was photographing. Unfortunately we do not have the ambassador's comments on *I Was Cicero*.

2 See Nicholas Elliott, *Never Judge a Man by his Umbrella*; London, Philip Russell, 1991, p. 133.

3 Eden wrote to Churchill about Hugessen: 'I consider it best to keep [him] where he is. There is another reason not mentioned in this telegram, namely that I want [Hugessen] to be in Angora [sic] when the officer we sent out to investigate charges [of insecurity] arrives there.' Memo dated 13 February 1944 in PRO FO371/44066. On Dashwood's return from Ankara he contacted the head of British diplomatic decryption in Berkeley Street who recorded this encounter in his appointments diary for 1944. 'Dine with Dashwood' was entered for 22 May 1944. It would be interesting to know what they talked about. As to where the thefts took place, Hugessen himself suggested they might have been from the chancery buildings – i.e. neither from the residence nor the embassy.

4 Allen Dulles, *The Craft of Intelligence*; New York, Harper and Row, 1963 and Dulles (ed), *Great True Spy Stories*; London, Robson, 1984, pp. 15ff, and his *The Secret Surrender*; London, Weidenfeld and Nicolson, 1967, pp. 22–24; Kim Philby, *My Silent War*; London, MacGibbon and Kee, 1967, p. 63: 'The telegrams exactly matched the intercepted telegrams already deciphered, and others, proving of the utmost value to [Denniston's] cryptographers in their breakdown of the German diplomatic code.' Elliott, op. cit., p. 133. See also Elliott's *With My Little Eye*; London, Phillip Russell, 1993, p. 122.

5 Nigel West, *Unreliable Witness: Espionage Myths of the Second World War*; London, Weidenfeld and Nicolson, 1984, pp. 99ff. David Kahn, *Hitler's Spies; German Military Intelligence in World War Two*; London, Hodder and Stoughton, 1978, pp. 340–46 and 591. On p. 342 he reproduces one 'of the documents that the spy CICERO photographed in the British

Embassy [*sic*] in Ankara (Angora) Turkey and telegram 1751 from the FO to Ankara quoting T-120, the National Archive designation for microfilms of German records. See also Anthony Cave Brown, *The Secret Servant: The Life of Sir Stewart Menzies, Churchill's Spymaster*; London, Michael Joseph, 1988, pp. 476ff; also Cave Brown, *Bodyguard of Lies*; London, Michael Joseph, 1978, pp. 399–401.

6 Bradley Smith, *The Shadow Warriors: OSS and the Origins of the CIA*; London, Andre Deutsch, 1983, pp. 131–33.

7 F.H. Hinsley, et al, *British Intelligence in the Second World War: its Influence on Strategy and Operations* vol. 3 pt 1; London, HMSO, 1984, pp. 501ff and 616; ibid, vol. 3 pt 2, London, HMSO, 1988, p. 1016; and ibid, vol. 4, London, HMSO, 1990, pp. 213–15, 230 and 506. 'Cicero certainly photographed a vast amount of material, some of it of the highest secrecy.' See also Howard, Michael; *Strategic Deception in the Second World War*; London, Pimlico, 1990.

8 Hinsley, op. cit., vol. 4, p. 214.

9 Moyzisch, op. cit. Anthony Cave Brown relies heavily on Moyzisch in his account of Cicero in *Bodyguard of Lies*, p. 400. Some of the more exotic details must have been lies told by Basna to Moyzisch, since Basna himself omits them in his own book.

10 Moyzisch, op. cit., p. 113.

11 Ibid p. 103.

12 Von Papen, op. cit., pp. 512–13.

13 Ibid p. 514.

14 Ibid p. 517. Telegram No. 36 of 7 January 1944 – Hugessen to FO – appears in von Papen's *Memoirs* – C.H. Fone in FO371 44064 pp. 23–26 (Moscow Conferences of October 1943); pp. 44–45 (approached German embassy on 26 November 1943; p. 58 (Moscow Conference) Telegram No. 875.

15 Basna, op. cit., p. 21.

16 Telegram No. 875 Ankara to London.

17 These, though undated, were written in 1963, as Hugessen refers to 'the whole episode, now twenty years old'. There are three papers: A) Cicero (4 pages); B) notes on Operation 'Cicero' (7 pages); and C) (no heading) (6 pages).

18 Basna, op. cit., pp. 35, 38. This is confirmed by private information from Rachel Maxwell-Hyslop.

19 Cave Brown, quoting some disenchanted British diplomats as saying he played extremely badly, is wrong here: all the evidence amassed by this diplomatic research suggests the contrary. His daughter, however, reported that Lady Hugessen was not the most appreciative of audiences.

20 Though with counterfeit British money.

21 Ibid, p. 60.

22 Kahn, op. cit., p. 343.

23 Schellenberg thought the plain texts of the telegrams might be useful to the *Forschungsamt* in reading the British diplomatic cipher, but as the FO routinely used the OTP which was by definition unreadable, Cicero's material was not usable.

24 Nigel West, *Unreliable Witness: Espionage Myths of the Second World War*; London, Weidenfeld and Nicolson, 1984, p. 104. Hitler definitely learned that Operation 'Overlord' would take place on the Normandy beaches from Cicero material, as one of his aides records his astonishment not that the Allies had made this decision but that the British FO had thought it necessary to inform its ambassador in Turkey of the fact. (Information from David Irving.)

25 Dulles, *The Craft of Intelligence*, op. cit., p. 153.

26 PRO HW1/2292, decrypted 18 December 1943. Preamble scrambled to Duty Office Hut 3 (BP) 7.10 p.m. same date. 'Following for ?Robertson from "C": Pass following to Martin for Colonel Warden [Churchill] from "C". Following from Duty Officer Hut 3 from CSS secretary. All copies to be destroyed after passing to addressee.' The full text of Oshima's report was distributed to twenty regular recipients of BJs, including of course Churchill who would not have been content with the FO's summary sent by Eden.

27 Kermit Roosevelt, *The War Report of the OSS*, p. 278.

28 Ibid.
29 Information supplied to Rupert Allason, MP, and quoted in, op. cit., p. 106.
30 The 1942–43 Venona intercepts from the Internet were kindly lent me by Rupert Allason.
31 See Appendix 7.
32 See P.W. Filby, 'Floradora and a Unique Break into One-time Pad Ciphers', in *Intelligence and National Security*, vol. 10, no. 3, 1995, pp. 408–22, for a recent technical account of how Floradora and the German diplomatic cipher OTP system were solved.
33 DENN 1/4 in the Churchill Archives; also PRO HW3/32, as well as the edited version in *Intelligence and National Security*, vol. 1, no. 1, 1986, p. 56.
34 'Later events suggest that Allen Dulles of OSS Berne and Philby of Section V provided technical evidence in 1943 that led to the large-scale decryption of Floradora from late 1943 onwards.' Cave Brown, *The Secret Servant*, op. cit., p. 406.
35 Philby, *My Silent War*, op. cit., p. 63.
36 Ibid p. 63.
37 PRO HW1 2743 (6351) dated 26 April 1944.
38 See F.H. Hinsley's entry on Denniston in *The Dictionary of National Biography*, supplementary volume 1950–59; Oxford, Oxford University Press, 1979.

Chapter 9

1 J. Ehrman, *History of the Second World War – UK Military Series* (ed J.R.M. Butler): *Grand Strategy*, vol. 5; London, HMSO, 1956, especially pp. 88–103 on the Dodecanese fighting in autumn 1943. G.E. Kirk, 'The War and the Neutrals' in *Survey of International Affairs 1939–46*; Oxford, Oxford University Press, 1956. W.N. Medlicott, *The Economic Blockade*, vols 1 and 2, from *History of the Second World War*. United Kingdom Civil Series (ed Sir Keith Hancock): vol. 1 chapters on Turkey pp. 269–79 and 18 pp. 601ff; vol. 2 chapters 8 and 18; also pp. 236–54 and 525ff; London, HMSO, 1952 and 1959.

2 Brig E.T. Williams, Montgomery's chief intelligence officer, reported on 5 October 1945: 'Very few armies went into battle better informed of their enemy and it is recognised by those who ostensibly provided the information that they were but useful hyphens between the real producers at Bletchley Park and the real consumers, the soldier in the field whose life was made that much easier by the product.' War Office WO/208/3575 'Birth of Ultra'.

3 Hennessy, *Whitehall*, op. cit., p. 79.

4 E. Basna (with Hans Nogly), *I Was Cicero*; London, Andre Deutsch, 1962, p. 72.

Bibliography

Primary Sources

Public Record Office

ADM1	Admiralty and Secretarial Papers.
ADM223	Naval Intelligence Division.
AIR40	Directorate of Air Intelligence.
CAB23	Cabinet Minutes.
FO195	Embassy and Consular Archives Turkey: correspondence.
FO198	Embassy and Consular Archives Turkey: miscellaneous.
FO226	Embassy and Consular Archives Turkey: Beirut correspondence, etc.
FO366	Chief Clerk's Dept Archives.
FO371	FO general correspondence: the main series of FO papers.
FO837	Industrial Intelligence Centre and MEW.

For DIR/C (HW1) and other HW files see Appendix 1.

FO371

These are FO general correspondence, arranged by date, nation, topic. Since recipients burnt their BJs immediately after use, the FO371 series contain no wartime diplomatic sigint though plenty of summaries, paraphrases, 'gists' and general references.

Other PRO Sources

Premier Series

PREM1	Correspondence and papers of the PM's office.
PREM3	Operational papers of the PM's office. PREM3/446 contains almost all the relevant Turkey material: also PREM3/448.
PREM4	Confidential papers of the PM's office. These include unsent drafts of memos and internal correspondence between Churchill and his staff, often very informal.

DEFE	
DEFE3	Intelligence from enemy radio communications: SCU/SLU signals to Allied commands conveying special intelligence reports based on intelligence from German naval and air force traffic; teleprinted translations of decrypted German and Italian naval radio messages (3.2. 963). These are Enigma messages processed through the Special Liaison Units for commanders in the field. There is overlap between the teleprints in DIR and those in DEFE3.

WO
WO32/4897, WO204/893 and WO208/3573.

Other Locations

Churchill College, Cambridge (Churchill Archives)
DENN1/3 (also in HW3/2).
DENN1/4 (see Appendix 7).
HALL papers.
Hughe Knatchbull-Hugessen diary for 1943 (manuscript).
Ian Jacob war diary covering the Adana Conference (typescript).

House of Lords Library
Lloyd George papers: F/209 7/10/1922 contain intercepts of Turkish diplomatic messages from the Turkish ambassador in Paris to Constantinople, as a result of reading which Churchill, with Lloyd George, Curzon and Lord Lee, instigated the Chanak crisis of 1922.

India Office Library
Prewar product of GCCS, including L/WS/1/73 and 72 – weekly letters from MI WO in 1939.

Canada: National Archives of Canada (NAC)

RG25: see Appendix 2

Internet
Venona 1943: see Appendix 4.

Unpublished histories, private papers, memoirs and diaries
Lord Alanbrooke papers, LHCMA, King's College, London.
Sir Alexander Cadogan papers, PRO and Churchill College, Cambridge.
Winston Churchill papers, Churchill College, Cambridge.
Clarke, W.F.; *From Room 40 OB to Bletchley Park*; Churchill College, Cambridge.
Hugh Dalton's typescript diaries of the war: held at the London School of Economics.
Alastair Denniston's papers in Churchill College, Cambridge.
Oliver Harvey's manuscript diary in BM.
Sir Hughe Knatchbull-Hugessen papers, PRO and Churchill College, Cambridge.
Lt-Gen Sir (Edward) Ian Jacob GBE, CB, DL 1899–1993. A number of his reports in 1942–43 of his travels with Churchill were deposited in the Churchill College Archives in 1994.
Sir Patrick Reilly: unpublished wartime memoir with useful material on the role and function of the MEW: pp. 2–9, 12, 17, 18, 24, 26–30, 32–3, 34–6, 38–42, 45–50, 54, 58–63, 65–7, 71–5, 85–92 (kindly lent me by its author).

Published Documents
Cantwell, John D.; *The Second World War: a guide to documents in the PRO*; London, HMSO, revised edn 1993.
Documents on British Foreign Policy 1919–1939, 2nd and 3rd series; London, HMSO, 1955–84.
Foreign Relations of the United States, Diplomatic Papers 1941; vol. 111; Washington, DC, Government Printing Office, 1943–64.
Documents on German Foreign Policy, 1918–45. War Years, 1940–41 Series D; vol. 10 (23 June–31 August 1940); vol. 11 (1 September 1940–31 January 1941); vol. 12 (1 February–22 June 1941); vol. 13 (23 June–1 December 1941).
Documents on British Foreign Policy, 1919–1939, Series 3; vol. 5 (4 April–8 June 1939); vol. 8 (15 August to 3 September 1939).
Gilbert, Martin; Companion volumes to vol. V of *Winston S. Churchill*; (i) 1922–29 London, Heinemann, 1979. (ii) 1929–35 London, Heinemann, 1981.(iii) 1936–39 London, Heinemann,

1982. Also two companion volumes: *The War Years* (i) *First Sea Lord September 1939–June 1940*; (ii) *Prime Minister: June–December 1940*; London, Heinemann, 1993 and 1994.

Irving, David (ed); *Breach of Security: The German secret intelligence file on events leading to the Second World War*; London, Kimber, 1968, pp. 123–166 and 175–184.

Kimball, W. (ed); *Churchill and Roosevelt: The Complete Correspondence*, vol. 2 'Alliance Forged' November 1942–February 1944; Princeton, Princeton University Press, 1984.

Principal War Telegrams and Memoranda, 1940–3 'The Middle East'; London, Kraus, 1976.

Führer Conferences: German Navy 1940, 1942.

Review of the Foreign Press 1939–45, Series A; vol. 5 nos 93–117 7/7–22/12–41; RIIA/Kraus, p. 504.

Keesing's Archives: 1943–5.

Who Was Who; London, A. and C. Black.

Published Memoirs and Diaries

Annan, Noel; *Changing Enemies: The Defeat and Regeneration of Germany*; London, HarperCollins, 1995.

Basna, Eleysa; *I Was Cicero*; London, Andre Deutsch, 1962.

Bond, Brian (ed); *Chief of Staff: The Diaries of Lieutenant General Sir Henry Pownall*, vol. 1 1933–40; London, Leo Cooper, 1972.

Brooke-Rose, Christine; *Remake*; Manchester, Carcanet, 1995, esp. p. 108.

Bryant, Arthur (ed); *The Turn of the Tide: Alanbrooke 1939–45*; London, Collins, 1957.

Chandler, A.D.(ed); *The Papers of Dwight D. Eisenhower: The War Years*, vol. 2; Baltimore, 1970.

Churchill, Winston S.; *The Second World War:*

  Vol. 2 *Their Finest Hour*; London, Cassell, 1949.

  Vol. 3 *The Grand Alliance*; London, Cassell, 1950.

  Vol. 4 *The Hinge of Fate*; London, Cassell, 1951.

  Vol. 5 *Closing the Ring*; London, Cassell, 1952.

  Vol. 6 *Triumph and Tragedy*; London, Cassell, 1952.

Ciano, Galeazzo (ed M. Muggeridge); *Diplomatic Papers*; London, Odhams, 1949, p. 456.

—— (ed Hugh Gibson); *Diaries* ; New York, Doubleday, 1946.

Clayton, Aileen; *The Enemy is Listening*; London, Hutchinson, 1980.

Colville, Sir John; *Downing Street Years*; London, Collins, 1985.

Cooper, Duff; *Old Men Forget*; London, Heinemann, 1946.

Dilks, David (ed); *The Diaries of Sir Alexander Cadogan O.M. 1938–45*; London, Cassell, 1971.

Dixon, Piers; *Double Diploma: The Life of Sir Pierson Dixon, Don and Diplomat*, compiled from diary entries edited by his son (Foreword by R.A. Butler); London, Hutchinson, 1968.

Doenitz, Admiral K.; *Memoirs: 10 Years and Twenty Days*; London, Weidenfeld and Nicolson, 1958.

Dulles, Allen; *The Secret Surrender*; London, Weidenfeld and Nicolson, 1967.

——; *The Craft of Intelligence*; New York, Harper and Row, 1963.

—— (ed); *Great True Spy Stories*; London, Robson Books, 1968.

Eccles, David; *By Safe Hand*; London, Bodley Head, 1983.

Eden, Anthony; *The Reckoning: 1938–45*; London, Cassell, 1965.

Halder, Franz (ed Charles Burdick and Hans-Adolf Jacobsen); *The Halder War Diary 1939–42*; New York, Greenhill Books, 1988.

Harvey, Oliver; *The War Diaries of Oliver Harvey 1941–5*; London, John Murray, 1978.

Hitler, Adolf; *Table Talk 1941–4*; London, Weidenfeld and Nicolson, 1953.

Hoare, Sir Samuel (Lord Templewood); *Diplomat in Spain*; London, Collins, 1954.

——; *Ambassador on Special Mission*; London, Collins, 1946.

Hollingsworth, Clare; *There's a German Just Behind Me*; London, Secker and Warburg, 1942.

Howarth, David (ed); *Intelligence Chief Extraordinary: The Life of the Ninth Duke of Portland*; London, Bodley Head, 1986.

Ismay, Gen Sir Hastings; *Memoirs*; London, Heinemann, 1969.

Knatchbull-Hugessen, Sir Hughe; *Diplomat in Peace and War*; London, John Murray, 1949.

Macmillan, Harold; *War Diaries: Politics and War in the Mediterranean January 1943–May 1945*; London, Macmillan, 1984.

Maisky, Ivan; *Who Helped Hitler?*; London, Gollancz, 1964.

Marshall-Cornwall, Gen Sir James; *Wars and Rumours of Wars*; London, Leo Cooper, 1954.

Massigli, René; *La Turquie devant La Guerre – Mission a Ankara 1939–49*; Paris, Plon, 1962.

Meynell, Francis; *My Lives*; London, Bodley Head, 1971.

Moran, Lord; *Churchill: the Struggle for Survival*; London, Constable, 1966.

Moravec, Frederic; *Master of Spies*; London, Bodley Head, 1975.

Moyzisch, Ludwig; *Operation Cicero*; London, Wingate, 1947.

Muggeridge, Malcolm; *The Infernal Grove*, vol. 2 of 'Chronicles of Wasted Time'; London, Collins, 1973.

Papen, Fritz von (translated by Brian Connell); *Memoirs*; London, Deutsch, 1952.

Philby, Kim; *My Silent War*; London, Macgibbon and Kee, 1967.

Schellenberg, Walter; *Memoirs*; London, Deutsch, 1959.

Welchman, Gordon; *The Hut Six Story: Breaking the Enigma Codes*; London, Penguin, 1983.

Wilson, Field Marshal Sir Henry Maitland (Lord Wilson of Libya); *Ten Years Abroad*; London, Hutchinson, 1948.

——; *Operations in the Middle East from February 1943 to January 1944*, supplement to the *London Gazette,* 12 November 1946.

Winterbotham, Frederick W.; *The Ultra Secret*; London, Weidenfeld and Nicolson, 1974.

Secondary Sources

Unpublished Theses and Lectures
Bailey, J.; *The Lion, the Eagle and the Crescent*, Western Allies in Turkey in 1943; PhD Georgetown, 1969.

Catherwood, C.; *Turkey in British Foreign Policy 1935–41*; Cambridge.

Koymen, O.; *A Comparative Study of Anglo-Turkish Relations 1830–70 and 1919–39*; Strathclyde, 1967.

Leavey, W.; *Hitler's Envoy Extraordinary; Fritz von Papen*; Ann Arbor.

Lippe, J.M. Van der; *Decade of Struggle: Ismet İnönü and Turkish Politics*; Austin, Texas PhD, 1993.

Miner, S.; *Stalin's Minimum Terms; the USSR and Great Britain 1940–42*; Indiana PhD, 1987.

Pearton, Maurice; *Britain and Turkey 1939–41*; text of a lecture delivered at the SSEES, kindly supplied by the author.

Roberts, Geoffrey; *The Unholy Alliance; Stalin's pact with Russia*; Indiana UP, 1989.

Robertson, J.; *Anglo-Turkish Relations*; LSE/Garland, 1982.

Trask, R.R.; *Relations Between the USA and Turkey*; Penn State, 1959.

Ulam, A.; *Expansionism and Co-existence: Soviet Foreign Policy*; NY, 1968.

Journal articles
Andrew, Christopher (ed); 'The Government Code and Cypher School Between the Wars' by A.G. Denniston, in *Intelligence and National Security*, vol. 1 no. 1 (1986).

——; 'The British Secret Service and Anglo-Soviet Relations in the 1920s: Part 1: from the trade organisation to the Zinoviev Letter' in *Historical Journal*, vol. 20 no. 3 (1977).

——; 'British Intelligence and the Breach with Russia in 1927' in *Historical Journal*, vol. 25 no. 4 (1982).

——; 'Churchill and Intelligence' in *Intelligence and National Security*, vol. 2 (1986).

Benton, Kenneth; 'The ISOS Years: Madrid 1941' in *Journal of Contemporary History*, vol. 3 no. 4.

Denniston, Robin; 'Yardley's Diplomatic Secrets' in *Cryptologia*, vol. 18 no. 2 (1994).

——; 'Fetterlein and Others' in *Cryptologia*, vol. 19 no. 1.

——; 'Yardley on Yap' in *Intelligence and National Security*, vol. 9 no. 1 (1994).

——; 'Diplomatic Eavesdropping 1922–44: A New Source Discovered' in *Intelligence and National Security*, vol. 10 no. 3.

Deringil, Selim; 'The Preservation of Turkey's Neutrality in World War Two: 1940' in *Middle Eastern Studies*, vol. 18 no. 1 (1982).

Dovey, H.O.; 'The Intelligence War In Turkey' in *Intelligence and National Security*, vol. 9 no. 1.

Farrell, B.F.; 'Yes, Prime Minister: Barbarossa, Whipcord and the Basis of British Grand Strategy Autumn 1941' in *Journal of Military History*, vol. 57, no. 4 (1993).

Ferris, John; 'Whitehall's Black Chamber: British cryptology and the Government Code and Cipher School, 1921–29' in *Intelligence and National Security*, vol. 2, no. 1 (1987).

——; 'From Broadway House to Bletchley Park: The Diary of Captain Malcolm Kennedy, 1934–46' in *Intelligence and National Security*, vol. 3, no. 1.

——; review article on Hinsley, F.H. and Stripp, A. (eds); *Codebreakers*; Oxford, Oxford University Press, 1993, in *Intelligence and National Security*, vol. 9, no. 2 (1994).

——; 'Indulged in All Too Late: Vansittart, Intelligence and Appeasement' in *Diplomacy and Statecraft*, vol. 6, no. 1 (1995).

Filby, P.W.; 'Bletchley Park and Berkeley Street' in *Intelligence and National Security*, vol. 3, no. 2.

——; 'Floradora and a Unique Break into One-Time Pad Ciphers' in *Intelligence and National Security*, vol. 10, no. 3.

French, David; 'The Dardanelles, Mecca and Kut: Prestige as a Factor in British Eastern Strategy, 1914–16' in *War and Society*, vol. 5, no. 1 (1987).

——; 'The Origins of the Dardanelles Campaign Reconsidered' in *History* (1983).

Geiser, L.; 'The Turkish Air Force 1939–45' in *Middle Eastern Studies*, vol. 26, no. 3 (1990).

Handel, M.I.; 'Strategic and Operational Deception in the Second World War' in *Intelligence and National Security*, vol. 2, no. 3 (1987).

Harrison, E.B.R.; 'Some Reflections on Kim Philby's My Silent War as a historical source' in *Occasional Papers in Politics and Contemporary History*, no. 3.

Neilson, K.; 'Pursued by a Bear: British Estimates of Soviet Military Strength and Anglo-Soviet Relations 1922–39' in *Canadian Journal of History* (1992).

Stafford, David; 'Sigint Secrets (1)' in *Canadian Journal of History* (forthcoming).

Russian, Turkish, Czech, German and Bulgarian Scholarly Articles
Czech

Teichman, Miroslav; *Turecko a velmoci fasusticke osy a antihitlerovske koalice v letech druhe svetove valky* [Turkey and the anti-Hitler coalition during the Second World War] in *Slovansky Prehled* [Czechoslovakia] 1983 69(3) 36B: 3128. abstract: During WW2 Turkey declared its neutrality but despite that continued to supply Germany with food, *matériel* and chrome.

German

Bonjour, Edgar; *Turkische und Schweizerische Neutralitaet waehrend des Zwei Weltkrieges*; Geneva: Institute University de hautes Etudes Internationales, 1981, pp. 199–213.

Heinz, Hurmhofel; *Die Tuerkei und die Sowietunion 1939–54 in Osteuropa 5*; (1955) pp. 21–33.

Hoppe, Hans-Joachim; *Neutralen Staaten in Suedosteneuropa* in *Les Etats entre European et la Seconde Guerre Mondiale*; Neuchatel, Editions de la Baconniere, 1985, pp. 229–42.

Krecker, Lothar; *Deutschland und die Tuerkei in Zwei Weltkriegen*; Klostermann, 1964.

Soenmez, Erguen; *Die okou political in militarische Abhaugigheit der Turkei von den entwickelten Kapitalist*; Berlin, 1978 (dissertation).

Turkish

Gurun, Kamuran; *Turkiye'yi 11. dunya savas'na sokma cabalari* [efforts to pull Turkey into WW2]; Belleten, Turkey, 1988.

Melzig, Herbert; *Turkiye Hatiralari* (Memoirs of Turkey) in *Tarih ve Toplum* (1989), p. 65.

Bulgarian
Petrov, Liudmil; *Voennata Politika Na Turtsiia i Otnoshenieto i Kum bulgariia prez vtorata svetovna voina 91939–44) Godina* [Turkish military policy and relations with Bulgaria in WW2] in *Voennoistoricheski Sbornik*; Sofia, (1988) 57/4 pp. 34–52.

Other Secondary Sources
Andrew, Christopher; *Secret Service: The making of the British Intelligence Community*; London, Heinemann, 1985.
—— with Dilks, David; *The Missing Dimension: Governments and Intelligence Communities in the Twentieth Century*; London, Macmillan, 1984.
—— with Noakes, J.; *Intelligence and International Relations 1900–45*; Exeter Studies in History no. 15, 1987.
—— with Gordievsky, Oleg; *KGB: The Inside Story of Its Foreign Operations from Lenin to Gorbachev*; London, Hodder and Stoughton, 1990.
Turkkaya Ataov; *Turkish Foreign Policy 1939–45*; Ankara, 1965.
——; *Turkey and NATO*; Ankara, 1970.
Barker, Elisabeth; *British Policy in South East Europe in World War Two*; London, Secker and Warburg, 1978.
——; *Churchill and Eden at War*; London, Secker and Warburg, 1982.
Beesly, Patrick; *Room 40: British Naval Intelligence 1914–18*; London, Hamish Hamilton, 1982.
Bennett, Ralph; *Ultra and Mediterranean Strategy 1941–5*; London, Hamish Hamilton, 1989.
——; *Behind the Battle: Intelligence in the War against Germany 1941–5*; London, Sinclair Stevenson, 1994.
——; *Ultra in the West*; London, Hutchinson, 1979.
Best, Anthony; *Britain, Japan and Pearl Harbor: Avoiding War in East Asia 1936–41*; London, Routledge, 1995.
Blake, R. and Louis, R.L. (eds); *Churchill*; Oxford, Oxford University Press, 1993.
Borovik, C.; *The Philby Files*; London, Little, Brown, 1994.
Boyd, Carl; *Hitler's Confidant: General Oshima Hiroshi and Magic Intelligence 1941–5*; Kansas, Kansas University Press, 1993.
Bryden, John; *Best-Kept Secret: Canadian Secret Intelligence in the Second World War*; Toronto, Lester, 1993.
Butler, J.R.M.; *Grand Strategy*, vol. 2 September 1939–June 1941; London, HMSO, 1957.
Calvocoressi, Peter; *Top Secret Ultra*; London, Cassell, 1980.
Carlton, David; *Anthony Eden*; London, Allen Lane, 1981.
Cave Brown, Anthony; *Bodyguard of Lies*; New York, Harper, 1967.
——; *The Secret Servant: The Life of Sir Stewart Menzies, Churchill's Spymaster*; London, Michael Joseph, 1988.
——; *Treason in the Blood*; London, Robert Hale, 1994.
Charnley, John; *Churchill: The End of Glory*; London, Hodder and Stoughton, 1993.
Clark, Alan; *Barbarossa: The Russian-German Conflict 1941–5*; London, Hutchinson, 1965.
Clark, Ronald; *The Man Who Broke Purple*; Boston, Little, Brown, 1977.
Collingwood, R.G.; *The New Leviathan*; Oxford, Oxford University Press, 1940.
Costello, John and Tsarev, P.; *Deadly Illusions: The First Book from the KGB Archives*; London, Random House, 1993.
Cowling, Maurice; *The Impact of Hitler: British politics 1933–40*; Cambridge, Cambridge University Press, 1975.
Dallin, David; *Soviet Russia's Foreign Policy*; Hertford, Yale University Press, 1942.
Deighton, Anne (ed); *Britain and the First Cold War*; London, Macmillan, 1990.
Deist, W. et al.; *Germany and World War Two*, vols 1 and 2; Oxford, Oxford University Press, 1992.
Deringil, Selim; *Turkish Foreign Policy During World War Two*; Cambridge, Cambridge University Press, 1989.
Ehrman, John; *Grand Strategy*, vol. 5; London, HMSO, 1956.

Elliott, Nicholas; *Never Judge a Man by his Umbrella*; London, Philip Russell, 1991.

Ericson, John; *The Soviet High Command 1918–41*; London, Macmillan, 1962.

Farago, Ladislas; *The Game of the Foxes*; London, Hodder and Stoughton, 1971.

Feis, Herbert; *Churchill Roosevelt Stalin: The War They Waged and the Peace They Sought*; Princeton, Princeton University Press, 1957.

Ferris, John (ed); *The British Army and Signals Intelligence During the First World War*; Stroud, Alan Sutton, 1992.

Fox, A.B.; *The Power of Small States: Diplomacy in World War Two*; Chicago, Chicago University Press, 1959.

Garlinski, Joseph; *Intercept: Secrets of the Enigma War*; London, Dent, 1979.

Gilbert, Sir Martin; *Winston S. Churchill: Vol. 6 1939–41: Finest Hour*; London, Heinemann, 1983.

——; *Road to Victory*; London, Heinemann, 1986.

Granatstein, J.L. and Stafford, David; *Spy Wars: Espionage and Canada from Gouzenko to Glasnost*; Toronto, Key Porter, 1983.

Gwyer, J. and Butler, J.R.M.(eds); *Grand Strategy*, vol. 1 pt 1; London, HMSO, 1964.

——; vol. 5; London, HMSO, 1956.

Hennessy, Peter; *Whitehall*; London, Cape, 1990.

Higgins, Trumbull; *Winston Churchill and the Dardanelles: A Dialogue in Ends and Means*; New York, Macmillan, 1963.

——; *Winston Churchill and the Second Front: 1940–3*; New York, OUP, 1957.

—; *Soft Underbelly*; London, Macmillan, 1968.

Hinsley, F.H. et al; *British Intelligence in the Second World War: Its Influence on Strategy and Operations*, vol. 1; London, HMSO, 1979.

——; Vol. 2; London, HMSO, 1981.

——; Vol. 3 pt (i); London, HMSO, 1984.

——; Vol. 3 pt (ii); London, HMSO, 1988.

——; Vol. 4; London, HMSO, 1990.

——; One vol. (abridged); London, HMSO, 1993.

——; *Hitler's Strategy*; Cambridge, Cambridge University Press, 1951.

Hinsley, F.H. and Stripp, A.(eds); *Code-Breakers*; Oxford, Oxford University Press, 1993.

Hodges, Andrew; *Alan Turing: The Enigma of Intelligence*; London, Hutchinson, 1983.

Holland, Jeffrey; *The Aegean Mission: Allied Operations in the Dodecanese, 1943*; New York, Greenwood, 1988.

Howard, Michael; *The Mediterranean Strategy in the Second World War*; London, Weidenfeld and Nicolson, 1968.

——; *Strategic Deception in the Second World War* (published as *Strategic Deception in the Second World War*, vol. 5 of the Official History of British Intelligence in the Second World War); London, HMSO, 1990 and Pimlico, 1992.

Irving, David; *The Rise and Fall of the Luftwaffe; The Life of Erhard Milch*; London, Weidenfeld and Nicolson, 1973.

——; *Churchill's War*, vol. 1; Australia, Penguin, 1987.

——; *Hitler's War*; London, Falcon, 1975 and 1991.

——; *Goring*; London, Macmillan, 1989.

——; *Goebbels: His Life and Death*; London, Falcon, 1996.

——; (ed with Watt, D.C.); *Breach of Security; The German Secret Intelligence Files on events leading to the Second World War*; London, Kimber, 1968.

Kahn, David; *The Code-Breakers*; New York, Macmillan, 1967.

——; *Hitler's Spies: German Military Intelligence in World War Two*; London, Hodder and Stoughton, 1978.

——; *Seizing the Enigma: The Race to Break the German U-Boat Codes 1939–43*; Boston, Houghton Mifflin, 1991.

Kennedy, Maj-Gen Sir John; *The Business of War*; London, Hutchinson, 1957.

Kirk, George; *The Middle East and the War*; Oxford, Oxford University Press, 1954. (RIIS series edited by Arnold and Rosalind Toynbee.)

Kozacuk, Wladizlaw; *Enigma: How the German Machine Cipher was Broken and How it was Read by the Allies in World War Two*; Warsaw, Ksiazka i Wiedza, 1979.

Krecker, Lothar; *Deutschland Und Die Tuerkei in Zweiten Weltkrieg*; Frankfurt, Klostermann, 1964.

Lamb, Richard; *Churchill As War Leader*; London, Bloomsbury, 1992.

Langer, William and Gleason, S. Everitt; *The Undeclared War*; London, Andre Deutsch, 1977.

Lash, Joseph; *Roosevelt and Churchill 1931–41: The Partnership that Saved the West*; London, Deutsch, 1977.

Lawlor, Sheila; *Churchill and the Politics of War 1940–1*; Cambridge, Cambridge University Press, 1994.

Lewin, R.; *Ultra Goes to War*; London, Hutchinson, 1979.

——; *The American Magic*; London, Hutchinson, 1986.

Lippe, J. M. Van der; *Decade of Struggle: Ismet Inönü and Turkish Politics 1935–50*; Austin, 1993.

Maclean, Alistair; *The Guns of Navarone*; London, Collins, 1953.

Mangune, Gerard (ed); *The International Straits of the World*; Dordericht, 1987.

Medlicott, W. N.; *The Economic Blockade*, vol. 2; London, HMSO, 1959.

Miner, S. M.; *Between Churchill and Stalin: The Soviet Union, Great Britain and the Origins of the Grand Alliance*; Chapel Hill, 1988.

Molony, Brig C.J.C., et al; *The Mediterranean and the Middle East vol. 5 The Campaign in Sicily and the Campaign in Italy – 3 September 1943 till 31 March 1944*; London, HMSO, 1973.

Müller, K-J. A.; *A German Perspective on Allied Deception Operations in World War Two*; Intelligence and National Security special volume, vol. 2, no. 3.

Newton, Verne; *The Butcher's Embrace: The Cambridge Spies*; New York, Madison Books, 1991.

Parish, Michael Woodbine; *Aegean Adventures 1940–3 and the end of Churchill's Dream*; Lewes, The Book Guild, 1993.

Parrish, Thomas; *The Ultra Americans: The US role in breaking Nazi codes*; New York, Stein and Day, 1986.

Petrov, Vladimir; *Soviet Historians and the German Invasion*; Columbia, South Carolina, 1968.

Playfair, G.; *The Second World War: The Mediterranean and the Middle East, vol. 4 The Destruction of the Axis Forces in Africa*; London, HMSO, 1973.

Reynolds, David et al (eds); *Allies at War: The Soviet, American and British Experience 1939–45*; London, Macmillan, 1991.

Rhodes, Robert James; *Anthony Eden*; London, Weidenfeld and Nicolson, 1986.

Richelson, Jeffrey T.; *A Century of Spies: Intelligence in the Twentieth Century*; Oxford, Oxford University Press, 1995.

Robertson, K.G.; *British and American Approaches to Intelligence*; London, Macmillan Press, 1987.

Rothwald, Ariel; *Estranged Bedfellows: Britain and France in the Middle East During World War Two*; Oxford, Oxford University Press, 1990.

Rothwell, Victor; *Britain and the Cold War 1941–7*; London, Cape, 1982.

Schoonheur, Klaus; *Neutralitaet Nonbelligerence oder Krieg: Die Tuerkei in spannungsfeld Europ. Maechte 1939–41*; Germany, Piper, 1991.

Skillen, Hugh; *Spies of the Airwaves: A History of Y Sections during WW2*; London, Skillen, 1989.

——; *The Enigma Symposium 1994*; London, Skillen, 1994.

Smith, Bradley; *The Ultra Magic Deals: The Codebreakers' War and the Most Secret Special Relationship 1940–6*; Novato, Presidio, 1993.

——; *The Shadow Warriors: OSS and the Origins of the CIA*; London, Deutsch, 1983.

Smith, Peter and Walker, E.; *War in the Aegean*; London, Kimber, 1974.

Stevenson, William; *A Man Called Intrepid: The Secret War 1939–45*; London, Macmillan, 1975.

Taylor, A.J.P.; *English History 1914–45*; Oxford, Oxford University Press, 1965.

Teichman, Miroslav; *Turkey and the Anti-Hitler Coalition in World War Two*; Czechoslovakia, Slovansky Prehled, 1983.

Toynbee, Arnold and Rosalind (eds); *Survey of International Affairs, vol. 6 (i) The War and the Neutrals by G.E. Kirk*; Oxford, Oxford University Press, 1956.

Ullman, Richard; *Anglo-Soviet Relations 1917–21, vol. 3 The Anglo-Soviet Accord*; Princeton, Princeton University Press 1972.

Wark, Wesley; *The Ultimate Enemy*; London, I.B. Tauris, 1985.

Wasserstein, Bernard; *Britain and the Jews of Europe 1939–45*; Oxford, Oxford University Press, 1979.

Watt, D.C.; *How War Came: The Immediate Origins of the Second World War, 1938*; London, Heinemann, 1989.

Weber, Frank G.; *The Evasive Neutral: Germany, Britain and the quest for a Turkish Alliance in the Second World War*; Missouri, Missouri University Press, 1979.

Weisband, L.; *Anticipating the Cold War: Turkish Foreign Policy 1943–5*; Princeton, Princeton University Press, 1973.

Welchman, Gordon; *The Hut Six Story: Breaking the Enigma Codes*; New York, Magraw Hill, 1982.

West, Nigel; *GCHQ: The Secret Wireless War 1900–86*; London, Weidenfeld and Nicolson, 1986.

——; *MI6: British Secret Intelligence Service Operations 1909–45*; London, Weidenfeld and Nicolson, 1983.

——; *Unreliable Witness: Espionage Myths of the Second World War*; London, Weidenfeld and Nicolson, 1984.

Winterbotham, F.W.; *The Ultra Secret*; London, Weidenfeld and Nicolson, 1973.

Woodward, Sir Llewelyn; *British Foreign Policy in World War Two*; London, HMSO, 1962.

Wright, Peter; *Spycatcher*; Sydney, Heinemann, 1988.

Zhikova, Ludmila; *Anglo-Turkish Relations 1933–9*; London, Secker and Warburg, 1976.

Newspapers

Review of the Foreign Press; 1939–45. Series A, vol. 5 nos 93–117 (RIIA Kraus) 504.

The Daily Worker; September 1942–March 1943 (Colindale).

The Economist; 23 August 1941.

Keesing's Contemporary Archives, vol. 5 (1943–45) (Keynsham, ND).

Brasseys Naval Annual: Führer Naval Conference 1939–44.

Index